ART PRACTICE
AS RESEARCH

For Ruby, Savannah, Jack, and Emma—artful minds that know no boundaries

ART PRACTICE AS RESEARCH

INQUIRY IN THE VISUAL ARTS

GRAEME SULLIVAN

TEACHERS COLLEGE, COLUMBIA UNIVERSITY

SAGE Publications
Thousand Oaks ▪ London ▪ New Delhi

Copyright © 2005 by Sage Publications, Inc.

All rights reserved. No part of this book may be reproduced or utilized in any form
or by any means, electronic or mechanical, including photocopying, recording, or by
any information storage and retrieval system, without permission in writing from the
publisher.

For information:

 Sage Publications, Inc.
2455 Teller Road
Thousand Oaks, California 91320
E-mail: order@sagepub.com

Sage Publications Ltd.
1 Oliver's Yard
55 City Road
London EC1Y 1SP
United Kingdom

Sage Publications India Pvt. Ltd.
B-42, Panchsheel Enclave
Post Box 4109
New Delhi 110 017 India

Library of Congress Cataloging-in-Publication Data

Sullivan, Graeme, 1951-
Art practice as research : inquiry in the visual arts / Graeme Sullivan.
     p. cm.
Includes bibliographical references and index.
ISBN 1-4129-0535-4 (cloth : acid-free paper) — ISBN 1-4129-0536-2
(pbk. : acid-free paper)
   1. Art—Research. 2. Art—Study and teaching. I. Title.
N85.S84 2005
707'.2—dc22

                                        2004015960

Printed on acid-free paper in the United States of America.

06   07   08   09   10   9   8   7   6   5   4   3   2

Acquisitions Editor:	Diane McDaniel
Editorial Assistant:	Marta Peimer
Production Editor:	Tracy Alpern
Copy Editor:	Richard H. Adin
Typesetter:	C&M Digitals (P) Ltd.
Indexer:	Jean Casalegno
Cover Designer:	Michelle Lee Kenny

CONTENTS

ACKNOWLEDGMENTS

Acknowledgments as written can never match gratitude expressed as deeds. Being around to shape the space and share the search is an act of artistry that Mary Northey continues to craft in ways that amaze. For this I am forever in her debt. Expressions of heartfelt support were also close at hand, even when from afar, as Brett Sullivan, Fiona Smith, Ben Sullivan, and Rebecca Cleary offered continual encouragement. My effort to push the boundaries and to look anew was prompted by their belief that being artful means making ideas happen.

Others gave support through a generosity of spirit that was edgeless. Colleagues at Teachers College Columbia University created a climate of change that helped me remain awake to possibility. The intellectual imagination of our students also made sure ideas were always questioned, issues contested, and diagrams debated. And throughout this process, Ami Kantawala Worah managed to make light of endless tasks that made the difficult seem simple.

My gratitude for critical conversations extends to the manuscript reviewers. Dipti Desai (New York University), Pradeep A. Dhillon (University of Illinois), and Rita Irwin (University of British Columbia) offered very insightful commentary in the transition from proposal to publication; Donald Blumenfeld-Jones (Arizona State University), Elijah Mirochnik (George Mason University), and Nicholas Paley (George Washington University) were generous in their response to the initial ideas. In their reviews of the draft manuscript, Jessica Hoffmann Davis (Harvard University), Doug Blandy (University of Oregon), and Arthur Efland (The Ohio State University) helped me add perspective and precision. There are traces of this dialogue throughout the text, and any confused concept or tortured term that remains means that I still struggle with my part of the task. In a similar collaborative way, Hugo Ortega López was able to envision graphic forms that helped bring some key ideas to life, while the call of Ken Marantz to "say it straight, mate" still rings in my ears after all these years. Numerous others, in their own way, assisted to make the book far better than it otherwise might have been. I am especially thankful for the help of Rose Viggiano, Hwa Young Choi Caruso, Lori Kent, Stephen Lane, Fern Lerner, and Sherry Mayo.

For permission to reproduce their artwork I am especially grateful to Brandon Ballengée, Rina Banerjee, Graham Blondel, Chakaia Booker, Christo and Jeanne-Claude, Angiola Churchill, Zhang Dali, Jayne Dyer, Fiona Foley, Will Grant, Jeff Heatley, Natalie Jeremijenko, Michael Leunig, George Longfish, Hugo Ortega López, Nikki McCarthy, Yong Soon Min, Tracey Moffatt, Aphrodite Désirée Navab, Damián Ortega, Maurizio Pellegrin, Patricia Piccinini, Maria Magdalena Campos Pons, Lucio Pozzi, Robert Solso, Mark Tansey, and Fred Wilson. Several museums, galleries, and institutions gave assistance, including the Avery Architectural and Fine Arts Library, Columbia University; Gagosian Gallery, New York; Graphic Press, Connecticut; Kurimanzutto Gallery, Mexico City; Massachusetts Museum of Contemporary Art (MASS MoCA); Roslyn Oxley9 Gallery, Sydney; Yale Center for British Art, Yale University; and Howard Yezerski Gallery, Boston.

● COVER

Graeme Sullivan, *Object Knowledge (Streetworks)* (2002). Encyclopedia, dragonfly, Plexiglas. 11 × 9 inches. Cover Photograph by José Bettancourt.

Object Knowledge was part of a series made from things retrieved from the streets of New York that were installed throughout the city. The work was placed in a New York library in August 2002. Its whereabouts is unknown, although an anonymous postcard was received a few weeks later with the following message:

Dear Streetworks,

I enjoyed my time at the Library—but I was checked out by a nice couple in Murray Hill. So I am now staying on their bookshelf. Hope to see you again.

The Dragonfly Book

INTRODUCTION: REVIEWING VISUAL ARTS RESEARCH

*A**rt Practice as Research: Inquiry in the Visual Arts* argues that the imaginative and intellectual work undertaken by artists is a form of research. As an area of individual, social, and cultural inquiry, the visual arts have, for the most part, remained outside the mainstream of community debate. They are often seen as arcane and use obscure personal symbols that are difficult to interpret. Although no stranger to controversy because of their capacity to arouse and divide public opinion, as a serious social phenomenon, the visual arts remain mostly sequestered within a limited cultural and political orbit. At worst, they are seen as elitist; at best, visual arts are misunderstood. Even when included in schools and institutions of higher education, visual arts programs struggle for acceptance as important areas of the curriculum. In this book I argue that existing misconceptions about the intellectual status of learning in visual arts means that the scholarly, cultural, and social significance of art is grossly undervalued. To redress this, a detailed analysis is undertaken that explores the theoretical basis of artistic practice to position it within the discourse of research. What is presented is a theory of visual arts practice as research.

The approach I take is to examine visual arts as a form of inquiry into the theories, practices, and contexts used by artists. The critical and creative investigations that occur in studios, galleries, on the Internet, in community spaces, and in other places where artists work, are forms of research grounded in art practice. Rather than adopting methods of inquiry from the social sciences, the research practices explored here subscribe to the view that similar research goals can be achieved by following different yet complementary paths. What is common is the attention given to rigor and systematic inquiry, yet in a way that privileges the role imagination and intellect plays in constructing knowledge that is not only new but has the capacity to transform human understanding.

● CHANGING DEMANDS OF VISUAL ARTS THEORY AND PRACTICE

As an area of undergraduate and graduate education, the visual arts have long been included in higher education programs. Yet the way the field is defined invariably influences how it is perceived within institutional settings. The traditions of the academy give rise to many different conceptions of the visual arts. When seen as a desirable experience in the liberal arts, the teaching of the visual arts rests on the capacity of an expert cultural tourist to enliven and enlighten students about art. In the humanities class, the methods are pedagogical, the data are observations, and images are experienced mostly as "art in the dark." When seen as historical inquiry, the study of visual arts builds on links between art history, fine arts, and the humanities, which means that established methods of research can be used and this ensures a level of institutional credibility. In the art history class, the methods are investigative, the data are antiquities, and the results mostly appear in heavily footnoted chronicles. When seen as the domain of the gifted or eccentric individual, the visual arts may be viewed with deference or indifference. In the studio class, the methods are iconoclastic, the data are idiosyncratic, and the outcomes are often viewed as social oddities. If seen as a form of cultural reproduction, the visual arts are seen as part of artworld practices that determine merit and worth. In the art theory class, the methods are often ideological, the data are constructed by figures of authority, and the outcomes are historical and social critiques.

In many countries, discrete art schools provided discipline-specific programs that mostly drew on the atelier traditions of the academy, or upon the internationalism of Bauhaus-inspired formalism and other modernist perspectives. The belief that artists cannot be "made" and therefore nothing much beyond skills can be taught prevailed throughout most of the 19th and 20th centuries. Although art schools remained mostly separate from the mainstream of higher education, the demands of accountability could be met within the professional and vocational expectations of the artworld. However, with the changes in worldwide economic structures and the rationalization of industry and information services, no educational or professional discipline can remain isolated. By the beginning of the 21st century, art schools and teacher-training institutions in most countries had been incorporated into a university structure. As art practices become part of broader systems of higher education, new questions emerge. For instance, while the sciences have their research paradigms, what is the equivalent of these in the arts, if any? How might visual arts practices be theorized as research?

While most undergraduate and graduate visual arts courses are located in universities in the United States, for the most part they remain discrete programs. However, with the need to institute "user pays" policies, the allocation of funding is becoming increasingly linked to productivity demands. This translates to a form of competition for resources and visual arts programs and art education programs consequently need to justify the research work done in academic terms. A challenge for many teachers in art programs is to define their studio-based teaching and art-learning practices not only as a form of professional training, but as scholarly inquiry. One argument I make in this book is that studio-based inquiry in visual arts will have greater institutional credibility if it is built on sound theoretical principles that can be shown to satisfy basic criteria for research practice.

Within the current professional, vocational, and educational demands there is an increasing expectation that visual arts and art education faculty and students are able to undertake research that has credibility within the academy and within the artworld. Consequently, approaches to visual arts research need to be positioned within existing frameworks but not be a slave to them. The thesis presented in *Art Practice as Research* is that visual research methods can be grounded within the practices of the studio and that these are robust enough to satisfy rigorous institutional demands.

LIMITATIONS OF CURRENT ● VISUAL RESEARCH METHODOLOGIES

In recent years, several discipline specialists published texts that deal with the topic of "visual" research and related approaches to inquiry. Generally there are three strategies followed by the authors of these texts. First, there are approaches that build on discipline-based research that have a tradition of using visual means of gathering and interpreting data. These titles draw on areas such as sociology, anthropology, and cultural studies. The second uses a discipline approach but draws on areas of visual arts such as art history, art theory, and criticism. These research traditions are based on historical inquiry, literary-based interpretive strategies, and postmodern critical perspectives. A third kind of research genre is arts-based educational inquiry. Those who promote this approach see the arts as comprising a set of practices that helps broaden the way we understand things and thus can be used to expand how information is gathered and represented.

Several titles were published in recent years that focus on the use of visual means of data collection and analysis within social science disciplines.[1] Earlier efforts emphasize the way visual approaches such as photography and film are used in sociology and anthropology that mostly relied on descriptive documentation and content analysis. An inherent problem is the continued misconception about the perceived objectivity of visual recording tools such as cameras and videos (Ball & Smith, 1992). Some sources position the discussion of visual inquiry within research traditions in the social sciences, particularly in the area of social anthropology (Banks, 2001). The visual means discussed include those pervasive forms of cultural representation such as film, video, photography, television, and the like. In other texts, the relatively new areas of visual sociology and visual anthropology are introduced within a context of previous approaches and the arena of research practice is expanded (Prosser, 1998). These authors document a variety of ways that the "visual" is defined to include photographs, cartoons, and graffiti, as well as time-based media of film, video, and television and how visual information is used in research projects.

The problematic nature of how the researcher knowingly or unknowingly interprets images in the construction of meaning is an issue of ongoing debate. What is instructive is how visual information is compiled as part of research activity. Methods draw mostly from those techniques found in anthropology and sociology and therefore do not fully satisfy the interests and concerns of the visual arts researcher. Other texts locate theories and practices about "researching the visual" within trends in the social sciences and argue against the marginalization of visual data in research. For instance, Emmison and Smith (2000) argue that the "visual" is a much more complex social construct than that which can be captured in photographs. The conceptual framework they build is informative in the way it includes visual images, objects, events, and "visual traces" that carry meaning and therefore can be subject to analysis. A sense of the debate about issues such as the validity, reliability, and trustworthiness of visual data is evident, yet these are never fully resolved or positioned in a way that could be applied in other contexts.

Other texts offer broad frameworks for considering the nature of images and how they can be researched and interpreted (van Leeuwen & Jewitt, 2001). A central theme is the way social and cultural practices are used to convey meaning using visual information. This raises issues about the kind of evidential bases that can be used to analyze how we might make meaning from these images. A useful heuristic is the way that the "interpretive space" used for analysis is located among several sources, including the text itself, the producer of the images, the surrounding context, and the position of the viewer. Although the politics of image making and interpretation are dealt with within the realm of visual culture, they do not meet the needs of researchers interested in looking more closely at the visual arts. Often, both the interpretation and critique of meaning are seen as research goals. Consequently, the kind of knowledge produced by visual anthropologists and visual sociologists emphasize the researcher as "editor" rather than artistic "practitioner."

Texts such as Gillian Rose's *Visual Methodologies* (2001) bring together research traditions used in the social sciences and some areas of the humanities and position them within discussions of visual culture. Here visual culture refers to those pervasive forms of imagery, texts, and technologies that are produced and interpreted within individual, cultural, and political contexts. Rose expands the notion of research outcomes and explores how goals such as "truth" and "critical understanding" can be defined within a flexible interpretive framework of cultural and political practice. Rose's text emphasizes a methods-driven rather than an issues-driven approach to research that limits its application across broader discipline boundaries. By contrast, Sarah Pink's *Doing Visual Ethnography* (2001) offers a broader theoretical framework around which issues of visual data collection and interpretation are covered. Central to the author's argument is "reflexivity" whereby the researcher becomes part of the emerging text, and this has an impact on how visual information is interpreted. Pink shows how reflexivity can be a conceptual asset in revealing information, but also an operational liability that can raise concerns about issues such as ethics. The important areas of visual technologies and visual culture are well positioned within existing discipline areas and paradigms of inquiry so that what Pink sees as distinctive about emphasizing the visual can be seen in context. Although *Doing Visual Ethnography* is an imaginative resource for inquiry, it is limited to the concerns of researchers in critical studies, media studies, and social sciences and does not accommodate the needs of those working in the visual arts. Pink's text follows a strategy common to most research in critical and visual cultural inquiry in that it emphasizes the *critique* and analysis of phenomena, but has very little to say about the *creation* of new knowledge using visual means that might be undertaken within a research perspective.

There are many sources, old and new, that base their methodologies on practices more directly related to traditions in the visual arts. Methods of inquiry used by researchers in the arts and humanities tend to align more clearly with practices drawn from art history, art theory, and cultural studies (Berger, 1972; Cheetham, Holly, & Moxley, 1998; Edwards, 1998). Traditional stances describe the methodologies used in art history to investigate artworks, artists, and cultures (Adams, 1996; Fernie, 1995; Minor, 1994). The approach is to review the basic strategies for conducting inquiry that emphasizes particular forms, themes, or issues. Methods covered include those that are part of longer traditions in art historical inquiry, such as formalism, iconography, and iconology, and critical approaches, such as Marxism, feminism, semiotics, poststructuralism, hermeneutics, and phenomenology. These research methods reveal how various historical protocols can be useful interpretive tools that help construct and deconstruct visual arts in the studio as in well as in the library.

Other sources serve as a bridge that brings together methods often used in visual arts as ways of interpreting image forms such as those found in areas of art history, and the more recent excursions into visual culture that incorporate sociopolitical contexts (Bal, 1996; Barnard, 2001; Bloom, 1999; Heywood & Sandywell, 1999; Pollock, 2001). These generally explore the complexities of vision as a perceptual and cultural phenomenon based on the idea that while different ways of seeing are evident, these forms can be analyzed for valuable cultural and political ends. The discussions are often set within a framework that contrasts modernist and postmodern perspectives that open up broader research possibilities. Some issues and ideas that are central to contemporary art practice are covered, yet the full dimension of how visual arts can be seen within and beyond existing research traditions is often left unexplored.

The text edited by Al Rees and Frances Borzello, *The New Art History* (1986), captured the critical mood of the times and the understanding of the constraints that hampered a comprehensive reading of visual arts as cultural history. The authors highlighted how the research methods favored by the academy were part of a broader methodological structure that was questionable in light of the dubious theoretical assumptions on which it was based. This sparked a more socially centered and politically responsive attitude that included Marxist and feminist critiques, semiotic analyses, neopsychoanalytic perspectives, and methods of poststructuralism and deconstruction. To review this radical tilt at art history, Harris (2001) examined a sample of influential texts from recent decades that each captured a critical moment in this widespread theoretical soul-searching. Harris's analysis reveals that, well before the claim of "new art history" was made, as a methodological practice, art historical study was acknowledged as a process of theory-driven inquiry shaped by position and value. Furthermore, art history was seen as a field of discussion about arguments and principles, rather than content and methods. The opening up of areas of art historical investigation to include an ensemble of artworks, viewers, and contexts, not only introduced a greater range of critical methods, but saw content expand to embrace all areas of visual culture.[2]

Within educational settings, a trend to emerge in recent years is a similar attempt to expand the domain of inquiry, this time to more adequately accommodate discipline interests in the arts. Loosely labeled "arts-based" research, those advancing this view call for a broadening of research practices that can take advantage of the way the arts offer unique insight into the human knowing and understanding (Barone & Eisner, 1997; Diamond & Mullen, 1999; Eisner, 1991; Jipson & Paley, 1997). Elliot Eisner, for instance, grounds his vision of inquiry in curriculum theory, artistic forms of knowing, and practices from the arts and humanities in his quest to extend the methodological scope of educational research.[3] The methods deployed are mostly language-based, and like art criticism, rely on the power of the evocative word-image to capture the reality of the classroom. In his publication, *The Arts and the Creation of Mind* (2002), Eisner presents a more thorough exposition of his ideas. Although there is a consolidation of the cognitive claims made about artistic experience, his sensory-based learning and the insights that artistic knowing brings to the individual and the culture remain as a legacy of his writing from past decades and carry his structuralist and essentialist stamp. It is the persuasive arguments Eisner makes about the transformative power of art learning that comes closest to the thesis I present in this book.

In mapping an agenda for educational inquiry, most arts-based researchers in the United States locate new directions within the domains of education and the social sciences. Some proclaim the integrity of the artistic product as a site of knowledge (Barone, 2001), while others argue that the arts can enhance the direction and breadth of data representation and thus more adequately align research with complex realities (Cahnmann, 2003). Generally, however, the arts continue to be seen as agencies of human knowing that are drafted into service according to educational practices already in place. Jessica Hoffmann Davis (2003), for instance, in drawing on Sara Lawrence-Lightfoot's notion of "portraiture" (Lawrence-Lightfoot, 1983; Lawrence-Lightfoot & Hoffmann Davis, 1997), describes how this arts-based methodology embraces ethnographic traditions, case study perspectives, and inductive forms of analysis. Yet for Hoffmann Davis it is the power of the "aesthetic whole" that is key to revealing a coherent, unified interpretation whereby "the research portrait is the result of a subtle synthesis of rigorous procedures that unite in an expressive aesthetic whole" (2003, p. 215).

The approach I take makes the case that informing theories and practices are found in the art studio, and the image of the artist-theorist as practitioner is taken as the locus of action rather than the arts teacher. Therefore visual arts research has to be grounded in practices that come from art itself, especially inquiry that is studio based (Sullivan, 2004). In addition, an axiom of research needs to be followed which accepts that different paths can be used to get to the same place.

● ART PRACTICE AS RESEARCH

The content covered in *Art Practice as Research* is divided into three main parts: *Contexts for Visual Arts Research, Theorizing Visual Arts Practice,* and *Visual Arts Research Practices. Part 1: Contexts for Visual Arts Research* provides the necessary historical context that positions the visual arts as a culturally grounded and institutionally bound area of artistic and educational inquiry. *Part 2: Theorizing Visual Arts Practice* argues that visual arts practice is a theoretically robust area of inquiry and a transformative approach to research. *Part 3: Visual Arts Research Practices* provides readers with a range of strategies and approaches to planning and conducting visual arts research.

Part 1: Contexts for Visual Arts Research establishes the historical and cultural basis upon which the thesis of the book is set. The opening chapter, "Pigment to Pixel," reviews the changing social and educational patterns of visual arts traditions from the private and public arena of the academy of the past, to the institutional and artworld academies of today. Topics covered include the changing ideas about art theories and practices. The status of the artist as a cultural lamplighter, human visionary, and educator is traced, along with approaches to the professional development of the artist and the challenge faced today in a world of cultural, institutional, and digital divides. Although the cultural relevance of art is firmly bound to different perceptions about its sociopolitical role, as an academic discipline and a basic form of educational engagement, the visual arts continue to be open to renovation.

Chapter 2, "Paradigms Lost," reflects on the powerful practices of inquiry that emerged as a consequence of the institutionalization of knowledge in the 19th and 20th century. The hegemony of the sciences is described in terms of the politics of authority and the rationality of progress that made it difficult for the visual arts to keep pace as a reliable source of knowledge and insight. However, the challenges brought forth by postmodernism, critical theory, and socially grounded conceptions of qualitative research offer new opportunities to reconfigure research practices. Consequently, in an uncertain world where assumed structures no longer serve as adequate explanatory models, the argument is made that different avenues to human understanding need to be pursued and that these are intrinsic to artistic practice.

Part 2: Theorizing Visual Arts Practice establishes a basis upon which visual arts practice is a form of inquiry that is sound in theory and robust in method and that can generate important creative and critical outcomes. Chapter 3, "Explanation, Understanding, and Beyond," examines the process of "theorizing," which is a basic procedure of inquiry and hence a core element in research. An accepted role of theorizing is to use conceptual problem-solving strategies to analyze and synthesize things in order to explain them in ways that help to implement new practices. The argument made in this chapter is that explanation is an important goal of inquiry, yet there are aspects of human understanding that are beyond the scope of explanatory systems where insight is not the consequence of causal, inferential, or predictive means. Different kinds of theorizing are described that use methods that range from instrumental means–ends approaches to practitioner-based approaches grounded in reflexive thought and action. Debates about practice-based research and the institutional conditions that are shaping the emergence of visual arts research practices are reviewed. From this analysis a framework for theorizing art practice as transformative research is proposed. A "braided" metaphor is used to identify characteristics and structures around which visual arts research practices are described.

Chapter 4, "Visual Knowing," examines the cognitive foundations of artistic practice. Simplistic dichotomies that align kinds of thinking and particular ways of knowing with the sciences, and forms of feeling with experience in the arts are rejected. It is argued that visual arts practice is a form of human understanding whose cognitive processes are distributed throughout the various media, languages, and contexts used to frame the production and interpretation of images. This is described in a framework for visual arts knowing. Drawing on research that examines the studio activities of artists, I identify a wider set of cognitive and contextual factors that influence visual knowing and describe this as *transcognition*.

The last chapter in Part 2, "Artist as Theorist," argues that artists' studios, and other such places used for the creation and critique of new knowledge, are theoretically powerful and methodologically robust sites of inquiry. In drawing together the arguments about ways of theorizing visual arts practice, I make a case for practitioner research where the artist-theorist can be seen as both the researcher and the researched. This chapter also focuses on the ever-expanding practices used by artists to advance our understanding of who we are, what we do, and what we know. Settings such as those opened up by digital environments, cultural collaborations, and community spaces are creating new places for creative and critical inquiry that offer opportunities for different forms of research and scholarship. I argue that artists explore these places in ways that disrupt assumed boundaries. The chapter also looks at how practice and theory merge as critical, curatorial, and cultural perspectives that are considered within the context of visual arts research practice.

Part 3: Visual Arts Research Practices has two purposes. First, visual arts research is characterized as inquiry that embraces cultural contexts, institutional settings, the digital environment, information arts, indigenous perspectives, and other realms that open up new avenues for study. As such, visual arts research practices are presented as creative and critical investigations from which many other areas of inquiry can be pursued. Another aim is to provide strategies to assist with planning visual arts research projects. The challenge is to be able to provide useful guidelines yet resist the tendency to prescribe methods. For the artist-theorist, however, working within constraints, be they technical means, design briefs, or problematic positions, is a long accepted practice in the creative construction of new knowledge.

Chapter 6, "Practice as Theory," builds on information in Part 2, and argues that research, theory and practice needs to expand to cope with the way ideas, information, and communicative forms defy existing discipline boundaries. Artists, scientists, teachers, and others who see structures that define theories and practices as bridges, are open to ways of exploring hybrid forms of imaginative inquiry. This chapter also provides a framework for conceptualizing visual arts research projects that build on structures described in previous chapters. Dimensions of visualization are described using objects, data, texts, and ideas. Critical and creative practices for reviewing and designing research projects are also outlined that use visual experiences, exercises, encounters, and enactments.

The final chapter of the book, "Conclusions and Beginnings," draws together the arguments presented in the book. The point is made that if visual arts practice is seen as research, it will resist codification and methodological prescription *only* if any inquiry "starts with art." Furthermore, the individual, cultural, and educational significance of the visual arts means that artists, art writers, and art educators need to be vigilant advocates and artisans of multiple forms of inquiry to ensure what it is we do is understood, appreciated, and acted on by others.

● STRATEGIES FOR USING ART PRACTICE AS RESEARCH

The meanings made from this book are not dependent on the way it is structured. There is logic to the three-part organization as the arguments build on historical, conceptual, and practical issues in order to present a coherent theoretical framework that describes art practice as research. Yet these areas can be considered as independent positions, much in the way that a series of paintings can be both a discrete investigation that is context specific and also be part of an ongoing series that is part of a larger pattern of inquiry. Consequently the information presented in the book encourages readers to revisit and reconstruct their own meanings in ways that are personally relevant. Questions about historical contexts, research traditions, theoretical quibbles, comparative critiques, or more practical guidelines for conducting visual arts research will lead to different ways of interpreting the text.

To encourage this kind of conversation each chapter includes sidebar components to supplement the text. The purpose is to provide examples and explanatory notes that will help to ground some of the ideas presented and offer points of departure for further discussion. In most cases these are anchored to illustrations of artists' work. It is seen as necessary to include examples as a way to confirm the depth and breadth of artistic practice, to illustrate the variety of ways that ideas are given form, and how projects are planned. Other components include diagrams that help illustrate concepts and their relationships. One of the central themes in the text is to promote the use of visual research strategies. Part of the challenge is to be able to show examples of how theories and ideas can be conceptualized and operationalized. Therefore several visual references are included, especially in *Part 3: Visual Arts Research Practices*.

The inclusion of the sidebars is based on my experience as a teacher and on my appreciation of how visual arts faculty and students access and use information. Like "reading" the artwork of others, there is a tendency to read chapters in several ways with the initial scan serving to give a "captioned" or instinctual overview of the information. Providing several points of entry throughout the chapters where the reader can absorb pockets of material and "talk back" to the information serves this orientation purpose. Thus there are several word-based and image-based areas in each chapter that contain discrete information, yet are also referenced to the chapter content. This dialogical emphasis should have the reader scratching pencil notes, drawings, and diagrams in the margins of the book as issues are raised, experiences challenged, or confirmed, and possibilities pondered. This element of discussion and debate is characteristic of visual arts inquiry, whether undertaken in the studio or in the public space of the classroom, gallery, or community.

The approach to visual arts research presented in this book is based on my experience conducting research with contemporary artists, teaching in higher education institutions, and knowledge gained from working in my own way as a practicing artist. Several research projects undertaken in collaboration with artists over the past 15 years ground the arguments presented and these are discussed throughout the text. Parallel to this work is my teaching at the university level. I have developed courses in visual arts research and currently supervise doctoral students working on dissertations that are extending the boundaries of research methodology and incorporate many of the approaches discussed here. Finally, there are things I do as an artist. An important point to be made that applies to me, and that has probable relevance to many others, is that one's art practice, teaching profession, and research projects, all operate within a similar set of informing conditions and a sense of inquiry, and you are never quite sure of the outcome.

Let me conclude with a brief story of uncertain inquiry. Since the early 1990s I have been making Streetworks that are conceived, constructed, and confined to specific sites. These works are made from materials found in the street and begin as a reaction to things and places, proceed as a partial reconstruction and eventual resiting, and continue to unfold in unknown ways as other processes take over. The task of retrieval and renewal of found objects has a long tradition, and returning works made from these materials to the street maintains a process of change that is pleasantly obscure. As artworks they become nice friends to live with. Despite their change, however, their existence on white walls slowly drains them of their streetwise energy. Therefore, to place these works back on the streets, to attach them to walls, beneath bridges, along alleyways, in parks, or on rocks, allows them to be stumbled on by others. For me this reflects part of the educational role of the visual arts, because even if the life of the artwork is short, or the encounter brief, one never really knows the outcome. This uncertainty is by no means futile, for it is at the heart of what the visual arts have to offer if we dare to see things differently.

● NOTES

1. Several titles are published in sociology and anthropology as visual research methods texts. See, for example, Banks (2001); Emmison and Smith (2000); Heywood and Sandywell (1999); Pink (2001); Prosser (1998); Rose (2001); and van Leeuwen and Jewitt (2001).

2. For an informative review of this transition from art history to visual culture and visual studies see Elkins (2003). The anthology edited by Heywood and Sandywell (1999) examines the expanded notion of the "visual," while the essays edited by Bloom (1999) explore visual culture from the perspective of gender and race.

3. In an article published in the *Educational Researcher,* Elliot Eisner (1993) argues for a broader conception of how research data might be represented to more adequately accommodate different forms of understanding. For an overview of the emergence of arts-based qualitative methods and a series of caveats considered in relation to the parameters common to psychological research, see Eisner's (2003) chapter in Camic, Rhodes, and Yardley (2003). See also a special edition of *Curriculum Inquiry*, 2002, *32*(2), dealing with arts-based research. Retrieved on May 11, 2004, from http://home.oise.utoronto.ca/~ci/32.2.html.

PART 1

CONTEXTS FOR
VISUAL ARTS RESEARCH

CHAPTER 1

PIGMENT TO PIXEL

I n modern times, four historical conditions characterize the emergence of visual arts practice. The first is critical vision. Artists continue to inquire into issues of everyday life and to disrupt our perceptions through studio art practices. The second is reflexive action. This is characterized by the way artists and theorists influence, and are influenced by, the changing dynamics of experience and knowledge. The third is technological agency. This describes how studio art practices get absorbed into the visual culture around us by the expansion of image-making technologies. The final historical theme is art instruction. Over the years, the cultural and educational basis upon which the visual arts was grounded shifted in response to ways that artist-teachers varied their pedagogical practices. As these conditions took effect, an ambivalent sense of art learning was set in place as new ideas clashed with the desire to forge a canon on which instructional programs could be built. Lines of authority were drawn as radical practices created in the garret competed with pursuits crafted in the academy. Yet binding these uncertain traditions was a passion for practice that glorified the mind for its imaginative and intellectual power.

This chapter reviews some of the practices used by artists in modern times as they responded to the challenge of the "new." These innovations are tracked alongside patterns of teaching in higher education as the training of the artist and the artist-educator became institutionalized. A range of models of practice evolved as history moved from the academy to the café, from the classroom to the studio, and into the virtual world. Particular periods changed ideas about the role of the artist. In the early years of the Enlightenment, the idea of the artist-as-analyst, or artist-as-technologist, flourished. By the middle of the 20th century the artist-as-teacher was prominent and the vision and voice of the creative iconoclast held sway. In recent decades, the giddy theoretical landscape uncovered by postmodernism all but ambushed studio art teaching as the canon crumbled and the tradition of the new was seen to be mostly a fiction for the few. And throughout all these periods debate continued about the purpose of the visual arts in educational settings. In his early 1990s critique of ever-complaining postmodernists, Robert Hughes eviscerated his mates in the art academies for the way they resided over a crumbling artifice that promoted "theory over skill, therapy over apprenticeship, strategies over basics" (1993, p. 193).

Yet there is resilience about art practice as a form of inquiry that is evident in the way it continually adapts to the demands of the various "artworlds" (Young, 2001), be it the artworld of contemporary art, or the artworld of educational institutions. There is also a resistance in the way the visual arts continue to give form to new ideas and images within the aesthetics of cultural practice (Carroll, 2001). The contemporary artist these days is part theorist, performer, producer, installer, writer, entertainer, and shaman, who creates in material, matter, media, text, and time, all of which takes shape in real, simulated, and virtual worlds. These characteristics of contemporary art practice change the way we think about the visual arts, which influences what we do in educational settings.

Approaches to visual arts inquiry in higher education institutions in several countries is variously labeled *arts-based research, arts-informed research,* or *practice-based research*[1] and highlights the capacity of the field to respond to the challenge of change. Developments like these are part of a rich historical legacy that can be traced through modernism to postmodernism and beyond. This helps position contemporary art as the critical and creative basis upon which artistic, cultural, political, and educational arguments can be made in support of a fresh conception of visual arts research.

● THE ENLIGHTENMENT AS A RESEARCH PROJECT

The ideas of the Enlightenment set in place a grand research project that sought to explain the workings of nature in a way that confirmed human ascendancy. The new paradigm reflected a worldview that saw the emergence of rational philosophy, among other things, as a form of knowing that revolutionized theory and practice in all disciplines. Radical views in the natural sciences about empirical inquiry and social theories challenged medieval conceptions of the mind and the place of humans in the world. The need to "know" meant that the Enlightenment project became a collaborative enterprise where methods had to be invented in order to answer the kinds of questions then being asked, and this required the imaginative insight of both the thinker and the doer. And the legacy of this time meant that theory held sway and shaped the arc of practice. Yet what some saw as impressive human progress, others mulled over as a loss of heart and soul.

The critical vision advanced by the philosophers of the 17th and 18th centuries touched almost all forms of human understanding. Radical dichotomies wrestled the mind and body apart, and debates saw experience come to overshadow authority. These were elegantly argued battles where skepticism challenged certainty as the basis for reasoning. The sense of doubt introduced by René Descartes into discussions about truth and reality was one of the most important insights to emerge at the time. The strategy of considering how something might be false, rather than trying to confirm it to be true, became a key tenet of both scientific inquiry and critical theorizing. And the implications were profound. The universe was within reach and truth could be found through the use of rational processes and empirical methods.[2] Not only was the natural world seen to be rule-governed, predictable, and able to be controlled, but also so were humans. And the same could be said for art, which was seen to be governed by its own rules. The template that described what it was to be human was drawn with mechanical precision but the explanatory power of what it was like to feel, think, and act eluded complete capture.

The patterns of practice that emerged during the Enlightenment saw the scientist and the artist share a common goal where ideas informed actions. The scientist of the day saw an ordered visible universe rendered in fine representational detail of points, planes, and perspective. Being able to deploy a prescriptive practice meant that the scientist could readily claim a place within a community of inquiry. The artist, on the other hand, was not so comfortable seeing the world through the crosshairs of the new age. For many artists who watched what was happening around them the human condition could not be partitioned into life slices of reality neatly seen through a lens. Yet from this uncertainty came intense personal visions that did, indeed, help us understand the life and mind of the times.

The ongoing question of *how* nature is designed and *who* is responsible occupied the best philosophical, scientific, and artistic minds. The ideas and images produced obviously reflect conceptions of the time. This debate has been going on for a long time. Presenting his aesthetic and moral convictions in an earlier century, Vasari for instance, was unequivocal in his causal explanation. In the preface to *Lives of the Artists* (1568/1993),[3] his reality-based Renaissance documentary, Vasari presents his version of the origin of the creative process. For Vasari, artistic thought was an act of divine providence and artists had "nature for their guide, the purest intellects for their teachers, and the world as their beautiful model" (p. 9). The images created thus mirrored this world of godly design through the use of newer technologies that gave full perspective to visual truth and idealized form. Charged with this lofty inspiration, the 15th century Italian artist personified an approach to teaching that saw the revered artist set forth as the model to emulate. The task of imagining what surrounded us, however, was ultimately found not to be adequately explained by theology, but by formalisms of encyclopedic scope. As Diderot and d'Alembert (1751/1965)[4] show in the allegory at the beginning of the volume on surgery, what it was to be human could be learned by studying nature, and this inspired the design of techniques and tools that became part of new systems of knowledge.

Mindful Inquiry in Art and Science

New methods of inquiry meant that conceptual systems were best seen in dichotomous terms: Reality existed within a split mind-body world of objective and subjective states, of idea and image, of theory and practice. So by the time the research agenda of the Enlightenment was fully enacted, the way knowledge could be conceived, perceived, and visualized gave rise to a new religion of rationality. Patterns of practice meant that the artist and scientist shared a common goal in the quest to better understand nature and the place of humanity within it. In many instances this capacity was found within the genius of the individual who could create knowledge, giving the artist status and authority within the social order. The sophisticated new visual practices and image-making technologies meant that art, like science, expanded its disciplinary scope as new forms of production, exhibition, and interpretation emerged.

The changing mindset of the European Enlightenment gave rise to different roles for the artist, especially in relation to technological advances and the institutionalization of knowledge. In this era of progress where individual liberty was constitutionally proclaimed, new social responsibilities and opportunities for art teaching arose. With access to education seen as a right for all citizens, at least in theory, this gave new importance to the arts as well as the sciences as agencies for human understanding. Patterns of art teaching continued to be built on the model of the academy. Efland (1990) describes this in its original conception as a setting "where knowledge of the theory and philosophy of artistic practice, based on the search for universal

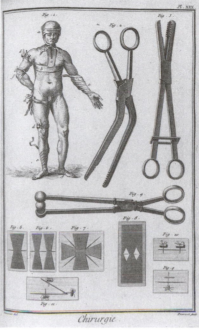

Denis Diderot (1713–1784) and Jean Le Rond d'Alembert. Entries from *Encyclopedia*, or *A Systematic Dictionary of Science, Arts, and the Trades. Surgery* (Chirurgie). Avery Architectural and Fine Arts Library, Columbia University in the City of New York. Courtesy of Columbia University.

Origin of the arts and sciences. In pursuit of his needs, luxury, amusement, satisfaction of curiosity, or other objectives, man applied his industriousness to the products of nature and thus created the arts and sciences. The focal points of our different reflections have been called "science" or "art" according to the nature of their "formal" objects, to use the language of logic. If the object leads to action, we give the name of "art" to the compendium of the rules governing its use and to their technical order. If the object is merely contemplated under different aspects, the compendium and technical order of the observations concerning this object are called "science." Thus metaphysics is a science and ethics is an art. The same is true of theology and pyrotechnics.

Speculative and practical aspects of an art. From the preceding it is evident that every art has its speculative and its practical aspect: The former consists in knowing the principles of an art, without their being applied, the latter in their habitual and unthinking application. (Diderot & d'Alembert 1965. *Encyclopedia* [Nelly S. Hoyt & Thomas Cassirer, Trans.], 1:713)

knowledge of the science of art, could be developed and shared by teachers and students working in concert" (p. 29). The practice of formalized instruction in art around canonical content meant that art knowledge was codified, and although it was based on nature, it was sifted through the theories of master teachers.

Within the influential tradition of the French Academy of the 17th century art lectures and studio teaching, especially life drawing classes, not only clearly defined what content was discovered, but also who already had it, and who could access it. Even the depiction of human emotion and passion through facial expression was indexed to standards of practice.

Drawing the Passions, from *The Elements of Drawing in All Its Branches*, Plate IV, etching after Charles LeBrun. Yale Center for British Art, Paul Mellon Collection.

The onset of the machine age saw the academic tradition become more of a service agency for the new manufacturing industries where drawing became aligned with design skill. Art techniques, therefore, were much like writing and could be taught to everyone as a life skill and not be seen as merely a cultural pursuit. This vocationalism saw artistic practice broaden considerably to embrace new roles such as the artist-as-technologist, analyst, illustrator, communicator, and researcher. As a visual recorder the artist used new techniques, such as engraving, aquatint, and printing, to document and order the wonders of new discoveries as well as depictions of antiquities and mythic histories. These detailed dioramas were didactic as they also described a way of thinking and helped others get a sense of the inductive world of newly classified things. In discussing the extraordinarily detailed etchings of Giambattista Piranesi, Barbara Stafford (1996) explains that

> he [Piranesi] trained the observer, as he trained himself, in the fine art of probability, that skill in estimating the unknown by knowledgeably judging a maze of seemingly isolated and dispersed objects. The architect-etcher began by anatomizing, or visually separating, parts, and ended by organically synthesizing what he dismembered into a heroic span of views. (pp. 32–33)

Stafford makes similar connections in the way that artistic practice mirrored the mindful activity of these times. For instance, the study of anatomy saw the artist-as-analyst at work in much the same way as the rational philosopher where "dissection interrogated the inert body by violently laying it bare—much like the deductive dismembering of a coherent thought by a syllogism" (pp. 36–37). So art was a visual tool for reasoning.[5] And as the range of artistic practice expanded, the relationship among the art object, artist, and the viewer also changed. Those in control of the cultural production promoted the social and educational function of art whereby viewing, collecting, and contemplating, art enjoyed a new status. As Stafford explains, "eighteenth century technology encouraged the privatization of pleasurable beholding" (1996, p. 24). This privileged-class belief in the cultural capital of art from the past differed from the practices of the journeyman artisan who satisfied local utilitarian needs. As a result, the distinction between art as a scholarly study, versus art as practical pursuit, was further ruptured.

The fledgling mindset that emerged during the Enlightenment as an exploring, explaining, and expressive icon of the times radically changed the way we saw our place in the grand scheme of things. The *procedural* mind became habit-forming yet constrained by the unerring belief in a rule-governed world. The *probing* mind, on the other hand, was sharpened by intellect and intuition and expanded the idea of what inquiry was all about. The *provincial* mind traveled and trekked around the globe but was mostly blind to the perspective of others. And while the *pious* mind sought refuge in the safe haven of moral certitude, its zealous cousin, the *polemical* mind, often confused argument with blind faith. Yet it was this diversity of dispositions that propelled us toward modernism.

● PROMISE OF PROGRESS

By the 19th century, a legacy of cultural practices, institutional procedures, and individual passions created a kind of bipolar world of ideas, images, and ideologies. The excitement of modernity and the pursuit of progress by European ambition were muted by social upheaval and dispossession experienced by non-Western cultures on an unprecedented scale. The triumph of science was tempered by moral campaigns that often featured denial rather than debate. New alliances continued to be forged between scientific and artistic inquiry, yet these later became unstable when they were institutionalized educational practices. The evolving modern age of ideas therefore can be seen as a time of competing canons. Even within the visual arts, pivotal distinctions became reified as art was variously seen as an individual gift, a cultural collectible, a social nicety, a vocation, or a profession in need of a home.

Identity Crisis in Art and Culture

An insight into the uncertainty facing artists and social commentators in the mid-19th century can be discerned from the popular commentary of the time, as well as from textbook descriptions that rationalized topical issues for general education. In the eastern United States, small-scale newspapers such as *The Independent* and *The Christian Union* captured the dilemmas faced as modernism challenged conceptions previously seen to be immutable. Reflecting this breadth of discussion were educational texts of the time. On the one hand, scientific treatises such as Draper's *Text-Book on Chemistry: For the Use of Schools and Colleges*[6] (1852) presented a comprehensive exposition of current knowledge in lecture and question format where the primacy of the scientific method was exalted. On the other hand, *Paley's Moral and Political Philosophy* (Valpy, 1838) continued to be popular, yet it took a different stance. This was a standard theological text used in schools and colleges for classes in philosophy and civil debates where the predominant feature was the use of the authority of the Scriptures as the basis on which to guide reasoning. Of interest is the way philosophy was defined as a science based on logical reasoning, yet the principles of ethical human behavior were based on religious doctrines and integrated into laws of the land as systems guiding moral and political action.[7]

Debates about morality, society, and education, and the impact on foundational knowledge as explained by science and represented by art were as deep as they were divisive. In discussing the moral nature of belief, *The Independent*[8] newspaper (1875) editorialized that logical reasoning and skeptical inquiry were incapable of adequately defining the basis of truth. Argument was seen to have its place, but the resolution of doubts and debates could only be found in an appeal to the conscience, not in logical critiques. The Church took a leading role in exploring and explaining phenomena, whether scientific, philosophical, or spiritual, by claiming the moral high ground. The editor of *The Independent,* Henry C. Bowen, put it this way:

> Speculatively, religion is in no worse plight than the most assured of the sciences; and if it prove itself powerful to cast out devils and reform the devilish it will need no other defense. And this it can never do by argument; but only by direct appeal to the moral nature, which is always on God's side. (December 30, 1875, p. 15)

This moral stance that posed a dilemma of sorts for religion was seen as both conservative in its obvious invocation of the past, yet liberal in the necessity to deal with the realities of the day. But for some, it was not a problem at all. The Reverend Julius H. Ward of Massachusetts[9] found fault, not with liberalism's aim of seeking truth, but with the method he described as "free inquiry," which ignores the creeds and doctrines of the church and as such discounts the past as a way to inform the present and the future. The use of a moral imperative to support arguments about the role of the arts in coming to understand everyday life was, of course, a central theme of the times and loudly proclaimed by many. For instance, the impact of the views of leading advocates such as John Ruskin is easy to underestimate. His particular passion and rhetoric traveled far, and while his advocacy for the moral function of art slowly ebbed under the iron weight of mechanization, his scrupulous faith in nature never did.[10]

The austerity and provincialism of Victorian views toward art gave rise to broader perspectives ushered along by an inquisitive middle class. This was brought into focus in part by exhibitions of collections and other curiosities and the popularity of public lectures. The widespread availability of books, newspapers, and magazines also brought to prominence images to match the ideas and did much to unite and divide popular opinion on all sorts of topics. The role of artists as reporters and recorders of events, and respondents and advocates of wider visions, placed them well within social and cultural debates.

Discipline Dilemmas

Although the model of the art academy popularized in Europe was only adapted in a few places in the young American republic (Hubbard, 1963), later industrialization and cultural seepage did prompt the development of formalized education. As Howard Singerman (1999) points out, the fine arts entered higher education in the form of art history and often in association with disciplines such as anthropology and classical studies.[11] Even when introduced as drawing in elementary schools, art served mostly an instrumentalist role where its value lay in the expected impact on the design of manufactured goods.[12] As the concept of higher education became more readily established within American society, the role of art became less clear amid the competing interests. Whether it was the ideals of a broad knowledge base provided by liberal arts colleges, the more technical and professional scope of state institutions, or the fundamental knowledge sought by the research-oriented private universities, artists and art educators could not quite decide what they should be doing.

The prevailing attitude around the mid- to late 19th century that had a tenacious hold, and generally still does, proclaims that because artists cannot be "made," all that can be taught is method or other professional pursuits. In some contexts this meant the standardization of theory and practice as enacted in the academies (Pevsner, 1973). For others the structure of formalized art history made it relatively easy to graft the study of art onto the institutional frameworks of classical inquiry that variously focused on the art object or the experience of it (Minor, 1994). Then there were those who saw studio practice as a form of cultural expression and the opportunity to bring the art studio onto the campus was a way to broaden its relevance beyond the usual roles as a solitary pursuit, or a social nicety, or as a form of technical training. But despite the many forms by which visual arts were introduced into educational institutions, the profession remained hung up on the old question about whether art was something that was learned, or made.

At issue here is the question of how visual arts contributed to the cultural production of knowledge. The vexed question of the provisional status of knowledge was precisely what was worrying the theorists at the time, whether in theology, science, technology, or art, and this meant that no discipline could ignore the relentless challenge to the most basic of assumptions. Daniel Dennett (1995) gives one such example with his reminder of the value of the systematic and rigorous search for alternative hypotheses, the classic example being Charles Darwin. At the time of Darwin's musings over his collections it was believed that only a God could be responsible for such impressive design as that found in nature. But, as Dennett notes, by looking at the *same* dataset, Darwin came up with a highly plausible, but distinctly *different* explanation: natural selection. Darwin's insight confirmed the ideas of like-minded scientific observers and the impact across disciplines was dramatic. Cultural theorists took claim over this model of development whereby individual growth was believed to "recapitulate" that of the species, yet this gave rise to spurious views when linked to developmental profiles of races (Gould, 1981). Education also gained a sequential model of human development so that by the end of the 19th century, Herbert Spencer was able to articulate the view that educating children should proceed from the "simple to the complex . . . from the indefinite to the definite . . . from the particular to the general . . . from the concrete to the abstract . . . from the empirical to the rational" (cited in Egan, 1999, p. 86).[13]

Nineteenth Century Artworld

Although the presence of influential advocates such as John Ruskin and others had a naturalizing impact on art education, the heavy hand of authority was also felt in other areas. The ubiquitous voice of Ruskin was also used as a warranty to convince provincial minds of the importance of innovative cultural practices. Arthur Danto (2001a) describes how the Pre-Raphaelite Brotherhood, a small group of American artists and supporting critics active around the 1860s, made expert use of Ruskin's ideology of moral and visual truth as a marketing strategy to advance their position as innovative artists of the time. Their actions set in place many of the practices that would later come to characterize the artworld. According to Danto, the Victorian artworld "more or less invented the idea of the hot artist, the art movement, the breakthrough, the press release, the manifesto, the buzz of sensational openings, and the idea that art must be set upon a new path" (2001a, p. xxii).

The idea of the art connoisseur as an artistic dilettante was not new, but the idea that an art critic not only had a review role, but also could help direct trends was a modernist conception that endured well into the next century. The art reviews published in *The Nation* (Meyer, 2001), a weekly magazine that began publication in 1865 and is still being printed, serve as a documentary that maps how art struggled to define itself amid the onslaught of so much new art that appeared in the latter part of the 19th century. Once the yoke of the reactionary mindset was revoked, the task of addressing issues of value made it hard to assess what art was good and not so good. The tendency not to be able to see beyond rather simplistic dichotomies persisted for a long time so that a critic, when confronting an unusual image or object, could only ever see it for its lack of skill rather than consider it, perhaps, in terms of innovation. A case in point is the way Rodin confounded the Paris critics in 1898 with the monumental simplicity of his sculpture of Balzac, which, for many, could only be seen for what it was *not:* it was *not* a skillfully modeled representation.

Some critics, however, really did take a close look. In a review of a large exhibition of the French Impressionists shown in London in 1905, the critic "N. N.," which was a *non de plume* for Elizabeth Robins Pennell, gave a new sense of how the art of a new age might be considered. Seeing the work on view with the benefit of brief historical distance and her insightful eye, she was able to reassess the innovative contribution of this loose group of artists in a way few other critics of the time could. In particular, she sought to dispel the myth that the Impressionists were incompetent artists. Elizabeth Pennell pointed out other, larger issues, and it is worth quoting her at length:

> But the most defiant Impressionists, in their eagerness to see Nature for themselves, to avoid known types, to express their own personality— in their determination never to compose a picture, never to arrange Nature—rebelled against everything that had gone before, in theory at least. . . . To see Nature for themselves meant inevitably to record it for themselves in their own way, and the methods they evolved in the attempt to put upon canvas effects no one had before attempted, bewildered the critics, who could not look below the method, and the then startling results, to underlying principles. That was why Impressionism was denounced as a short cut, a labor-saving device for the artist who was too indolent or conceited to go through the usual training and apprenticeship as student. That such a reproach should have been made against it seems incredible, now that the excitement has calmed down. In an exhibition like the present, nothing strikes one so much as the fact that knowledge, experience, and technical skill are the solid foundation for the most daring experiments of the men who wanted to use their eyes for themselves, and to say what they had to say in their own fashion. (Cited in Meyer, 2001, p. 82)

In an article in the *New York Times* in 1999, Richard Panek nicely captures the mood of this time when art and science seemed to be indistinguishable in their empirical explorations using the senses. Yet their methods differed, and "to the scientist fell the purely objective, the masses and motions that led to universal laws; to the artist, the purely subjective, the individual responses that spoke to universal truths" (p. 1). By the late 19th century it seemed the inevitable deterministic conclusion was in sight: Artists were focusing on irreducible elements such as Seurat's pixels of paint, Cezanne's underlying structures, and a little later, Malevich's squares and Kandinsky's lines, points, and planes. In science, the microscope and telescope were tracking and cracking basic structures and later Ernest Rutherford's splitting of the atom took us further than ever into the new world of pure form. This followed a pattern where "for hundreds of years, scientists had been investigating the natural world and artists interpreting those results on a human scale" (Panek, 1999, p. 39).

But knowledge was making uncertain progress. The physicists followed the mathematicians to search out abstract theoretical worlds. They were looking to construct theories that might correspond to the increasingly uncertain observations of the natural world that had previously been able to be quantified. This was a world where

> a wave could be a particle, mass was energy and space was time. Music lost its melody, literature its linearity, painting—once again providing the most revealing illustration—its perspective. . . . When scientists abandoned sense evidence for the pure ether of theory, they left the rest of us behind. (Panek, 1999, p. 39)

The parallel quest of artists and scientists sought to see the world in new ways, but when science turned to theory, art could not keep up, and things split.

FRACTURED REALITIES ●

The indecision about inquiry in the 19th century that shook faith in the old and saw uncertainty in the new was eclipsed by an aggressive confidence that sharpened the conceptual, creative, and cultural divides in the 20th century. Embedded in this was the unresolved role of the artist as a professional and an academic along with the uneasy relationship between the artworld of commercial interests and the institutional artworld. Even at the beginning of the 20th century, those teaching in colleges and art schools were barely beginning to apply the insight about art expressed so eloquently by Ralph Waldo Emerson in 1841.

> Because the soul is progressive, it never quite repeats itself, but in every act attempts the production of a new and fairer whole. . . . Thus in our fine arts, not imitation but creation is the aim. . . . The artist must employ the symbols in use in his day and nation to convey his enlarged sense to his fellow-men. Art is the need to create. . . . Art should exhilarate, and throw down the walls of circumstance on every side, awakening in the beholder the same sense of universal relation and power which the work evinced in the artist. (cited in Logan, 1955, p. 43)

An ongoing quest that shaped the way visual arts was formed into institutional regimes was the professionalization of the field during the 19th century. As had been the pattern observed in the past, the consolidation of views around agreed visions meant a nod in the direction of standardization of theory and practice. The early efforts at finding a space within higher education often meant the visual arts were variously seen as a place to practice art history, a hamlet in the humanities, a technical vocation, or a form of cultural cleverness that carried with it a moral signature. Even as a curriculum subject in schools, art education could never quite rid itself of its instrumental appeal as drawing first became industrialized, pictures had the capacity to move morals, and art was an activity for the hand and not the mind. It was not until the innocence of vision found among the art of children and non-Western cultures was aligned with the need for artists to see the world anew that expression challenged impression as a favored educational philosophy. Eventually the relentless quest among artists and scientists to get to the heart of the matter meant that the new formalisms of vision had an essence of their own.

Artists Are Found, Not Made

Debates among art factions in the early decades of the 20th century could not quite resolve how best to define art learning. For the art historians, art practice meant learning about art, while artists needed to make art. Lurking just below the surface, however, was the imponderable problem that remains in the minds of many: Artists are found, not made. Consequently any attempt to institutionalize art learning could at best offer technical and professional training, or broaden the liberal sprinkling of art historical awareness, or open pathways seen as less creative such as art teaching. For professional organizations such as the College Art Association (CAA),[14] the choice was clear: The educational future of visual arts study at the university level lay in the contribution to be made to knowledge and thereby adapted the conventions of scholarly practice. The college survey course in art history became the signature imprint of what it was to study art. To train those who made art, on the other hand, was best left to art schools and liberal arts colleges.

What was obvious to advocates that sought an active role for artists within the burgeoning field of higher education was that the practicing artist had the necessary expertise to cover content that bridged studio experience, art historical themes, and philosophical issues. This, after all, was what the contemporary artist was seriously engaged in; therefore the preferred pedagogical approach was to surround the artist-teacher with aspiring students who would benefit from substantive exchanges on topics about art and life. This version of the expert-novice model relied on the image of the artist as a social outsider

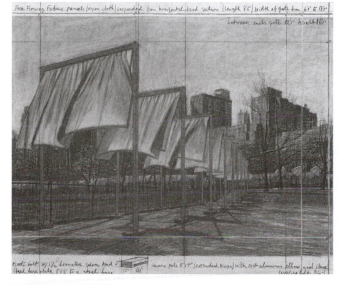

Christo, *The Gates Project for Central Park, New York City* (Collage, 2003). In two parts: 30.5 × 77.5 and 66.7 × 77.5 cm. Pencil, fabric, charcoal, wax crayon, pastel, enamel paint, hand drawn map, fabric sample and tape. Photograph by Wolfgang Volz. © Christo, 2003. Reproduced courtesy of the artist.

In words that echo Ralph Waldo Emerson, who in 1841 said that "the artist must employ the symbols in use in his day and nation to convey his enlarged sense to his fellow-men . . . Art should exhilarate and throw down the walls of circumstance on every side," Christo and Jeanne-Claude (2000) offer their response in talking about their artworks:

The temporary quality of the projects is an AESTHETIC DECISION. In order to endow the works of art with the feeling of urgency to be seen, and the tenderness brought by the fact that it will not last. Those feelings are usually reserved for other temporary things such as childhood and our own life, those are valued because we KNOW they will not last. These feelings of love and tenderness Christo and Jeanne-Claude want to offer to their works, as an added value, (dimension) as a new aesthetic quality. (p. 24)

There is an inherently educational experience located within the art practice of Christo and Jeanne-Claude. Like their art, personal meaning is negotiated through a process that is partly charged by immediate experience, but all the while built around ongoing growth and change. (Graeme Sullivan and Lisa Hochtritt, 2001)

engaged in an intense pursuit of a personal vision. As such, curriculum content could not be specified in any formal way, nor techniques introduced as prerequisites for creativity; teaching became conversation, and learning focused on individual aesthetic problem solving. Consequently the criteria for "newness" was not seen in relation to past or existing image banks or stylistic brands, but by the extent of radical difference. The drive toward the illusion of "things never seen" reached mythical status that kept the social constructedness of art practice at bay, at least until the theoretical onslaught of postmodernism.

By the mid-20th century the image of the artist-teacher was being battered on several fronts and yet the place of the visual arts in higher education continued to expand, even if the studio spaces remained mostly far removed from mainstream academic life. In the wake of regular reviews of the cultural and educational role of visual arts, the CAA saw the necessity to control the professional profile of artists amid the rapid expansion of campus programs. The image was built on the basis that the artist was indeed an autonomous professional who possessed cultural capital that could be traded in educational settings. The association monitored peer practices so as to maintain accreditation responsibilities and political patronage. Part of the stipulation governed the teaching qualifications of university bound artist-teachers whereby the master of fine arts (MFA) was deemed the entry credential into university teaching, while any form of educational degree was a distinct liability. Even by the latter decades of the 20th century, artists were still believed to be "found" in bachelor of arts (BA) and MFA programs, but certainly not among the general art education crowd, so the role of teaching in any strict sense of the term was irrelevant. To assume that teaching might be a requirement for viable institutional programs in visual arts was an anathema for many who saw the elusive language of the "crit" and the art of writing an artist statement as about as formal as instruction could get (Kent, 2001). In terms of inquiry, the student in this setting became a "searcher" seeking artistic identity, rather than a "researcher" in any broader way. Other theoretical, cultural, and political changes, however, further challenged the reified practices surrounding institutionalized art education.

Art Meanings Are Made, Not Found

Several metaphors characterize the patterns of change that occurred as the visual arts responded to modernist moves, and later to postmodern perspectives. These images chart the elusive impact of theory as paradigm principles and discipline links were first secured, and then separated. Three dominant themes relate to conceptions of *seeing,* notions of *structure,* and the discourse about *context,* and these map how visual arts expanded as a profession, as a site for cultural production, and as a discipline.

From Seeing to Knowing

Seeing, of course, has always been central to the sensory-based traditions of the visual arts and arguments about educational purpose. For instance, changing notions about seeing moves from ideas about the "innocent eye" to the "trained eye" to the "knowing eye." This transition might be described as a move from a time when vision involved seeing things in new and fresh ways, to a period where the process of visualization could be formalized and educated, and on to the present where it is necessary to know how vision is mediated and constructed.

The notion that the eye was capable of capturing innocent visions that could be expressed in artistic abstractions took many versions. For some, childhood was a site of profound cultural symbolism as might be seen in the art of Marc Chagall; or a universal language as described by Wassily Kandinsky; or as an ideographic form as explored by Paul Klee; or later as a liberating creative process as modeled by Jean Dubuffet.[15] Many of these conceptions, however, were as much a product of the social attitudes of the time as they were believed to be radical ways of seeing. For instance, early interest in the naïve simplicity and exuberant essence of child art was linked to the expressive power of non-Western image making. Yet this convenient coupling merely satisfied the view that child art, like that produced by "primitive" cultures, was shaped by a compulsive urge to create in ways that were innocent and imaginative. This version of ethnocentrism took its dubious moral warrant from recapitulationist theory that saw the pattern of individual growth as mirroring the development of the species. As such, the innocence of childhood matched the simplicity of non-Western cultures and both were presumed to occupy a space at the low end of a stagelike model of progress. The impact of such views on artistic mythology and educational practice cannot be underestimated and was felt well through to the mid-20th century as various explanatory psychological theories were drafted into service to ground the expressive paradigm.[16]

The pervasive interest in all things visual that was part of historical, empirical, and artistic inquiry saw the emergence of the artist as a cultural lamplighter. In his text, *The Mirror and the Lamp,* Abrams (1971) describes the modernist artist as an innovative change agent whose imaginative practice illuminates in ways that encourages others to see things differently. This model of the visual artist was used to claim a new professional status that linked modern art to notions of innovation and progress. Whereas the characteristic stance of those interested in the historical traditions of the fine arts by necessity involved looking back, those creating art amid the heady days of modernism were excited by the prospect of seeing ahead. Insights into the physiology of vision and the psychology of perception meant that the science of sight and the creativity of the eye were related, as were the practices of the scientist and the artist. Therefore by aligning the process of artistic inquiry with the reductive methods of science, elements of the visual arts could be identified, structured, and formalized, and the title of influential texts clearly defined how *composition* (Dow, 1899/1998) and *design and form* (Itten, 1964) came to constitute a *language of vision* (Kepes, 1944).

The linking of fine arts with art historical inquiry, and the visual arts as a term to describe studio practices, made it easier to maintain distinctions among institutional programs in universities, colleges, and art schools. The prominence of formalist aesthetics taking hold in classrooms and studios gave new impetus to theory and practice. Conceptualizing art as a language of forms meant that content could be defined and curriculum designed. What became internalized was a framework of art knowledge based on a formalist language of art that everyone could learn. Aesthetic principles were explicit. As professionals steeped in studio experience, the artist-teacher, working in studio classrooms, could engage students in visual explorations and problem solving. Teaching principles were also clear. The dual demands of formalist inquiry and expressionist insight could be resolved in the studio classroom whereby the structure and language of form served as a vehicle for individual discovery. In a paradoxical way, it was asserted that principles and formalisms could be used to give voice to individual vision, as captured in Paul Klee's image of the artist as a natural creator of new forms.

Paul Klee on Modern Art

May I use a simile, the simile of the tree? The artist has studied this world of variety and has, we may suppose, unobtrusively found his way in it. His sense of direction has brought order into the passing stream of image and experience. This sense of direction in nature and life, this branching and spreading array, I shall compare with the root of the tree.

From the root the sap flows to the artist, flows through him, flows to his eye.

Thus he stands as the trunk of the tree.

Battered and stirred by the strength of the flow, he moulds his vision into his work.

As, in full view of the world, the crown of the tree unfolds and spreads in time and space, so with his work.

Nobody would affirm that the tree grows its crown in the image of its root. Between above and below can be no mirrored reflection. It is obvious that different functions expanding in different elements must produce vital divergences.

But it is just the artist who at times is denied those departures from nature which his art demands. He has even been charged with incompetence and deliberate distortion.

And yet, standing at his appointed place, the trunk of the tree, he does nothing other than gather and pass on what comes to him from the depths. He neither serves or rules—he transmits.

His position is humble. And the beauty at the crown is not his own. He is merely a channel.

. . . The creation of a work of art—the growth of the crown of the tree—must of necessity, as a result of entering into the specific dimensions of pictorial art, be accompanied by distortion of the natural form. For, therein is nature reborn. (1948, pp. 13–19)

Making Connections

The transition of ways of conceiving visual imaging that moved from notions of the innocent eye, to the trained eye, to the knowing eye was confirmed by two different sources in the later decades of the 20th century. Evidence from clinical studies in cognitive science gave a fuller picture of the science of vision. And insights from literary discourse and cultural inquiry gave a more comprehensive understanding of how the interpretation of visual images as texts is framed and mediated by personal and social contexts.

The outcomes of neuropsychological and behavioral studies of visual cognition rejected the concept of isomorphism, which maintained that images were perceived holistically as a "gestalt." This principle influenced the way vision was seen as a process of perceptual organization that was adopted by art teachers who saw visual training as exercises in the language of vision. However, the brain gives meaning to what the eye sees. For those who study connections among the senses, thoughts, and feelings, perception is a cognitive process of active, mindful, meaning making (Arnheim, 1969; Scheffler, 1991). As Nelson Goodman (1978) reminds us, "conception without perception is merely *empty,* perception without conception is *blind*" (emphasis in the original, p. 6). Therefore, the world we see is given meaning by the world we know. But rather than the serial processing of visual forms as symbols that deploy some neural structural software, the process is much less rule governed and more dynamic as networks of potential meanings are sourced. This "connectionist" (Bechtel & Abrahamsen, 1991) model of information processing is activated by an encounter with sensory input where a problem is perceived, and interpretations produced from an array of parallel neural activity as meanings are made. Robert Solso (1994) explains:

> If our brain knows the external world—the world that exists outside of human cognition and imagination—through sensory experiences (among which vision is very important), then our impressions are funneled through the narrow band of electromagnetic energy to which the eye is sensitive . . . our cognitive life—the life that exists within the mind—is largely a composite of sensory experiences and the unique way those experiences are combined through the exchange of neurological signals by the brain. (p. 45)

Other scientists, who John Brockman (1995) defines as "third-culture thinkers" (p. 18),[17] also describe the dynamic way that information is processed and speak to ideas and images that cut across discipline boundaries, not only in the content covered, but also in the flexible way interpretations and meanings are made. In most of these cases, the scientists could well be talking about the visual arts. For instance, the computer scientist Roger Schank says that information processing is about surprises and it is from the unexpected that we learn. When Marvin Minsky and Seymour Papert were looking for images to conceptualize their ideas about artificial intelligence, they realized there was no single structure on which they could model their smart machine. Their "society-of-mind" theory made use of multiple structures and variable resources. As Minsky says, "Maybe you can't understand anything unless you understand it in several different ways, and that the search for the single truth—the pure, best way to represent knowledge—is wrongheaded" (cited in Brockman, 1995, p. 163). According to Minsky you need several different ways to represent something in order to understand it and to be able to apply it because things around you change all the time. Using mathematical examples, Ian Stewart's book, *Nature's Numbers* (1995), discusses how mathematics goes beyond "rigid laws" to embrace "flexible flux" (p. 47). The implication is that knowing laws and formula about how something might work is not enough. As Stewart would say, "fix and flux" coexist.

Framing Interpretations

Another area that gives credence to the knowing eye as a contemporary conception of how visual images are produced and understood comes from language-based theories of interpretation. Along with the neuropsychological construct of the seeing brain, and psychological descriptions of cognitive scripts (Schank & Abelson, 1977) that highlight the importance of prior knowledge as an agent that shapes meaning, similar notions are used in literary criticism and cultural discourse to explain how interpretations are framed. Scripts, schemas, or "frames" are available and accessible in meaningful chunks that help join the dots in coming to understand an event, action, or artifact. The principle at play is the flexible flux that Ian Stewart describes whereby meaning making is negotiated as interpretations are formed. In other words, meanings are made, not found. To explain the elegant economy in how we make judicious use of what we know to help make sense of what we see, literary and cultural theorists reframe the boundaries that influence how interpretations are made. By drawing attention to the varying ways that meanings can be recognized within textual sources and the references and contexts that surround them, the dynamic, interactive nature of the interpretive process is revealed. This differs markedly from a more modernist perspective that sees interpretation as an explanatory process that assumes meaning is inherent to a text or artifact and can be revealed if the reader or viewer has the requisite knowledge and perceptive skill.

Let me give an example from visual arts. One of the distinctions argued by the New Critics in literary theory around the middle of the 20th century that had such an impact on art criticism was that it was a fallacy to judge a work of art according to the meaning intended by the artist, be they poet or painter. Described and debated as the "intentional fallacy" (Wimsett & Beardsley, 1946/1971), the views suggested that meaning is invested in the capacity of the work itself and is inherent in its form and structure, which is independent and self-validating. In art circles, judgment of this kind in the eyes of astute and knowledgeable critics and teachers could be summed up in the authoritative claim, "It works!" But this instance of moving the interpretive focus away from the artist to the viewer remained mired in the mud of privileged reading. It wasn't until the formalist legacy was nudged aside that the full ensemble of meaning-making agencies and informing contexts could be appreciated. This dynamic view of interpretation is based on the assumption that the contexts that influence the way meanings are made are not a passive set of coordinates that situate an artwork in any prescribed time or place or point of view. Rather than being a "given," contexts themselves change according to the perspectives, connections, and settings surrounding the interpretive encounter. MacLachlan and Reid (1994) explain it this way:

> A text does not have a single meaning determined by a single context; given the interplay of different framings, contexts and therefore meanings are multiple. Thus the term "context" is often unsatisfactory, not only because it is too broad and imprecise to be of much use in clarifying what is at issue in interpreting texts, but also because its static connotations tend to obscure the dialectical nature of the text-context relationship. (p. 8)

Invented Realities

A similar distrust of the principle that contexts are static and meanings are found embedded within a phenomenon and able to be retrieved by astute analysis is evident in cultural theory. Changes in the positionality of those who study the human sciences reveal how cultural representations are constructions that rely as much on politics and poetics as they do on dispassionate descriptive accounts (Clifford & Marcus, 1986; Said, 1978). The rationalist model that sees cultural inquiry, even when enlivened by the view of the participant observers, is unable to maintain the myth of the insightful recorders who can see without themselves being seen. Instead, those who consider the field encounter as a site of problematic relations recognize "the centrality of the subjectivity of the researcher to the production and representation of ethnographic knowledge" (Pink, 2001, p. 19). These are dialogical accounts that give voice to the observed as well as the observer, and transform the research artifact "into a speaking subject, who sees as well as is seen, who evades, argues, probes back" (Clifford & Marcus, 1986, p. 14).

Conceptions of how inquiry needs to "speak back" are clearly evident in arguments presented by indigenous cultural theorists. Historically, those working with indigenous First Nations, Native Peoples, and Aboriginal cultures were unable to free research from the specter of colonialism and imperialism. In asking the basic question, "Whose research is it?" indigenous cultural theorists set in train a process of "decolonizing" Western research traditions in order to "escape the gaze" and to recenter the interpretive lens on indigenous conceptions. In doing so, the purpose is to take control of the survival of peoples, cultures, and languages. Linda Tuhiwai Smith (1999) explains:

> From an indigenous perspective Western research is more than just research that is located in a positivist tradition. It is research which brings to bear, on any study of indigenous peoples, a cultural orientation, a set of values, a different conceptualization of such things as time, space and subjectivity, different and competing theories of knowledge, highly specialized forms of language, and structures of power. (p. 42)

In reviewing an agenda of research projects undertaken by indigenous communities Linda Tuhiwai Smith identifies a pattern of practice that is action oriented, inclusive, and dynamic and that combines elements of mainstream methodologies and indigenous practices. The themes investigated, however, are decidedly invested within indigenous perspectives and present with eloquent power conceptions that deal with claiming, naming and remembering; negotiating, reframing and restoring; discovering and envisioning; creating, representing, and narrating; gendering, democratizing, and protecting; and connecting and networking.

The way knowledge might be visualized is now unable to be contained within the conceptual frameworks of rationalistic inquiry. The elusive scope of the digital landscape offers an intriguingly complex conceptual space that captures part of the metaphysical possibilities known to indigenous cultures, and the theoretical imagination for new ideas in science and art (Wilson, 2002). On the Internet many of the intriguing problems identified in postmodern discourse become more manifest as, for example, is the case with body politics, the de-centered self, cultural ruptures, and transdisciplinary excursions (Turkle, 1995). Digital technology serves as a site for inquiry where information is clearly no longer a form within which knowledge is found, nor a unit

Chakaia Booker uses old rubber tires to give form to social commentaries that address issues from black identity to urban ecology . . . Booker, however, extracts an intense concentration of meanings from the tires. Their black color signifies African skin, while their patterned treads resemble tribal decorations and the welts of ritual scarification. The tires' resilience and versatility represent, to Booker, the "survival of Africans in the diaspora" . . . Booker engages in a resourceful act of recycling, transforming one of today's most indestructible waste products into things of furious beauty. (Anderson, Auping, Cassel, Davies, Farver, Miller-Keller, & Rinder, 2000, p. 65)

In making meaning from the tires, their black color creates images of African skin while their patterned treads resemble tribal decorations and the essence of ritual scarification. (Chakaia Booker, personal correspondence, June 21, 2004)

Chakaia Booker, *It's So Hard to Be Green* (2000). 150 × 252 × 288 inches. Rubber tires and wood. Exhibited: The Whitney Museum of Art Biennial 2000. Reproduced courtesy of the artist and Marlborough Gallery. Photograph by Nelson Tejada.

of analysis that lends itself to neat manipulation or interpretation. Yet this uncertain realm of investigative opportunity is just the kind of place where artists, scientists, researchers, cultural theorists, and community activists are speaking to each other in a fresh language of images and ideas.

The radical mix of cultural, political, technological, and economic change now influencing research practice is therefore challenging visual artists, art teachers, and students in higher education to look more closely at what they do. No longer can the practices of the past that see the art studio as an isolated place in the academy be maintained. While cultural critics such as Robert Hughes (1993) can rail against the damaging ascendancy of theory over skill in art schools, these domains cannot of course be seen as mutually exclusive. Artists such as Chakaia Booker wrestle figuratively and physically with visual forms that embrace cultural and situational contexts as readily as they project formal skill and imaginative zeal. For Booker, the painter's multicolored palette has an inherent energy, and she sees tires as her palette. "On my palette," she says, "instead of having colors, it's the texture of tires. These textures, whether from the treads of the tires or how the tires have been ripped or torn, are my sources of energy to create my works of art." This idea that form could be content that goes beyond artistic areas helps extend our understanding of the challenge of living in a world beyond cultural borders, between debates about social roles, and within expressive technological means.

● CONCLUSION

The institutionalization of visual arts practice has a long and checkered history. In each era the formal training of the artist and art educator invariably created a schism between those within institutions who saw a need to uphold a canon, and those from without who challenged it. Many advocates of the training of artists see the marketplace of the commercial artworld as the arbiter that offers professional success, with institutions being mostly responsible for technical training. Those who seek academic status for the profession invariably have to respond to the challenge of setting creative practice on a more solid discipline foundation. As such, the university exerts its own agenda and in doing so helps shape an institutional artworld. The challenge is how to accommodate these demands yet also maintain a degree of integrity about what constitutes visual arts as a field of study. Yet questions surround the status of visual arts faculty within the academy, and this can be linked in part to a lack of credibility for the credential used to admit artists into higher education and the ambivalence in how they fulfill their role as teachers and researchers. For many, this is a perennial issue that continues to shape arguments about the relevance of the visual arts within institutions. The politics of what constitutes research in the visual arts lies at the heart of these dilemmas. The uncertainty of these times and the questions being asked about how the visual arts contribute to new knowledge suggest that there is no better time to act.

Economic globalization and political polarization continue to both unify and disrupt patterns of cultural change. The impact of widespread economic rationalist policies is keenly felt at the local level where the microeconomic reform of recent decades directly affects educational change. Whether through rationalization and accountability in higher education, or standardization in public schools, the model of education as a marketplace of performance continues to dominate.[18] If visions of education remain bereft of imagination, perhaps it is in cultural areas rather than factory models or management structures that hold the potential for profound and equitable change.

So where might an artistically challenging, socially relevant, economically viable, and culturally aware model of art education be found? A review of current systems yields several possibilities, and some of these are taken up later in this book. However, let me give two examples here. The Internet, of course, helped reinvent network communication that unleashed a flurry of "dot.com" activity as business ventures tried to capture the electronic marketplace. But it is the use of the Internet for nefarious purposes, such as zealotry, that exploit the capacity to set up secretive systems and market misinformation that is on the rise. Whereas the *McWorld* (Barber, 1996) of Western corporations maintain a hierarchical structure to carry their homogenized messages, the production of "ideology" takes place through an independent franchise that makes use of the rhizomatic nature of the Internet. And here the lure is emotional not economic, and it is an *idea* rather than an organization that carries the message. While not wanting to sanction the use of the Internet by extremists, there are many examples where the Web is used as an active network for communities such as artists, whereby a nonhierarchical structure actively encourages conversation at the local and global level.[19]

Another area where institutional and cultural practices are being reconceptualized in ways that offer promise for visual arts research is with curatorship in galleries and museums. Art curators, for instance, who seek to profile all perspectives, do not act as cultural poachers or postcolonial collectors. Rather, they see cultural and educational discourse as emanating from a multiplicity of centers where philosophical, economic, and political ideas form a basis for exchange, communication, and enactment. If theories and issues spark ideas, then a need to discuss them in order to create visions, structures, and methods becomes necessary. On the other hand, the need to deconstruct them is also critical, for perspective is knowingly or unknowingly framed around myths such as race, culture, gender, and class. This is the basis of "praxis," for theory without action is mere rhetoric, and action without theory is anarchy. And within this global perspective the logocentrism of the "center" as the primary source of insight and action is usurped. Shuddhabrata Sengupta, Dietz, Nadarajan, Bagchi, and Narula (2003) explain that those who believe they occupy the "center" are culpable of "asymmetry of ignorance." They add that "we, on the fringes of the global space, know more about the global space than those who are at its core know about us" (p. 49). So being on the edge rather than the center offers a better perspective. It is a discourse opened up by artists, curators, and the like who seek new forms of engagement with issues that nowadays not only explore the human condition, but who question the very design and function of the human body and mind, and this is raising the possibility for the visual arts to occupy a more central place in our world of knowing.

In the introduction to her "essays-manifestos" (1996, p. 9) that explore the new significance of visual images within the transdisciplinary cyber age, Barbara Stafford issues a challenge to art educators, historians, and artists to re-create a praxis of practice that is real and relevant. Eschewing the ennui of language-based regimes that reveal difficulties and dilemmas through a process of critique and deconstruction, Stafford argues that a more constructive stance is needed to "forge an imaging field focused on transdisciplinary *problems* to which we bring a distinctive, irreducible, and highly visible expertise" (p. 10, emphasis in the original). For Stafford, *not* to do so means that our image-based discipline as we know it is in danger of disappearing and "we confirm our irrelevance both within institutions of higher learning and in a decentralized electronic society" (p. 9). On the other hand, to act calls for some real risk-taking. And here Stafford issues her challenge:

> It is one thing to embrace the agendas, definitions, and theories provided by other disciplines—themselves, ironically, in the throes of blurring or dissolving—and quite another to reconceptualize visuality historically, and in the light of that past lens culture to devise crosscutting projects for the emergent cyberspace era. (pp. 9–10)

I take up Stafford's challenge in the remaining chapters of this book. The agendas, definitions, and theories that inform research methodologies in the social sciences and human sciences are not so much "embraced" but "embattled" as important similarities and differences in approaches to inquiry are contested and conceptualized. This provides a basis for arguing that the visual arts have an important contribution to make in the quest to know more, but that the approach to this shared goal follows a different path.

NOTES ●

1. For a discussion of arts-based research and arts-informed research, see Chapter 2.

2. A Monty Python skit from *The Quest for the Holy Grail* captures the tentative beginnings of scientific rationality that was soon to displace the medieval mind. An early scene shows a rabble of rowdy peasants hell-bent on burning a witch when they have the rationality of their actions questioned by Bedivere, a noble who later joined King Arthur on his trail for the grail. Bedivere asks the peasants, "What else burns besides witches?" to which they meekly respond, "Wood?" Therefore they deduce that maybe witches burn because they're made of wood. Bedivere asks *how* it might be determined if the witch is indeed made of wood. Various guesses are given before the peasants conclude that wood not only burns, but it also floats. And furthermore, a duck *also* floats. Therefore, they logically deduce that *if* the witch weighs the same as a duck, it means she *is* made from wood, and therefore she *is* a witch! Unfortunately for the young lady, when she is weighed the scales remain unmoved and medieval logic prevails, so she is taken off to be burned. This incident says something about the logical problem of false premises and false consequences. As their Greek predecessors knew, even if the mindful peasants didn't quite realize it at the time, "rational" thought can have irrational outcomes.

3. Giorgio Vasari's *Lives of the Artists* was first published in 1550 and a second enlarged edition was published in 1568. George Bull's translation was selected from the 1568 version and originally published in 1965.

4. Diderot and d'Alembert (1751/1965).

5. The need to communicate visually sometimes set in place myth and misconception as much as insight and imagination. Stephen Jay Gould (1991) provides a quirky example in his essay, *Petrus Camper's Angle*. Petrus Camper was an 18th century Dutch scientist whose career in anatomy saw him lauded as one of Europe's foremost authorities. But he was also a part-time painter. His interests in science and art led him to question the widespread depiction of religious iconography, such as the Black Magus, as a faithful copy with white European facial features. His annoyance with this visual inaccuracy led him to define specific guidelines for mapping the anatomical structure of the head of different races and nationalities. His primary indicator was the "facial angle" that represented a measure of the ratio of the differing flatness or extension of the profile of the head. What Gould also documents is the way that this cranial measure later became a quantitative index used for invidious purposes to depict inherent racial differences on a scale where the lowest facial angle was that of an ape, with mid angles being shown to be African, and the highest angle being a Grecian head. What was lost in historical translation in this insidious use is the original intent of Petrus Camper—his motive was artistic and his painterly and scholarly task was the definition of beauty.

6. The publishers, Harper & Brothers of New York, published an extensive series of school and college textbooks that included compilations in discipline areas

by prominent professors of the time. Some examples are *Professor Abercrombie's Philosophical Works; Professor Loomis's Mathematical Series;* and the extensive collection of *Professor Anthon's Series of Classics.*

7. An example of how this kind of thinking influenced ideas of the time is the view regarding the possession of land, considered to be "real" property because of the increasing resource potential and investment value. Those areas without documented details of ownership could be freely acquired for, "as God has provided the ground for all, he has given leave to any to take what he pleases, (if not previously possessed,) without any kind of consent from others" (Valpy, 1838, p. 73). This enabled the principle of *terra nullius,* for instance, to be enacted, which proclaimed that certain tracts of land were not owned by anyone. This had devastating consequences for indigenous cultures in particular because, according to Paley's tome, there were "no traces of property in land . . . amongst the savages of America or of Australia" (Valpy, 1838, p. 71).

8. *The Independent* was a weekly newspaper published in New York City by Henry C. Bowen, who was editor and proprietor. It had widespread circulation through yearly subscription and a regional agency in Chicago.

9. New England Liberalism, a column that paraphrased a sermon by Rev. Julius H. Ward, rector of St. Michael's church, Marblehead, Massachusetts, *The Independent,* August 10, 1876, p. 26.

10. John Ruskin enjoyed considerable influence on both sides of the Atlantic, as seen by an 1873 review of his small book on birds, *Love's Meinie*, published in the New York newspaper, *The Independent*:

> Eminent among recent books in interest is Mr. Ruskin's latest pamphlet, which is an essay on birds—their structure, their names, their modes of flying, and their use in nature and in art . . . it is in everyway charming reading, and is full of that acute observation and quick sympathy which makes no small part of Mr. Ruskin's genius. He has, more than other men, the gift of vision. He will pick up the commonest object, as here the robin's wing-feather, and point out features in it which are new to almost all of us, and wholly new as topics of interest in literature. His power of minute observation recalls that open secret which we see daily in our mirrors without seeing it—that the pupils of our eyes are not in the center of the iris, but a little inside of it. Whatever can be seen is noticed by Mr. Ruskin, and he knows how to tell what he has seen in the most attractive style. That he does not fall in with the popular majorities in his thought is a reason why we should read him more, rather than less. His writings are an invaluable minority report upon Christian civilization. (Minor Notices, November 13, 1873, p. 1418)

11. See Howard Singerman (1999), especially Chapter 1, "Writing Artists onto Campuses" (pp. 11–40). See also Chapters 3 through 5 of Guy Hubbard's (1963) doctoral dissertation.

12. For an account of the establishment of art as a subject in schools see Arthur D. Efland, (1990), especially Chapters 3 through 6. See also Don Soucy and Mary Stankiewicz (1990) and Peter Smith (1996).

13. There are alternatives to the dominant model of human development. In his delightfully titled book of essays, *Children's Minds, Talking Rabbits & Clockwork Oranges*, Kieran Egan (1999) recounts his argument that development moves from the complex to the simple. He places great faith in the capacity of children to understand complex things. This view highlights the significance of negotiating meaning through "story, metaphor, rhyme and rhythm, binary structuring and mediation, image formation from words, affective abstraction and so on" (p. 92).

14. The College Art Association (CAA) was established in 1912. For a brief history of its inception see Howard Singerman (1999).

15. See *The Innocent Eye* (1997) by Jonathan Fineberg. He traces parallels in the artistic practice of modern painters and the creative process of children by examining artists' collections of child art, related historical archives and accounts, and the innovative artworks of modernism.

16. The following quote from the New South Wales 1952 *Curriculum for Primary Schools* is a good example of how child-centered theories of artistic development subscribed to G. Stanley Hall's dictum of "ontogeny follows phylogeny" whereby individual growth repeats the developmental pattern of the entire species. In this case, early childhood is seen to be an immature or "primitive" phase of development:

> Primitive peoples, down the centuries, have achieved many fine examples of creative art. It is significant that this should have been done without the aid of formal teaching. The truth is that Art is more than culture; it is the expression, in particular in children and primitive people, of an otherwise inarticulate urge for self-expression. (p. 357)

17. The title of John Brockman's book, *The Third Culture* (1995), was coined in response to C. P. Snow's publication, *The Two Cultures* (1959/1993), which highlighted the cultural chasm between the humanities and the sciences that occurred during the early to mid-20th century as a clash between the "intellectuals" and the "boffins." Brockman's publication chronicles a series of conversations among a highly regarded group of scientists. Brockman describes them as "third-culture thinkers" (p. 18) who seem to be filling the gap identified by C. P. Snow decades ago and who speak directly to an interested public.

18. Conservative educational politicians and administrators believe that a social efficiency movement reminiscent of the early 20th century is a viable model for the early 21st century and that public education needs to be based on a form of neo-Fordism where standardized testing is the only way to control the quality of educational outcomes.

19. There are many artist-run, Web-based cooperatives whose common interests revolve around ideas, research, social action, community development, and the like. See, for example, www.sarai.net (last accessed on November 22, 2003).

CHAPTER 2

PARADIGMS LOST

As science became the manifesto of the Church of Reason,[1] a period was ushered in institutionalizing logical reasoning as the way to produce new knowledge. When mechanization began to shape our understanding of the physical world and human behavior, the arts were reduced to the role of mute bystanders. The hegemony of the sciences and the rationality of progress made it difficult for the visual arts to be seen as reliable sources of insight and understanding. Although there were radical flourishes as artists captured a vision of the new, to argue for novelty as an adequate outcome of the visual arts was seen as rather hapless.[2] Still, the creed of chic remained as dogged dogma in the art academies and in art schools, even though it had minimal influence on broader practices of inquiry. Yet by the close of the millennium the canons of science also faced debates and doubts that highlighted the need to conceive of more expansive notions of human understanding. For many, intriguing possibilities were to be found within the sociocultural collage of the arts and humanities and the virtual constructions opened up by the layered spaces of the new digital era.

This chapter explores two main themes. In the first section, *Method as Truth,* the principles on which the scientific method is used to codify knowledge is reviewed. Scientific inquiry proves to be a powerful and robust method for investigating the physical world and is readily adapted to the study of the social sciences once the normative nature of human behavior is accepted. But even as the study of human capacity remains difficult to capture using reductive models, a rational perspective on this otherwise unpredictable world can still be adapted according to the postpositivists (Phillips &

Burbules, 2000; Popper, 1968). A second theme covered in this chapter, *Doubting Doctrines,* examines and critiques positivist assumptions that were prevalent at the turn of the 20th century. Although questions about change and debates over practices (Kuhn, 1970; Feyerabend, 1993) continued to come from within the sciences, other direct and indirect challenges to the scientific paradigm come from postmodernism and critical theory. On a methodological level, qualitative research is seen as a philosophy of inquiry that challenges the reliance on positivism. These critiques base their argument on an interpretivist paradigm and offer new opportunities for researchers in the arts and humanities. However, if the importance of the visual arts as an agency of human knowing is to be fully understood, there is a need to seek an even broader conception of inquiry—one that is based on creative and critical perspectives.

To construct new ways to reconfigure old paradigms, it is argued that those in the arts need to be knowledgeable about methods of inquiry used in the sciences so that similarities and differences can be cogently articulated. This does not mean, however, that the methods of science are blandly accepted or blindly rejected. It means that insight is informed by perspective as much as it is by precision. In the early 19th century, Friedrich Froebel[3] proposed the principle of the "unity of opposites" to illustrate how knowledge is grounded in direct experience. For instance, children playing with wooden spheres and cubes come to understand a block is "square" by comparing these forms and realizing that it is *not* "round." This way of knowing sees things in oppositional form and is a useful heuristic that serves the visual arts well as a learning strategy and as a tool of inquiry. Although comparative analysis sharpens this kind of critical understanding and is the primary analytical device used in qualitative research, there is a need to maintain an even broader interpretive lens. By this I mean that changing contexts continually shapes how meanings are made. Artists and viewers, for instance, know that the "push and pull" of painterly forms creates a dynamic tension between the parts and the whole within and beyond the frame. Therefore, if the visual arts are to provide a way of coming to know the world that is real and relevant, any approach to inquiry should be compared with the methods of science, but not be a slave to them. As I state in the introduction to this book, rather than adopt methods of inquiry from the social sciences, visual arts research practices share similar goals in the quest to create new knowledge and understanding, but argue that these can be achieved by following different, yet complementary, paths. Consequently, there is a need to be aware of foundational principles of scientific methodology to fully understand and appreciate the many points of convergence and divergence between inquiry in the visual arts and the sciences.

METHOD AS TRUTH ●

Many subscribe to the view that the search for meaning becomes a tangible goal once the procedures used to determine truth are accepted and codified. While "meaning" may be an elusive construct that conjures up notions of "being" and relationships with the world of "things," the process of coming to know is generally understood as accessing and using new knowledge. The quest for knowledge consequently requires procedures to be put in place that serve as an agreed set of practices for a community of inquirers. Conceptions for codifying methods of scientific inquiry rest on basic philosophies and assumptions such as rationalism and empiricism. Like feuding cousins, these perspectives carry with them historical baggage that holds knowledge and truth to be either the outcome of rational deduction, or the inductive product of experience. Yet both serve as kindred spirits in maintaining a secure means for constructing knowledge.

Notwithstanding the revisionist tendencies of postpositivism in the latter half of the 20th century, the rationality of logical positivism has been the long-term trustee overseeing what is commonly known as the "scientific method." This approach to knowledge construction is perhaps the most powerful leitmotif of modernism and has high status as the emblem of progress. The firm focus on prescribed ways that knowledge is acquired means that methods of natural science can be applied to the social sciences. Deploying deductive logic allows arguments and testable propositions to be defined and investigated from which explanations, causal connections, or relational properties can be inferred and lawlike generalizations made. Within the scientific tradition it is readily accepted that things have causes, and while this notion may serve the natural sciences well, it is less convincing when applied to the human sciences. Identifying cause and effect has rich predictive power but human nature remains tantalizingly obscure in revealing underlying causal structures or discrete patterns of behavior. Cohen, Manion, and Morrison (2000) suggest that "where positivism is less successful, however, is in its application to the study of human behavior where the immense complexity of human nature and the elusive and intangible quality of social phenomena contrast strikingly with the order and regularity of the natural world" (p. 9).

Although the positivist paradigm is not without its critics much of the debates about inquiry rest on distinctions drawn between the scientific method in contrast to naturalistic or qualitative approaches. The latter, it is believed, provide a more realistic and relevant set of assumptions upon which research practice can be grounded. However, it is necessary to locate these conceptual differences within a framework that relies less on dichotomies of difference, or as somewhat pragmatic blends,[4] and more as connected forms of theory and practice if a way beyond the quantitative—qualitative debate is to be considered. The tendency to separate ways of thinking about the procedures of inquiry into opposing camps can be hard to dislodge if a more inclusive and holistic model of research is sought. As Natalie Jeremijenko's artwork, *Tree Logic,* shows, when our perceptions are radically disrupted, existing frames of reference are unable to account for the new experience. Although there is a need to consider alternative approaches to inquiry, a first step is to look more closely at certain beliefs that guide scientific inquiry so that areas of antagonism and alliance might be entertained.

Natalie Jeremijenko, *Tree Logic* (1999). Six live trees, metal armature, stainless steel planters, and telephone poles. Photograph by Douglas Bartow. Reproduced courtesy of MASS MoCA.

Natalie Jeremijenko is an artist-experimenter. *Tree Logic* displays the contrived growth responses of the trees over time. . . . Trees are dynamic natural systems, and *Tree Logic* reveals this dynamism. The familiar, almost iconic shape of the tree in nature is the result of gravitropic and phototropic responses: The tree grows away from the earth and toward the sun. When inverted, the six trees in this experiment still grow away from earth and toward the sun—so the natural predisposition of trees might well produce the most unnatural shapes over time, raising questions about what the nature of the natural is.

Our perceptions of trees change when we view them as a collection of growth responses rather than as immutable symbols of the natural world. The public for a work of art, and for *Tree Logic* in particular, is encouraged to interpret (and debate) motives and outcomes, though the opposite is often true of "real" science, which does not invite public discourse. Through her elaborate framing systems Jeremijenko revels in exposing the idiosyncratic manipulation intrinsic to combining facts to form "data." Retrieved on December 14, 2003, from http://www.massmoca.org/visual_arts/visual_arts.html.

There are at least four principles I would like to discuss in more detail, because they guide scientific understanding and constitute a method of inquiry that has a pervasive influence on scholarly practices. *Rationality rules* describes a principal feature whereby logical reasoning is used as the means by which knowledge is investigated and reconstructed. Within this system of inquiry, the *codification of empiricism* provides a strategy for applying rigorous interventions as forms of experience are described, analyzed, and verified. Although the objectification of reality accepts that forms and experiences can be described as observable phenomena, taking into account *objective and subjective realities* is important in discussions about inquiry, and I take these up later. Finally, *essentialist (mis)conceptions* subscribe to the view that things around us have an inherent nature or an "essence," which makes it possible to identify and study particulars from which general outcomes can be predicted once they are subjected to rational and empirical analysis. There is merit in exploring the central tenets, as they are often used to distinguish differences between research methodologies as systems of beliefs about reality, knowledge, and relationships. So what are these foundational principles that are so revered?

Rationality Rules

To fully understand scientific paradigms as something more than prescriptions for inquiry there is a need to be aware of the underlying conceptions upon which they are based. These parameters reflect beliefs about ontology (reality), epistemology (knowledge), and axiology (values). Ontological assumptions are concerned with the nature or essence of the social phenomena being investigated that deal with definitions of reality. In answer to questions about "what is real," a scientific rationalist will claim that things exist independent of any human connection and therefore can be identified and studied. Assumptions about epistemology revolve around a conception of knowledge that is seen to be "real" in that it is based on sense experience that is confirmed by observation and experiment and from which understanding is acquired, accrued, and communicated. Assumptions about human nature and relationships with the environment accept that a deterministic, rule-governed world exists whereby understanding causality gives a firm basis for prediction and control. Although the quest for absolute truths is problematic, Dewey (1938) identified "warranted assertability" as a suitable substitute. In this sense, a warrant amounts to a reasonable cause. So the challenge of researchers is the quest for explanations that are well supported. This requires the collection of empirical data from which theoretical propositions can be deduced that may be provisional, but explain things in a verifiable and generalizable way.

In addition to these conceptions can be added the element of experience that helps frame what we know and don't know. These systems of thought are set up as hierarchies of knowledge that become reference points of authority and peer critique. Research, therefore, is a combination of experience and reasoning and a most pervasive form is the scientific method. The power of the scientific method is attributed to several characteristics and assumptions. For instance empiricism functions on the expectation that data will confirm or refute hypotheses in terms of probability whereby it can be claimed that an outcome is *probably* the result of the designed intervention, and not the result of chance or error. The exercise of control and concerns of validity and reliability, reductive design, use of representative samples, and operationalizing concepts that allow for the manipulation and measurement of key variables provides a robust model that can be replicated and checked by others. This helps maintain a mantle of objectivity and contributes to the self-correcting feature of ongoing inquiry upon which the scientific edifice is built.

In considering the practice of research, there is a need to distinguish between "method" and "methodology." I subscribe to the view of Morrow (1994) among others, who see methodology in a philosophical sense as a broader explanatory system of theory and practice within which certain methods, or forms of inquiry, are nested.

> The term *methods* refer more specifically to individual techniques (e.g., surveys, participant observation), whereas *methodology* can be construed broadly to suggest both the presuppositions of methods, as well as their link to theory and implications for society. Methodology, in short, more clearly implies a concern, an overall *strategy* of constructing specific types of knowledge and is justified by a variety of metatheoretical assumptions. (Emphasis in original, p. 36)

These methodological principles and methods of practice are well described in introductory research texts and need not be repeated in detail here.[5] However, the way rationally argued propositions are investigated and tested by empirically grounded knowledge needs to be explored further.

Codification of Empiricism

The belief that experience and the senses are a source of knowledge that can be objectified and studied has an enduring legacy but is also open to ready caricature. For instance, the reliability of the senses as a site upon which knowledge is grounded has long been treated with suspicion, as it is easy to show that the senses play tricks on what we know. Another stereotype of empiricism is the assumption that empirical procedures are only used in conjunction with scientific inquiry and "is associated exclusively with variable analysis, as if ethnographic research was not empirical" (Morrow, 1994, p. 32). As a way of knowing, empiricism takes data grounded in human experience and makes sense of it by subjecting it to rituals of analysis and verification. Therefore empiricism not only offers a systematic method of investigating elements of experience and phenomena, but the outcomes can be readily assessed against the cumulative record of what is already known.

Modeled on various forms of logical reasoning empiricism was progressively refined by the who's who of Western philosophy when inductive inquiry was added to the discussions. This deceptively simple procedure now has canonical status as the means by which questions are raised, conjectures or hypotheses posed that can be empirically tested, and consequences confirmed or refuted as probable outcomes. Robert Pirsig's (1974/1999) travelogue of the mind describes this scientific method with elegant reference to his motorcycle metaphor. His description is worth quoting at length.

> Two kinds of logic are used, inductive and deductive. Inductive inferences start with observations of the machine and arrive at general conclusions. For example, if the cycle goes over a bump and the engine misfires, and then goes over another bump and the engine misfires, and then goes over another bump and the engine misfires, and then goes over a long smooth stretch of road and there is no misfiring, and then goes over a fourth bump and the engine misfires again, one can logically conclude that the misfiring is caused by the bumps. That is induction: reasoning from particular experiences to general truths.
>
> Deductive inferences do the reverse. They start with general knowledge and predict a specific observation. For example, if, from reading the hierarchy of facts about the machine, the mechanic knows the horn of the cycle is powered exclusively by electricity from the battery, then he can logically infer that if the battery is dead the horn will not work. That is deduction.
>
> Solution of problems too complicated for common sense to solve is achieved by long strings of mixed inductive and deductive inferences that weave back and forth between the observed machine and the mental hierarchy of the machine found in the manuals. The correct program for this interweaving is formalized as scientific method. (pp. 103–104)

An assumption embedded within scientific methods is that knowledge is gained through the speculation, accumulation, analysis, and confirmation of facts, and the utility of empirical approaches remain the cornerstone of scientific inquiry. This is also apparent with some of the empirical practices in qualitative research traditions such as grounded theory (Strauss & Corbin, 1990). Fieldwork researchers keep their theoretical predilections under wraps and begin with theory-neutral observations from which emergent themes are compared and categorized as theory is "discovered." But the status of what is a "fact" is itself open to question. Empirical understanding gleaned from observations and sensory perception does not function without the input of what we know, feel, and believe. Popper (1968) and others describe this as "theory-laden" observation, which means that our experiential knowledge base is continually informed by whatever preexisting conditions are in place that makes up our reality. Phillips and Burbules (2000) explain it this way:

> What an observer sees, and also what he or she does not see, and the form that the observation takes, is influenced by the background knowledge of the observer—the theories, hypotheses, assumptions, or conceptual schemes that the observer harbors. (p. 15)

Therefore, the indeterminate status of where knowledge actually resides—with the "object" (the known) or the "subject" (the knower)—dislodges the grip on rationalist inquiry as a cool and detached methodology. What is not fully acknowledged is the renegade status of intuition or other imaginative mindsets that resist codification and confirmation yet have the capacity to influence conceptual understanding.

Inextricably linked to empirical reasoning and the theory-laden nature of perception is the concept of falsifiability that is used to confirm the robustness of scientific inquiry. Eloquently argued by Karl Popper (Miller, 1985), the basic principle is that there is more merit in trying to expose something to failure rather than trying to confirm its probable truth. Morrow (1994) describes it this way:

> For Popper what is more fundamental to science than verifying empirical propositions is the attempt to prove them wrong—to *falsify* them. . . . After all, endless amounts of good evidence can be found for all kinds of theories. But one crucial piece of falsifying or disconfirming evidence can potentially demolish a given theory . . . in the light of the theory-laden character of facts, any fairly credible theory can amass a body of factual "proof." What was more important for scientific adequacy was whether propositions potentially could be proven wrong. (p. 70)

Being able to subject untenable propositions to rigorous testing is a way to uncover those that do not stand up to analysis, and those that can be confirmed that are the best theoretical fit. The steely eye of the science community and the methodological safety net of replication serve as an additional basis for monitoring the accumulation of knowledge. But even empirically supported theories and their potential refutation remained somewhat impoverished if an open-mind is not maintained. Paul Feyerabend (1993) explains:

> Science is much closer to myth than a scientific philosophy is prepared to admit. It is one of the many forms of thought that have been developed by man, and not necessarily the best. It is conspicuous, noisy, and impudent, but it is inherently superior only for those who have already decided in favor of a certain ideology, or who have accepted it without ever having its disadvantages and limits. (p. 295)

Objective and Subjective Realities

If a challenge of inquiry means that there is a need to find out new information about the universe of people, places, and things, then a legitimate question to ask is, "Whose universe?" Our conceptions of social reality shape most of what we think, say and do and are defined by assumptions about some of the most basic questions we ask when we inquire into human thought and action. When the question "What is real?" is asked, answers will be framed by a range of ontological beliefs: A realist will assert there is a singular reality, independent of individual interest or influence; a relativist will claim reality is socially constructed and exists in many forms. In a similar way, concerns about how knowledge is acquired and communicated will raise epistemological distinctions about objective states and subjective experiences. These differing conceptions are most often seen as opposing perspectives positioned along an objective–subjective continuum that highlight alternative ways the world is seen.

The tendency to try to reside on either side of the objective–subjective divide is to adopt an overly simplistic stance. For instance, to resort to extreme relativism ignores the idea that there are elements of an objective world "out there." Although we might view empirical reality through a personally constructed lens, there is no mistaking that we understand certain things better now than before because of accumulated knowledge. Reality may be relative and truth tentative, but making use of what is currently known about certain kinds of phenomena is a crucial perspective to ponder. To neglect such information is to ignore the necessary distinction between "a truth," knowledge, and opinion.

In assuming that one's worldview will constitute a perceived reality upon which personal truths are grounded, Phillips (1990) reminds us not to conflate truth with objectivity. What he means is that it is easy to dismiss demands for objective standards as fool's gold, but maintaining objectivity does not automatically mean that one is claiming certainty. Therefore, "objective truth" can be seen to be a convenient fiction if it is accepted that any measurement is an approximation at best—there is always error. Any quantitative outcome produced from a scientifically robust study may be expressed in statistical terms, but this is just a way of assessing whether or not the findings are probably a result of error. So, although truth is provisional and to objectify it doesn't make much sense, what is useful to keep in mind is that the process of inquiry itself, irrespective of the methodological perspective, needs to be kept in continual check, as does the "critical spirit in which it has been carried out" (Phillips, 1990, p. 35). This sense of critical spirit and its relationship to subjectivity is well captured in Angiola Churchill's elaborate paper installations that are made with detailed attention to form, structure, and measurement, yet the precision also reveals a perceptual space that is much harder to define.

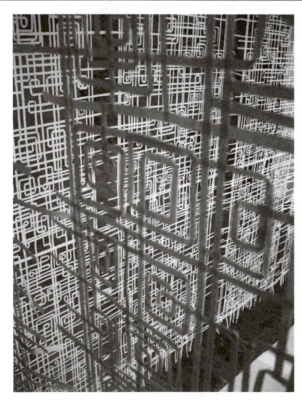

Angiola Churchill had her first one-person show in 1958. As an artist, teacher, and author, Churchill has shown her work extensively in Europe and the United States and whether through her painting, paperworks, installations, or her teaching, she moves continually to expose the space between form and content, structure and subjectivity.

What matters for Angiola Churchill is that the viewer learns to engage the subject matter with fresh eyes. To see something with fresh eyes means that we see it for the first time. Nothing is repeated according to a particular style or tradition. Or if the style or tradition is present, the subjectivity of the viewer makes it new, makes it fresh and appealing, even titillating. Churchill sustains the power of creative inspiration. (Robert C. Morgan, 1999)

Angiola Churchill, *The Labyrinth* (2003). Paper. Reproduced courtesy of the artist.

The critical attention given to methods of dealing with objectivity and subjectivity can also apply to the issue of intersubjectivity. By intersubjectivity, I am referring to Michael Parsons's definition that there exists a realm of "shared symbolically-mediated meanings" (1995, p. 12) that facilitate individual and community understanding. The principle involved is that interpretations are mediated by contexts and relationships as much as they are by personal perspectives and proclivities. For Nick Crossley (1996) this connection comprises "dimensions" he describes as "radical intersubjectivity," which sees experience and action as socially constructed, and "egological intersubjectivity" (p. 71), which acknowledges that the self and others are reflective and reflexive beings. This suggests that meaning is not contained within a form itself, say a person, painting, or a poem, but exists within a network of social relations and discourse. This interpretive landscape of "intertextuality" serves as the means by which meanings become distributed and debated. For Carter (1990), intertextual reference suggests "that there is never a unified set of 'true' meanings to a work because it will always appear within an intertextual field of some kind" (p. 135). Intersubjectivity is also often presented as a way to reconcile the objectivity-subjectivity dichotomy by assuming that agreement is a balanced indicator that offsets extreme views. Therefore intersubjectivity reflects a sense of consensus that characterizes how individuals and cultures construct meaning that is consistent and understood by all. Elliot Eisner's (1991) approach is to emphasize the "transactive account" that he sees as a way that humans negotiate a meaningful space for themselves within the objective-subjective divide. He draws on Dewey's account of transactional learning, and this emphasizes the way that human experience is the site upon which knowledge is constructed. He explains:

> Since what we can know about the world is always a result of inquiry, it is mediated by mind. Since it is mediated by mind, the world cannot be known in its ontologically objective state. An objective world is postulated both as a general and as a particular entity. Since what we know about the world is a product of the transaction of our subjective life *and* a postulated objective world, these worlds cannot be separated. (p. 52)

In a similar way, the sharing, corroborating, and validating of perspectives among individuals, groups, and communities helps establish a defensible and useful knowledge base.

In research applications an interest in intersubjectivity translates into different methods that are used to check the reliability of observations and interpretations. Intersubjective agreement is used as a protocol in quantitative research and presented as a measure of reliability of the assessments of a panel of judges or scorers. A high level of uniformity on an index suggests the instrument is doing its job and those using it are coming up with results that are consistent. In qualitative inquiry, a similar goal of consensus is sought by using triangulation so that different data collection methods and sources can be used to converge on a trustworthy interpretation. But much like the difficulty in establishing reliable means of scoring sporting events, the method itself will not guarantee confidence in the outcome. Having unquestioned belief in a quantitative measure makes as much sense as having blind faith in experts, who, it has been quipped, are people who know more and more about less and less. Rather, confidence in the use of any method that seeks agreement or consensus among individuals rests on its rigorous application.

Essentialist (Mis)conceptions

A pervading tenet in rationalist musings is that it is easier to identify and examine elements of reality if it can be assumed that things have essences, or at least a fixed nature. Although essential qualities are less-readily described in human nature than in physical nature, the belief that forms have inherent characteristics means that it is possible to define certain features that are able to represent these qualities. Hence, constructs, which describe components of theories, and concepts, which are abstract representations of ideas, may be identified that are essential components of some phenomena under study. Furthermore, these constructs and concepts can be operationalized in order to examine them in a systematic, empirical way. The claim is that a concept is meaningless unless the researcher can specify how it is to be measured, and as such these definitions become the framework for discussing the concept. Consider the psychological literature on creativity from the mid-20th century and the attempts to design psychometric tests. Creativity was seen as a critically important feature of human behavior at a time when scientific invention and the imaginative use of new technology were eagerly sought. Defining the creativity construct meant identifying concepts such as fluency in generating ideas, sensitivity to problems, flexibility, and novelty of ideas, and the capacity to synthesize and organize new information, as these were believed to describe essential attributes.[6] Subsequently, tasks could be designed whereby the way these concepts operated in creative behavior could be observed and measured and creative individuals identified. It was in later decades that the limitations of these kinds of essentialist views of creative behavior were challenged by arguments about creativity as a social construction (Feldman, Csikszentmihalyi, & Gardner, 1994).

If it is accepted that forms, thoughts, and actions have an essential nature, it makes it easier to logically claim that attributes are distributed across classes or genres of things. This not only gives a rational explanation for observable differences, but also allows for scientific analysis. This problematic notion is most apparent when applied to the study of human social psychologies and cultural contexts. For example, an essentialist methodological conception makes it feasible, but not defensible, to define racial profiles and ethnic traits as fixed entities that deny any conditions of ongoing change or variation. Similarly, an essentialist view of gender assumes that individuals can be described according to group characteristics. Although sexual differences may have a rational biological basis, when this serves as the basis for judgments about gender differences, problems arise. The outcomes of practices that essentialize human nature in this way means that decisions made are based on distinguishing features or perceived differences and, in these two instances, constitute racist and sexist perspectives. Essentialist views in educational philosophy result in similar crude ends and periodically appear as a way to shape the mission of schools and institutions based on the acceptance of intrinsic, underlying cultural, social, political, and economic values and beliefs.[7] Schooling is seen as a means of transmitting enduring truths and moral imperatives, which are acquired by learning skills essential to master prescribed content and thereby become a functioning citizen able to contribute to society. Yet the methods by which educational basics are pursued are necessarily reductive, outcomes-based, and normative. The assumption is that the essentials of learning in any discipline can be sequenced in prescribed curricula that can be efficiently taught and assessed using standardized means, which are accepted as valid and reliable measures of learning. If only life was so simple.

Essentialism, of course, has a long legacy in the visual arts, as an aesthetic tradition, a characteristic of artistic practice, and as a rationale for teaching. The assertion that the arts represent a unique way of knowing builds on the essentialist tradition and is used to advance arguments for aesthetic education, sensory-based learning, and visual literacy. Western philosophers have long been trying to articulate and explain the nature and power of the artistic experience. Even Plato, when he banished the poets from *The Republic* recognized the essential power of art. Aristotle was more supportive as he proclaimed that poetry offers insights into the human condition and thus foreshadowed some of the cognitive claims for the arts. It was Baumgarten, in the 18th century, who emphasized how experience of art could be an aesthetic form of knowing. This was grounded on the way the senses offered a particular perceptual understanding of phenomena that could have educational relevance. When applied to formalist aesthetics, a slightly different argument was advanced about how visual symbol structures could be encoded and decoded to reveal significant "truths." An element of this is captured in Clement Greenberg's spirited defense of Jackson Pollock,

William de Kooning, and Arshile Gorky whose work was soundly criticized when it was exhibited in the Venice Biennale in 1950.

> The kind of art that Pollock, de Kooning, and Gorky present does not so much break with the Cubist and post-Cubist past as extend it in an unforeseen way, as does all art that embodies a new "vision." Theirs represents, in my opinion, the first genuine and compelled effort to impose Cubist order—the only order possible to ambitious painting in our time—on the experience of the post-Cubist, post-1930 world. The formal essence of their art is penetrated through and through by this effort, which gives their works their individual unity. At Venice they must have looked too new—new beyond freshness, and therefore violent; and I can understand why the Europeans were puzzled, given also that the experience conveyed is American experience, and still a little recalcitrant to art. (Greenberg & Sylvester, 2001, pp. 229–230)

As a rationale for art education in schools, essentialist arguments highlight what the intrinsic value of art learning contributes to individual development, and how the distinctive quality of art content enhances the breadth and depth of the curriculum. Drawing on claims about the unique nature of art learning, advocates highlight the expressive capacity of art to give vision and form to thoughts, ideas, and feelings. Variations of this view see art learning as a process of visual symbolization whereby images are encoded and decoded within a structuralist regime that is used to create and communicate meaning in ways that no other human modality can (Gardner, 1973; 1990). Art knowing comprises elemental parts that make it relatively easy to conceive of art learning as a process of inquiry, and teaching as a developmental sequence. But as Arthur Efland (2002) points out, this symbol processing view of knowing is limited by the lack of attention given to contextual or situational factors that shape understanding. Perception and cognition involve a much more complex array of human capacities and circumstances, as Jeff Heatley's photograph of the floor of Jackson Pollock's studio suggests.

Beyond Method

Many of those who advocate a scientific approach to research acknowledge that far from being a rigid system of inquiry, the basic tenets are subject to continual philosophic debate and the application of principles in practice involve adaptation and change. Sometimes, however, rigid conceptions can

The floor of Jackson Pollock's studio, The Springs, East Hampton, Long Island. Photograph by Jeff Heatley, 1998. Reproduced courtesy of Jeff Heatley.[8]

In his essay for the Jackson Pollock retrospective, 1998–1999, Kirk Varnedoe describes his experience of being inside Pollock's studio barn on Long Island. He said, "physically Pollock's big canvases just fit; experientially they don't even come close" (p. 16).

The power of knowing something anew in the way Varnedoe describes it hit home when I saw the Pollock show. The Australian Government bought Pollock's highly acclaimed *Blue Poles: Number II* (1952) in 1972. I have experienced that work over the years displayed on a huge expanse of wall space in the National Gallery in Canberra. Yet it seems that by the time Pollock rolled out around 110 square feet of canvas on the floor in his Long Island studio he only had a few feet of working room around the perimeter—how *could* he create such a visual space in the painting within the confines in his studio space? To know *Blue Poles* as part of a museum collection; to know it as an emotional flickering from a charged-up life; and then to stand inside a replica of the studio to experience Pollock's floor palette, was to know the richness of the continual renewal of aesthetic experience.

stifle the flexibility of attitudes and actions. For instance, to assume that there are some psychobiological constructs that cause all human action is to place far too much faith in determinism. Social effects may be the result of multiple causes rather than a single cause, or be the product of human agency for individuals have the capacity to choose how they might respond in social situations. There are obvious links in the way humans are shaped in part by their neural architecture and their interactions in sociocultural settings. But to focus on causes seems unnecessarily reductive when the more interesting questions center on the kind of decisions people and cultures make that lead them to do the things they do. In a way, giving undue emphasis to the linear logic of causality is similar to assuming that an art work is merely the consequence of artistic intention when obviously there is an array of factors that influence the making and reading of visual images.

Other foundational principles are not limited to use in the sciences. For instance, although Popper's concept of falsifiability is used as a conjectural hedge to keep a critical eye on the context surrounding evidence, it would be wrong to assume that there are no traditions or practices in the arts whereby theories are not subject to empirical risk. As Efland (2002, p. 86) notes, the visual arts comprise an "ill-structured domain" and do not have the self-correcting features of replicability that characterizes inquiry in the sciences. If, however, we subscribe to the view that empiricism involves verifying things through observation, then those involved in the arts routinely put theories and practices up for empirical critique through a process of critical review. This is precisely what happens if the arts are seen as systems of engagement that include artworks, artists, cultural commentators, and educators. These agencies become arenas for debate, disagreement, and consensus through the use of the affirming processes of peer review and historical legacy.

The conventions of quantitative research provide a clear structure for generating questions based on accumulated knowledge. While it is readily acknowledged that hypotheses must be measurable and testable, they need not lack imagination. Yet the quest for verification and the demands of control and reductionism often leave little room for speculative maneuvers as Kirk and Miller note.

> When confirmatory research goes smoothly, everything comes out precisely as expected. Received theory is supported by one more example of its usefulness, and requires no change. As in everyday social life, confirmation is exactly the absence of insight. (1986, p. 15)

Radical insights in science, however, emanate as much from serendipitous events, happy accidents, or intuition as they do from following prescriptions (Feyerabend, 1991; Perkins, 2000; Weisberg, 1993). Situating inquiry that builds on previous research may be sound research practice but scholarship is also about ideas. Obviously, in science as in art, knowing one's craft heightens the awareness of not only what is probable, but also what is possible. But hypothesis testing is not the only way to go about systematic inquiry. Confirming or not confirming a null hypothesis only really allows the researcher to claim that certain effects or relationships are probably the result of chance or not. Levels of statistical significance provide a numerical indicator of the odds. Yet if the principle of subjecting predictions to the risk of empirical rejection is adopted, then there are several strategies that can be followed in arts inquiry.

The criterion for assessing the trustworthiness of findings is not so much a matter of whether an outcome is statistically significant, but whether it is meaningful. Therefore for those researchers seeking understanding rather than explanation, the emphasis on discovery requires one to maintain an especially vigilant pose in dealing with issues of validity and reliability (Eisner & Peshkin, 1990). This involves sound reasoning, systematic analysis and sustained focusing, along with the process of subjecting emerging findings to continual empirical challenge as new observations are framed by existing interpretations. As Bruner notes, the purpose is to achieve understanding rather than explanation, and in the process we construct meanings.

> The object of interpretation is understanding, not explanation; its instrument is the analysis of text. Understanding is the outcome of organizing and contextualizing essentially contestable, incompletely verifiable propositions in a disciplined way. . . . The requirement, rather, is verisimilitude or "truth likeness," and that is a compound of coherence and pragmatic utility, neither of which can be rigidly specified. (1996, p. 90)

Isn't this what thoughtful art critics do? This is precisely the suggestion Arthur Danto made in his response to reactions to Renee Cox's controversial five-panel photograph, *Yo Mama's Last Supper,* on display at the Brooklyn Museum in New York that prompted the then mayor, Rudolph Giuliani, to consider setting up a "decency committee." In describing how art critics might assist others who feel a need to assess art according to whatever prescribed criteria is set, Danto explains his way of using the null to reject the dull:

> I would be eager to point out the complexities of interpretation . . . and that the panelists should consider the art the way it [artwork] is considered by a critic, from the perspective of what view is being visually advanced. Seen that way, it becomes a matter of finding plausible critical hypotheses and then seeing whether they could *not* be true. (Emphasis added, 2001b, p. 33)

● DOUBTING DOCTRINES

Doubting doctrines examines critiques of the scientific paradigm as a hegemonic model of research. Traditions and perspectives that inform basic assumptions about reality, reason, truth, knowledge, and subjectivity come under scrutiny. Postmodernism, for instance, issues a broad challenge to the theoretical foundations of modernist philosophies and practices. On a methodological level, proponents of critical theory and qualitative research question the adequacy of relying on limited notions of rationality and empiricism to guide inquiry. These are reactions to the positivist conceptions described earlier in this chapter and present instead an interpretivist or critical perspective on research within which it is believed the visual arts can be best located as a form of individual, social, and critical inquiry. In this section, the discussion of *postmodern push and beyond, critical theories,* and *research remix* draws out particular themes, such as critical constructionism, positionality, reflexivity, and transformation. These issues are taken up later in the book as concepts that are used to theorize art practice as research.

Postmodern Push and Beyond

In the early 1990s, I, like many others, attempted to characterize postmodernism by referring to the ubiquitous description of the "postmodern condition" as something that captured the mood of the times.[9] Although definitions of postmodernism were mostly vague, it was often more instructive to get clues from the harshest of the critics. It is not difficult to get Walter Darby Bannard's point when he describes postmodernism as "aimless, anarchic, amorphous, self-indulgent, inclusive, horizontally structured, and aims for the popular" (cited in Jencks, 1989, p. 12). Others offered a more balanced stance.

> The postmodern view has features that evoke both optimistic and pessimistic responses. As we approach the twenty-first century, optimists would envision an art education in which local cultural practices are valued; the differences of those historically marginalized by virtue of gender, race, ethnicity, or class, are celebrated; and the cultural artifacts of all places and times are valid "texts" for study by art educators and students. Pessimists would see an aimless, fragmented, relativistic art education, cut off from standards of excellence. (Pearse, 1992, p. 251)

Postmodernism can be seen as a genuine attempt to offer a critique mostly directed toward basic assumptions underlying theories and practices of modernity and the invasive constraints of the Western canon.

For me, those times were characterized by a sense of meaning, a sense of connection, a sense of doubt, and a sense of perspective. These critical dispositions alluded to the socially constructed nature of meaning and the role of the interpretive "turn" whereby the viewer remade the artwork in order to understand it. Meaning making was theory laden and context dependent and redistributed the relationship among the artist, artwork, viewer, and the setting as agencies that inform understanding. The presumed structures that classified, ordered, and controlled how knowledge was seen and studied were shaken from their dichotomies, hierarchies, and typologies. Yet there was a surprising coherence evident among this conceptual collapse as theory was seen to be a part of practice; form was content; thought was action; mind was body; fact was fiction; and science was art. Redirecting the critical focus in order to dislodge comfortable and complacent attitudes and to challenge accepted practices meant that the landscape of ideas and actions became more intriguing, if unsettling. As Mark Tansey implies, all is not well with a rusty underbelly that purports to propel things forward if at best it maintains an illusion that cannot withstand a critical glare. This sense of doubt raised questions about received histories and dislodged power and privilege as the frame makers that controlled how the past was viewed. This broadened the perspective from the center to the periphery as marginalized voices unsettled the social, cultural, political, and economic claims made in the name of progress. The attention to diverse social realities meant that a more inclusive view of individuals, groups, and cultures could be cast. Being part of this picture, visual artists, building on traditions of social critique, made use of all manner of circumstances, settings, and technologies to ask questions that might affect the way people think, feel, and act as a result of their encounters with art.

The postmodern push is clearly felt in the area of educational research. Here the critiques tend to fall into three main categories. One strategy is to adopt a critical perspective by applying an explanatory thesis drawn from postmodern theories to an analysis of some phenomena. This approach questions the field of educational inquiry (some would say "problematizes" it) and deconstructs underlying theories and practices using particular postmodern concepts and ideas. The aim is to better understand what is "out there" by coming up with a more adequate theoretical explanation. James Scheurich (1997), for instance, adapts elements of Foucault's archaeological construct in his critique of the positivistic basis of educational research and shows how research themes and methods can be reconceptualized. A second kind of strategy used by postmodern educational critics is to apply a similar approach to that used by Scheurich and to deconstruct specific research methods. For example, Tony Brown and Liz Jones (2001) unravel the guiding principles of action research and show how practitioner-based inquiry that

Mark Tansey uses irony and surreal combinations of places and historical figures to make uncanny but coherent connections between ideas and events. The canvases are based on photocopied images and figures culled from the artist's library of popular, academic, and art-historical sources. Tansey mixes and matches this appropriated imagery, using a calculated system of opposition, reversal, and contradiction to create his seemingly realistic historical scenarios . . . Ultimately, these paintings are not just an opportunity to discover some hidden, complicated meaning. They are proof that representations, whether realistic or historical, are inherently problematic. (Jonathan P. Binstock, 1996)

Mark Tansey, *Pleasure of the Text* (1986). Oil on canvas, 65 × 54 inches. Reproduced courtesy of Gagosian Gallery, New York.

aims to empower the participants can sometimes be seen to result in a new type of control. This tactic is not unlike that taken by the curator or art writer who presents a retrospective or text about a particular artist that advances a revisionist position that may tell us more about the theorist than the artist. A third kind of postmodern account of educational research is more generative as conceptions of practice are not only deconstructed, but images and ideas are devised that offer frameworks to see things more clearly. Let me paraphrase one such example.

In their postmodern critique of educational research, Ian Stronach and Maggie MacLure (1997) describe postmodernism as a historical phenomenon that is more like a "nervous breakdown rather than a breakthrough" (p. 21). In looking to characterize the spirit of the times, yet also offer insights into the practicalities of inquiry, they see the "postmodern embrace" as a rupture that may be hard to pin down, but which puts us in a much stronger position to construct more relevant and telling ideas about the world we live in. Stronach and MacLure respond to the criticism that postmodernism is mostly a language game played by theorists that has little relevance in the real world by identifying how postmodern thinking has infiltrated everyday experience and commercial practices. Instances abound such as self-referentiality (Mona Lisa is smiling back), simulacrum (a photo of Mona Lisa as a young girl), and performativity (Mona Lisa is da Vinci in drag). They claim that "the contemporary worlds of architecture, literature, fashion, cinema, business management, market research and advertising are shot through with concepts drawn from postmodernism" (p. 15). This is clearly supported by a passing glimpse of the image blitz we encounter everyday, or a detailed analysis of visual culture, and has been well documented by others (Barnard, 2001; Gierstberg & Oosterbaan, 2002; Mirzoeff, 1999; Walker & Chaplin, 1997). Although Stronach and MacLure highlight this pervasive influence, they are critical of the way many theorists interpret the relationship between modernism and postmodernism, particularly when grafted into service as an applied structure in educational research. Their analysis of the main metaphors used to characterize postmodernism is instructive as it helps see connections among issues confronting theorists and practitioners across many disciplines and perspectives.

The dominant mapping metaphor used describes postmodernism in terms of boundaries and borders that set the center and the edge in opposition. Stronach and MacLure deconstruct this image to show how it unwittingly negates the kind of perspective most cultural commentators and educational theorists hope to achieve. They describe several ways that the boundary metaphor is deployed. Some theorists, for instance, see modernism and postmodernism as polarities or paradigms that maintain an "us/them" or "either/or" dichotomy that does little to address problems of power relations or position. A variation of this theme highlights the poverty of the border metaphor, for if one tries to locate the boundary at the center or the edge, there is a problem about whether one is looking in or looking out. There are commentators in visual arts and art education that like to see things in these extremes and prefer to argue from a preferred perspective. The description of "outsider art" as naïve and untrained, whose value can only be appreciated if seen to be beyond the mainstream, is a case in point, as is the tendency to see high culture and popular culture as mutually exclusive.

Another image of postmodernism critiqued by Stronach and MacLure sees the transition from modernism to postmodernism as more of a stagelike process that seeks to expand the perspectives taken yet this consequently smoothes out the rough, critical edges, especially when seen within educational contexts. This, for instance, is an ongoing dilemma faced by educational theorists advocating multiculturalism,[10] or writers of art education texts who position postmodernism as merely a stylistic phenomenon that replaces modernism within a neat historical sequence (Clark, 1996). A further use of the boundary image is evident in the way some theorists try to renovate or "rescue" limitations in modernist thinking by using postmodern strategies to deconstruct and then to envision a more inclusive conception. Suzi Gablik's (1991) effort to reinstill a sociocultural imperative in contemporary art in the early 1990s is an example of this kind of reconstructive stance.

In looking at the heuristic value of identifying practical connections between modernism and postmodernism Stronach and MacLure reject what they see as the more "masculine" oriented border-boundary metaphor. They prefer a feminine reading associated with a "field of metaphors" that draws on the idea of "folding" (1997, p. 28). In exploring the various ways the folding metaphor and the reference to clothes and the body reveals the relationship between modernism and postmodernism, they present a range of interpretive themes that help "weave" understanding or, as they prefer, to "mobilize meaning" (pp. 85–98).[11]

> In these sorts of ways, then, this metaphorical space engendered by "body/clothes" allows us to pose questions about inside and outside, origin and cause, and the relation of the individual to the cultural—but without being dragged towards a singular reading or an essential meaning or a static once-and-for-all interpretation. Such a bricolage of possibilities might not be an incongruent resource with which to begin to narrate postmodernism's "limits." It acts not as a definition or frame, but more as a series of semiotic chains, from, through and against which emerge different readings of the complex and shifting articulations and differences that attend the problematic relationship of modernism/postmodernism. (p. 30)

Critical Theories

Another widespread reaction that challenged the adequacy of the positivist position as a basis for research is found in the views of critical theorists. As a type of historical discourse that moves easily between the past and present, the basic tenets of "criticality" were put in place in Europe in the early decades of the 20th century (Geuss, 1981; Kellner, 1989; Morrow, 1994). The characteristic oppositional stance, interdisciplinary perspective, and political agency were geared toward individual empowerment and social change and came together under the loose rubric of critical theory. In later translations, the focus on individual and social critique and transformation brought critical theory more directly into the realm of educational praxis with the emphasis on the way theory informed practice and practice informed theory. This was evident in particular in the applications in practitioner-based research and critical pedagogy.[12] This genesis moved both in parallel and in opposition to postmodernism as a form of cultural inquiry and social critique. Sharing a family resemblance in their telling reactions to modernity, critical theory and postmodernism challenged practices that had become stultified and reified. Whereas postmodernism remained fixated on debates about the human condition, critical theory, in its various guises, retained a specific focus on social change. As a sibling rival to postmodernism, therefore, critical theory analyzes how social structures conspire to constrain human potential and imagination and theorists seek to empower individuals against alienation, domination, and the like. This, by necessity, addresses more specific, local domains, rather than the more totalizing specter of postmodernism. While acknowledging the different schools of thought that comprise critical theory, Kincheloe and McLaren (1998) nonetheless identify a critical theorist with an eclectic mix of features.

> We are defining a criticalist as a researcher or theorist who attempts to use her or his work as a form of social or cultural criticism and who accepts certain basic assumptions: that all thought is fundamentally mediated by power relations that are social and historically constituted; that facts can never be isolated from the domain of values or removed from some form of ideological inscription; that the relationship between concept and object and between signifier and signified is never stable or fixed and is often mediated by the social relations of capitalist production and consumption; that language is central to the formation of subjectivity (conscious and unconscious awareness); that certain groups in any society are privileged over others and, although the reasons for this privileging may vary widely, the oppression that characterizes contemporary societies is most forcefully reproduced when subordinates accept their social status as natural, necessary, or inevitable; that oppression has many faces and that focusing on only one at the expense of others (e.g., class oppression versus racism) often elides the interconnections among them; and, finally, that mainstream research practices are generally, although most often unwittingly, implicated in the reproduction of systems of class, race, and gender oppression. (p. 263)

In distilling elements from Kincheloe and McLaren's list of features of critical theory, the centrality of the impact of social inquiry on the individual is evident. Terms like "empowerment," "enactment," "praxis," and "critical reflection" refer to the reflexive practice required to drive the process forward. Here reflexivity is linked to notions of "positioning" that acknowledge the situated nature of the perspectives that frame the way we see things. As a construct initially identified in feminist discourse, positioning, or positionality, is of critical interest in identifying the frameworks that inform the way researchers interpret and present data. For Tetreault, "positionality means that important aspects of our identity, for example, our gender, our race, our class, our age . . . are markers of relational positions rather than essential qualities. Their effects and implications change according to context" (cited in Banks, 1996, p. 6). For Bronwyn Davies (1992), "positions are discursively and interactively constituted and so are open to shifts and changes as the discourse shifts or as one's positioning within, or in relation to, that discourse shifts" (p. 57). Another theme that is clearly associated with critical theory is the expectation that the outcomes have an impact on individuals and communities. This political focus is linked to the critical purpose that seeks to expose structural and systemic problems that deny voice, access, power, and privilege. The transformative goal is intended to better position individuals to be able to challenge and change inequities and oppressions, and to reclaim the means of cultural production used to give form to representations of cultural identity, as is so elegantly captured by Aphrodite Désirée Navab.

As a theoretical goal, seeking to challenge entrenched views is admirable but of mere rhetorical value unless it is backed up with thoughtful actions. This kind of quest for attitudinal change is similar to adopting a critical perspective to curate or critique an art exhibition so as to question assumptions, perspectives, and practices, something the Guerilla Girls, for instance, have been doing successfully since 1985.[13] There are several methodological implications that can be drawn from this discussion of reflexivity, positionality, and transformation. The first is that there is a need to consider the "observer" and the "observed" as legitimate sources of knowledge in any inquiry. Therefore reflexivity can be seen as an asset rather than a liability, and positionality can be seen as a necessity rather than a difficulty. A second implication is that there is a need to hold up knowledge, no matter where it comes from or how it is obtained, to continual scrutiny. As critical theory is grounded in individual and community action there is also a need to become aware of how critical practices can give rise to creative responses that have transformative appeal. These ends, however, rely less on the implementation of any defined method and more on insightful, responsive approaches. For although the tenets of critical theory as a form of social inquiry are extensive, there is no formal research method that neatly aligns with these beliefs. As the quote by Kincheloe and McLaren indicates, critical theory is an eclectic mix of principles and practices. Although it is less prescribed how critical theory translates into discrete research methods, there is agreement that inquiry is issues driven and context dependent. Therefore critical methods from different disciplines may be deployed in service of the research agenda. As constructs that are also centrally connected to visual arts research

In my photographic series, *I Am Not A Persian Carpet* (2001), I challenge the ways that the complexity of Iranian culture has been reduced to its commodities . . . At times it is difficult to tell where the "real" carpet on my floor ends and the "human" carpet begins. However, the full female body or self is never shown, only fragments. At the same time that I embody the stereotype, I challenge it by being disembodied, as each photograph shows bits and pieces of a female identity that defies neat categorization . . . As a woman born and raised in Iran and having lived in the United States for twenty years, I have had to negotiate between competing histories and practices that have often sought to undermine each other. With my camera and my pen I interrogate the visual productions and politics of both cultures. (Navab, 2004, pp. 131–132)

Aphrodite Désirée Navab, *I am not a Persian Carpet* (2001). Gelatin Silver Print, 16 × 20 inches Reproduced courtesy of the artist.

practice, I pick up this discussion of reflexivity, positionality, and transformation as methodological features in *Part 2: Theorizing Visual Arts Practice*.

Research Remix: Arts-Based Response

Although recent decades might be characterized as a period of dissonance and debate within cultural politics, the mood of change is much less active in the academy. Even with postmodern critics picking incessantly at the seams, and critical theorists seeking to recover omitted voices and perspectives, the direct impact of these incursions on methods of inquiry is much less dramatic than might be expected. Moves to meet the challenge of theory mostly come from within disciplines and fields of knowledge themselves. Let me briefly look at methodological dilemmas in educational research as an example of what might be called an institutionally based response to challenges of theory and method. This is played out around the border skirmishes between quantitative research and qualitative inquiry and much is written about the apparent differences in philosophy and practice and does not need to be reiterated here.[14] Generally seen as a rift between positivism and constructivism, staunch advocates lined up on either side of the ideological divide. Critiques of institutional practices reveal the problematic status of traditional boundaries, be they discipline divisions, arts areas, or cultural divides, and many see these as symptomatic of the apparent incompatibility of research paradigms. Eisner (1993) highlights this apparent impasse in his discussion of the tension between "what is individual and distinctive" and what is "patterned and regular" (p. 5). He asks:

How do we avoid the verificationist's constipation of conceptual categories on the one hand and the radical relativist's free-for-all, anything goes, no-holds-barred nihilism on the other? Or are these really untenable alternatives that nobody really believes? Maybe so. (p. 8)

The emergence of qualitative methodologies as viable approaches to research in the human sciences has, of course, not been without its critics (Gross & Levitt, 1994; Smith & Heshusius, 1986). Cizek (1995) questions the "crunchy granola" character of qualitative methods that favors "thick texture" rather than scientific analysis (p. 26). He asks:

If one accepts the notion that all understanding is contextualized, if all experience is embedded in culture, and if all knowledge is a personalized construction, and so on, then can any interpretivist claims be rejected? If not, then we are not only poststructuralist, postconstructivist, and postmodernist, but probably postscientific as well. (p. 27)

In qualitative inquiry the criteria for assessing outcomes relies on their plausibility, not their probability. Rather than explain phenomena in terms of differences in degree, the interest of qualitative researchers is to compare differences in kind. This rests on the premise that generalizing results from a representative sample to the general population is not the only way to configure research outcomes. Yet even if the need for a probability sample is critical, there are field-based strategies that are able to meet this requirement, such as the respondent-driven sampling method developed by Douglas

Heckathorn at Cornell University.[15] The important point, however, is that the plausibility of research findings grounded in observations of real world actions, events, and artifacts relies on the acceptance that outcomes can be interpreted as connections between the "specific and the specific." In other words, what is seen to be real in one observed setting can have a parallel relevance in a similar situation. Eisner (1991) calls these kinds of outcomes "prospective" and "retrospective." He adds, "generalizations [made] through art provide a heuristic or canonical image with which to see more clearly" as "they give you something to look for or to reflect on" (1999, p. 20).

In many cases the arguments about the relative merits of different research paradigms seem to offer theoretical barriers rather than guidelines to bridge them. There is, however, plenty of evidence to suggest that the reality of research practice readily blurs these distinctions. Amundson, Serlin, and Lehrer (1992) adopt a postpositivist perspective and suggest that unlike the positivists' past emphasis on observation and prediction, a realistic approach is to seek more global criteria, such as simplicity and theoretical consistency, as a means of monitoring rigor and control. Salomon (1991) offers a nested approach to research that identifies discrete and interdependent elements within complex educational phenomena that subsequently require different forms of inquiry. Although based on different conceptions of knowledge such as the distinction between specific outcomes and multiple meanings, the "analytic" and "systemic" (p. 13) approaches serve to complement each other in data analysis. Salomon's approach seeks to capture the complexity of learning environments whereby the precision of analysis helps to maintain focus, whereas systematic data management ensures that outcomes are authentic. These pragmatic approaches to blending methodologies from qualitative and quantitative research take various forms depending on the degree of integration and are described as "mixed methodologies" (Creswell, 2003), or "mixed model studies" (Tashakkori & Teddlie, 1998, 2003).

Another way of dealing with the limitations of more traditional modes of research is to expand the forms of representation that constitute how qualitative data can be collected, analyzed, and reported. As outlined in the introductory chapter, "arts-based research" is an example of practitioner-based inquiry where researchers investigate educational problems by using strategies for inquiry that are grounded in the arts, yet conform to methodological demands of qualitative research. Arts-based research takes the artistry of classroom teaching as its model of inquiry. An aim is to bridge perceived disconnects between quantitative and qualitative traditions of educational research and to attempt to face square on the underlying assumption held by many that the arts do not constitute rigorous areas of inquiry. Using Elliot Eisner's (1991) notion of educational connoisseurship that posits knowledge as sensory knowing and a form of critical engagement, arts-based research involves a process of analysis, reflection, and disclosure of meaning. Seen within this context, the genesis of Eisner's ideas about educational connoisseurship can be understood as elements drawn from art criticism whereby the educational "critic" becomes an expert by developing sensitivity to phenomena seen in classrooms. This perceptive understanding provides a basis for making judgments about educational change. Arts-based educational inquiry therefore describes and interprets phenomena whereby "seeing" and "sensing" is the basis for compiling thematic patterns of evidence from which meaning is made vivid. Arts-based researchers favor those features of qualitative research that encourage the use of a responsive approach to understand the complex realities of the classroom. In surrounding research problems in order to solve them, data gathering involves creating rich descriptive word portraits and visual documentation that reflect the insight of the insider and the critical focus of the dispassionate observer. While the mode of communication is language-based, the means of representation invoke many artistic forms that are used to capture, reflect, and critique the multiple textural realities being investigated.

Tom Barone and Elliot Eisner (1997) outlined the basic features of arts-based research and contrasted it to the more pervasive science-based research and claim that the kind of research advocated offers a distinctly different insight into educational phenomena. What distinguishes arts-based research is the multiplicity of ways of encountering and representing experience, and the deployment of forms of expression that can effectively communicate these phenomena. Thus intersubjectivity and interactivity are seen as agents in research that are assets rather than liabilities. Although claims are made for a broader range of inquiry methods, the proponents of arts-based research note the need to be able to attend to the rigor required for undertaking educational inquiry. Arts-based researchers make use of methods of inquiry found in the arts and humanities that emphasize literary traditions and therefore the "artistry" characteristic of the research is akin to art criticism and narrative storytelling.[16] Arts-based research, with its emphasis on constructivism, critical interpretation, and contextualism, is a form of qualitative inquiry that can readily draw on wider theoretical and technical support systems to further build its image as a methodology. For instance, computer-assisted qualitative data analysis with its language-dependent conventions and comprehensive data management schemes for online and offline data is well suited to enhance the reliability of arts-based research.[17]

There is a need, however, to be clear about what Eisner and others present as arts-based research. The argument of arts-based researchers is that the arts provide a special way of coming to understand something and how it represents what we know about the world. The claim, therefore, is that as research methods broaden within the domain of qualitative inquiry in the social sciences, there is a need to be able to incorporate the arts as forms that represent human knowing. For the most part, those researchers promoting arts-based research locate the theoretical parameters that shape their inquiry in the social sciences in general and qualitative educational research in particular. The approach taken argues for an expansion of inquiry practices, yet this is undertaken within existing theoretical paradigms. While Eisner and others make a strong case for educational change that is informed by the arts, there are limits to what can be achieved if the conditions of inquiry remain locked within the constraints of the social sciences rather than within art practice itself. There is a bland ontology evident whereby inherent qualities of phenomena, be they teaching practices or individual insight, are assumed to be able to be revealed through sensitive and perceptive analysis. Despite efforts to accommodate issues central to the discourse of qualitative research and postmodern critiques, some descriptions of arts-based research remains embedded within modernist conceptions of art. As such, essentialist concepts are reified rather than contested, and perspectives are passive rather than critical. Consequently the quest to embrace more artistic forms of representation results in decorative research[18] rather than deconstructive inquiry.

Other arts-based researchers and practitioner-based researchers[19] more consciously deploy a range of creative processes as research practices to fully investigate the contexts that surround complex human activities such as teaching and learning. The role of lived experience, subjectivity, and memory are seen as agents in knowledge construction, and strategies such as self-study, collaborations, and textual critiques are used to reveal important insights unable to be recovered by more traditional research methods. Researchers at the University of Toronto describe this approach as "arts-informed research."[20]

> Arts-informed research brings together the systematic and rigorous qualities of scientific inquiry with the artistic and imaginative qualities of the arts. In so doing the process of researching becomes creative and responsive and the representational form for communication embodies elements of various arts forms—poetry, fiction, drama, two- and three-dimensional visual art, including photography, film and video, dance, music, and multimedia installation. (Cole & Knowles, 2001, pp. 10–11)

Incorporating and embodying creative arts practices within research frameworks characterizes approaches taken by higher education researchers in Canada where discipline boundaries are not seen to limit the opportunity for collaboration and communication among institutions, communities, schools, and the public. For instance, faculty and students at the University of British Columbia are exploring innovative examples of arts-based research that incorporate studio explorations within rich theoretical and cultural contexts. Building on ethnographic approaches such as "autoethnography" (Reed-Danahay, 1997), they have developed an autobiographical research approach they label "A/r/tography" that references the multiple roles of **A**rtist, **R**esearcher, and **T**eacher, as the frame of reference through which art practice is explored as a site for inquiry (Irwin, Stephenson, Robertson, & Reynolds, 2001).[21] A characteristic of the arts-based research emanating from Canada is the strong element of reflexive engagement that makes good use of the creative and critical features of artistic knowing.

Reflexive Return

A review of debates about research methods not only highlights a desire to expand the representational language of research, but also reflects a broader disquiet about the lack of a critically reflexive attitude (Brown & Jones, 2001; Scheurich, 1997; Stronach & MacLure, 1997). "Reflexivity," as discussed within the context of critical theory, acknowledges the positive impact of experience as a necessary agency to help frame responses and to fashion actions. George Marcus (1998) observes that in general, "reflexivity is associated with the self-critique and personal quest, playing on the subjective, the experiential, and the idea of empathy" (p. 395). Yet when seen within the framework of research in the human sciences and humanities, reflexivity is a form of critical constructivism that affects the researcher and the researched. Those advancing a critical theory position, for instance, have advocated an emancipatory role for research for a long time (Kemmis & McTaggart, 1988; McTaggart, 1997). However, it is in the areas of *visual* research that the notion of reflexivity offers the most potential to improve our capacity to research and reveal fuller dimensions of human processes and actions.

The interest in how images might be interpreted as data and the status of still and moving images has a long history of debate, particularly in sociology and anthropology. Traditionally, the use of photography and film has been questioned, as these forms of data are believed by some to be too subjective and messy and resist systematic analysis. On the other hand, some researchers believe recorded images are an objective artifact. Ball and Smith (1992) note that "[p]hotographs of people and things stand as evidence in a way that pure narrative cannot. In many senses, visual information of what the people and their world looks like provides harder and more immediate evidence than the written word; photographs can authenticate a research report in a way that words alone cannot" (p. 9).

It is somewhat ironic that many researchers in disciplines that pioneered field-based research remain wedded to practices that see the image as a device for documentation, and the interpretation of visual forms mostly an exercise in content analysis (Prosser, 1998). For instance, the use of photography as merely a visual index as described by Ball and Smith severely misinterprets what a photograph is.

What is missing from much of the visual research methods literature is an acknowledgment that the interpretation of visual data is not so much about trying to describe visual content. Rather, the task of the researcher is to understand how those who make images—artists and other visual communicators—and those who interpret images—critics and other cultural commentators—construct their meanings as they present them in visual form. Obviously the visual researcher also creates and interprets visual data, so a central consideration is to address the need to be critical in assessing how the researcher makes meanings. This reflexive attitude is captured by Sarah Pink's (2001) description.

> The idea that subjective experience can be translated into objective knowledge is itself problematic for reflexive ethnography. Therefore an "analysis" through which visual data becomes written academic knowledge has little relevance. Instead, ethnographers need to articulate the experiences and contexts from which their field notes, video recordings, photographs and other materials were produced, their sociological or anthropological understanding of these ethnographic contexts, and their relevance to wider academic debates. (p. 97)

This critically reflective position implies that the visual image is more than a product that can be isolated and contextualized. The symbolic inferences in Will Grant's winged image, for example, typify how visual forms are rooted in cultural practices, symbolic processes, and information systems that are reflective of individual purpose and kindle reflexive cultural response. Within the wider realm of visual culture, images are located in an enormous array of spaces and places and subject to mediated processes and manipulated practices (Emmison & Smith, 2000; Rose, 2001; van Leeuwen & Jewitt, 2001). Particular research strategies that embrace a reflexive practice are explored in greater detail in *Part 2: Theorizing Visual Arts Practice*.

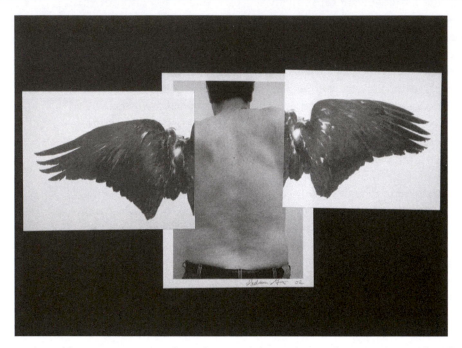

The winged parable attempts to paraphrase human ability and powerlessness. It is evident that the wings are separate elements as they are placed on the figure and tacked down. The arranged wings might be seen as something transitory. Each segment could be removable, taken away, discarded or lost. The placed airfoils suggest a duality, a binary message of what is lost is also something to be found. The image ponders what is in and what is out, what is sacred and what is profane. Therefore the winged image is an amalgam of many beliefs: the image of the angel, spirit, demon, sundancer, and shaman cross many cultural and religious boundaries. We all experience the hallowed and the irreverent. We all encounter a falling from grace and redemption over and over throughout our lives. The winged icon addresses itself to an individual's intangible needs. The placed wings create a manifestation of a fallen angel, unrequited spirituality, or a symbol of an elevated soul. (Will Grant, personal correspondence, January 18, 2004)

Will Grant, *Winged* (2002). Black and white photograph. 20 × 16 inches. Reproduced courtesy of the artist.

● CONCLUSION

Our worlds as we know them are changing. Gone are the presumed certainties and stable entities that make the process of finding out about things a relatively simple task. I was reminded of the way that nature eludes easy captivity in February 2000, when the first draft of the human genome was met by puzzlement by those who expected to find a neat and clean solution "down there." It seems that what we know as the complex reality around us is also messy at the level of genes and proteins. The genetic landscape is certainly no flat earth and the barcode image we are shown is not so much an endless two-dimensional label, but more of a multidimensional topographical map. It's lumpy and bumpy, patched and pasted together, and seems to function in both specific and complex ways. The results reported in the *New York Times* were unexpected. So how did the science writers make sense of it all? Initially they resorted to arts-based strategies of metaphor, analogy, and imagery. A report stated that "genetic archaeologists" had uncovered the "sticky, stringy, springy, dynamic, garrulous, gorgeous, and preposterous molecule of life." The genetic map was compared to the population distribution of urban and rural United States, as varied as neighborhood clusters and mountainous landscapes. The human genome was likened to lumpy oatmeal in the school cafeteria. This was not your usual science reporting. This was a struggle to interpret, a search for other ways of coming to understand something. The process is a natural way humans negotiate meaning. We create to understand. We imagine as we come to know. But this kind of image-rich instrumentalist crafting of experience is still seen to be in service of a greater need. The expectation is that to fully understand something we need to classify, organize, compare, and reference information so that it fits comfortably within an accepted system of knowledge. So artistic sensibility is sufficient but not necessary to *fully* understand something.

Although scientific inquiry has enormous status, the capacity to cater for the full dimensions of human need and knowing is shown to be limited. A greater intellectual and imaginative space that opens up options for inquiry is now part of the discussion. However, despite worldwide access to information sources that offer the possibility of different perceptions about the way knowledge is valued and used, little has changed within institutional walls that challenge the limitations of Western scientific conceptions. The way the visual arts can contribute to a fuller understanding of everyday reality is rarely heard within academic rhetoric, cultural commentary, or public debate, and this leaves artists, critics, theorists, and teachers talking among themselves.

Yet many claims continue to be made that seek to justify the visual arts as significant forms of human knowing. The task of gaining cultural and institutional credibility as a discipline of study mostly involves aligning the visual arts alongside other areas of sibling inquiry whereby the methods deployed are drawn directly from the accepted parent practices of the sciences. Despite the versatility of the visual arts as a form of human understanding that can be adapted to many settings and circumstances, reconfiguring such a diverse field into prescribed formats has limited chance of success. Another strategy used to gain cultural and educational acceptability is the claim made about the uniqueness of visual arts. Here the approach is to argue that visual arts is different from other forms of human knowing and therefore is valued mostly in terms of inherent properties and qualities. As such, this form of separatism maintains the boutique appeal of the visual arts as the province of the talented few, rather than a capability for all, and therefore the contribution to wider cultural and community development is limited.

Part 2: Theorizing Visual Arts Practice argues that the visual arts are a powerful cultural agency of human insight, and if the field is to be further developed and sustained, there is a need to argue from a perspective that is grounded in the theories and practices of the visual arts. The need to work within institutional parameters while maintaining professional credibility beyond them requires an approach that is distinctive and defensible. To achieve this, I take the position that the purpose of knowledge creation and the practice of research can be expanded by acknowledging the value of agreed ends, but arguing that these can be met by different means.

● NOTES

1. Robert Pirsig (1974/1999) describes the irony of proclaiming rationality as a guiding philosophy and how it results in a sense of dependency. He notes that "the Church of Reason, like all institutions of the System, is based not on individual strength but upon individual weakness. What's really demanded in the Church of Reason is not ability, but *in*ability. Then you are considered teachable. A truly able person is always a threat" (p. 402).

2. For examples of essays that respond to problems of "avant gardism" see Danto (1986a), "Bad Aesthetic Times," Chapter in Reflections section (pp. 297–313); Gablik (1984), "Individualism," Chapter 2 (pp. 20–36), and "Bureaucratization," Chapter 4 (pp. 55–73); and Eagleton (1992).

3. Norman Brosterman (1997) presents an engaging account of the theory and practice of Friedrich Froebel and the development and influence of the kindergarten movement, particularly on modernism.

4. See, for example, Creswell (2003) and Tashakkori and Teddlie (1998, 2003) for research strategies that promote mixed methodologies incorporating quantitative and qualitative approaches.

5. For general educational research texts see, for example, Cohen et al. (2000) and Jaeger (1997). For introductory texts that deal with conceptualizing qualitative research see Flick (2002), Marshall and Rossman (1999), and May (2002).

6. See, for example, the creativity research of J. P. Guilford (1950, 1956). For educational experimentation and application see Gowan, Demos, and Torrance (1967); and Torrance and Myers (1970).

7. See the similarity in the essentialist rhetoric in the educational report, *Nation at Risk* (National Commission of Excellence in Education, 1983), which was written during the time when economic rationalism and cultural literacy (Bloom,

1987; Hirsch, 1987) were powerful conservative forces shaping debates, and the No Child Left Behind (NCLB) legislation of 2001, which links educational progress with economic prosperity, national standards, and global performance.

8. The photographer, Jeff Heatley, provides another perspective. He explains that "to see the entire floor, practically speaking, is only possible by looking at the photograph itself. To visit the site, stand in the doorway or walk across the floor, it is not possible to 'see' the entire surface. This was true as well for me, the photographer, because the ladder and rafters prevented me from seeing what the camera and film would record once the ladder and photographer left the studio. So, seeing the final transparency was a revelation" (personal correspondence).

9. Articles published at the time argued that art education as conceived at the school and college level could take more direct reference from contemporary art practice as a guide to curriculum, teaching, and learning. The basic premise was that postmodernism provided the critical context and the practice of artists the frame of reference around which "art-based" art education could be argued. See, for example, Sullivan (1993, 1996, 1998).

10. See the description of educational responses to multiculturalism by Banks (1996) where he identifies a knowledge typology that describes a continuum of outcomes that range from personal/cultural knowledge to transformative academic knowledge.

11. Six themes are identified by Stronach and MacLure (1997, pp. 28–30): exclude–include, surface–depth, real–unreal, utility–excess, nature–culture, and history–myth. These distinctions offer ways of exploring possible connections among modernist and postmodern theories and practices in a way that exemplifies or translates a set of relationships rather than a static set of conditions.

12. For general texts on action research and practitioner-based research, see Kemmis and McTaggart (1988) and McTaggart (1997); for a postmodern perspective on action research, see Brown and Jones (2001). Prolific authors in the area of critical pedagogy include Apple (1990, 1993, 1996, 1999), Giroux (1981, 1983, 1997), and Giroux and McLaren (1989).

13. The Guerilla Girls are a group of feminist artists who describe themselves as the "conscience of culture." Their activist art uses arresting visual images, factual information, and biting humor to subvert cultural practices that reinforce inequities, bias, and discrimination. See http://www.guerrillagirls.com/ (last accessed on January 18, 2004).

14. For a summary of the paradigm debate, see Creswell (2003, Chapter 1), Tashakkori and Teddlie (1998, Chapters 1 and 2), and Reichardt and Rallis (1994). For an extended response to questions about methodological issues in qualitative research, see Eisner and Peshkin (1990).

15. The national Study of Jazz Musicians conducted by the Research Center for Arts and Culture, Teachers College, Columbia University, used respondent-driven sampling to reach a representative sample of jazz musicians in four U.S. cities. For more details, see *Changing the Beat: A Study of the Worklife of Jazz Musicians* (Vol. III) (Jeffri, 2002). See also http://www.tc.columbia.edu/academic/arad (last accessed on October 22, 2003).

16. See, for example, Diamond and Mullen (1999) for essays on arts-based research that deal primarily with literary-based inquiries, and McNiff (1998) for arts-based strategies applied to art therapy.

17. For a useful review of computer-based qualitative research resources, see Tesch (1990). For practical applications, see Gahan and Hannibal (1998) and Weitzman and Miles (1995).

18. The article by Fox (2001) argues that although arts-based research deploys the arts as agencies of inquiry, they are mostly used as decorative features of educational research. His strategy for invigorating a regime of educational research is to look toward contemporary art as a source of thematic content and issues that has the capacity to disrupt current complacencies and offer fresh visions that inform theory and practice.

19. The School of Art and Design, University of Hertfordshire, England, publishes a biennial online journal, *Working Papers in Art & Design*, which deals specifically with issues and debates about practitioner-based research. This approach to research in the visual arts is discussed in greater detail in Chapter 3. See http://www.herts.ac.uk/artdes/research/papers/wpades/vol2/intro02.html (last accessed on September 14, 2003).

20. The Center for Arts-Informed Research comprises a network of faculty, students, and arts researchers whose mission is to explore new methods of research that infuse arts practices within scholarly inquiry. The center is located within the Ontario Institute for Studies in Education of the University of Toronto. See http://home.oise.utoronto.ca/~aresearch/airchome3.html (last accessed on May 11, 2004). Another Canadian center that is pioneering arts-based research is the Image and Identity Research Collective established by Sandra Weber from the Department of Education at Concordia University (Montreal), and Claudia Mitchell from the Faculty of Education at McGill University (Montreal). The founding researchers work with other faculty, students, artists, and independent researchers on projects that use image-based approaches and interdisciplinary explorations to investigate a broad range of cultural and educational issues. See http://www.iirc.mcgill.ca/about.html (last accessed on May 14, 2004).

21. See the Department of Curriculum Studies, University of British Columbia, http://www.cust.edu.ubc.ca/whatsnew/salon.html (last accessed on May 6, 2004). For reviews of issues relating to self-study as a research method, see Bullough and Pinnegar (2001), Smith and Watson (2002), and Feldman (2003).

PART 2

THEORIZING
VISUAL ARTS PRACTICE

CHAPTER 3

EXPLANATION, UNDERSTANDING, AND BEYOND

Damián Ortega, *Cosmic Thing* (2001). Beetle, 1983. Steel wire, variable dimensions. Installed in The Everyday Altered, curated by Gabriel Orozco. On display in the Arsenale as part of the Venice Biennale, Dreams and Conflicts: The Dictatorship of the Viewer, June 15–November 11, 2003. Reproduced courtesy of the artist and Kurimanzutto Gallery. Photograph by Graeme Sullivan.

This chapter is introduced by an image. It is an artwork by Mexican artist Damián Ortega titled *Cosmic Thing* (2001). In pulling apart his own Volkswagen (VW) Beetle, Ortega manages to unpack a considerable amount of form, and in doing so stacks together a considerable amount of content. His aesthetic sensibility is anything but suspended, as it becomes a vehicle for his wry political commentary. The dismembered specimen is held in a ballet balance that becomes a social space where inferences are easily revealed. The exploded view is a bit like a three-dimensional political cartoon that doesn't need word balloons to make messages. This ubiquitous form of everyday life of a recent past, the VW Beetle, carries memories of a cheap get-around, hints of cultural repurposing, and traces of the postindustrial military complex as an original emblem of Nazi efficiency. But Damián Ortega's installation is also a theoretical system where the structural analysis clearly describes how the synthesis of parts comes together. What causes the car to work is partially explained by our knowledge of mechanics. However, the effects of driving have to be experienced to be understood. And here memories and prior knowledge of all kinds frame our responses as the immediacy of the visual impact of the floating Beetle takes hold.

As we can see from this brief encounter, several creative and critical capacities are invoked in visual experience. Like the gestalt of Damián Ortega's form in space, neither the parts nor the whole lose their mystery under the glare of analysis. Instead, something else is added as explanations are revealed, connections are made, and new forms of understanding emerge. These kinds of theorizing processes are at the heart of what it is we do when we create and respond to art and serve as the basis upon which the visual arts can be seen as a research practice. However, if an aesthetically grounded and theoretically robust approach is to emerge, then the methods used to study creativity, communication, and cultural commentary should be located within the domain of visual arts practice. To continue to merely borrow research methods from other fields denies the intellectual maturity of art practice as a plausible basis for raising significant theoretical questions and as a viable site for applying important cultural and educational ideas. While criteria for quantitative results are based on the probable likelihood of occurrences, and findings from qualitative inquiries are assessed by the plausibility or relevance of outcomes, the prospect of imaginative insight remains an elusive criterion for judging the significance of research. If a measure of the utility of research is seen to be the capacity to create new knowledge that is individually and culturally transformative, then criteria need to move beyond probability and plausibility to *possibility.*

The process of theorizing is a basic procedure of inquiry and hence a core element in research. We construct theories about how the world works all the time as we explain things and come to understand them. Some theories are based on how knowledge is applied to help solve problems. This kind of theorizing involves explanation, which is a logical process whereby observations are linked so that some are seen as causes and others as effects. In these instances, some perplexing issue or event is reconciled or resolved as we draw on known theoretical knowledge to help explain what we see. In other situations, theories are based on experience, which helps us understand more complex things. This kind of theorizing involves understanding, which is a cognitive process whereby who we are and what we know shape interactions and transform awareness. In these instances, intuition and intellect, grounded in context-specific circumstances provide an experiential base for constructing new frameworks of understanding. Therefore understanding is a powerful state of mind that allows us to see things differently. From an informed perspective we are able to form more adequate explanations and look with insight at other possibilities. It is argued here that the capacity to create understanding and thereby critique knowledge is central to the visual arts and that artists are actively involved in these kinds of research practices.

Debates about whether the goal of inquiry is to "explain" or to "understand" human behavior goes back at least to the 18th century. For early researchers, the intention was to explain human activity by adapting a similar paradigm as that applied to the study of the natural sciences. This contrasted to the belief among others that the purpose was to understand human agency and this necessitated quite a different, more naturalistic method of research. These perspectives were bound up in the epistemological arguments about objective knowledge and subjective experience. As such, explanations connect empirical observations to causal events and others can verify these outcomes. Understanding on the other hand is an adaptive process of human thinking and learning that is changed by experience.

Despite the emergence of qualitative approaches to inquiry that achieve a more adequate "goodness of fit" for the kind of learning seen in the studio and in the classroom, the need to construct theories that explain phenomena is still assumed to be the goal of research. The premise is powerful because if something can be explained then there is a high probability that effects are known in terms of their causes. Therefore a theoretically robust causal explanation means that we can make predictions and this can have significant implications. Consider the impact of a theory of learning that explains this aspect of human behavior: We would know what causes learning and could therefore re-create the conditions and predict with some confidence the outcomes. Many scientists of learning have been trying to do this for a long time. Yet the use of reductive methods to try to study and explain the workings of complex mechanisms of human thought and action is beginning to be seen as inadequate. Even a committed educational researcher such as Jerome Bruner ceased to ask the causal question, *How do children learn?* and began to ask, *How are meanings made?* It was this complex question that took him out of the clinical setting and into the "real" world in order to understand the culture of learning (Bruner, 1996).

If a purpose of research is to create new knowledge that increases our awareness of whom we are and about the world in which we live, then it seems plausible to argue that understanding is a viable outcome of inquiry. The possibility of gaining new understanding involves accessing, designing, and investigating issues of personal and public interest. Research of this kind is imaginative and systematic and includes the exploration of one's tacit knowledge and the insight of others as both experience and reasoning come into play. Generally the goal of research is to describe, interpret, or explain phenomena, but if the desire is to see inquiry as having the capacity to change human understanding, then our sight needs to be set on a bigger picture. To assert that understanding is as significant as explanation as a goal of research is especially feasible with inquiries in cultural and educational contexts, and this includes most of the research undertaken in the human and social sciences. If this is accepted, then this quest for understanding sees individual and social transformation as a worthy human enterprise for "to know" means to be able to think and act and thereby to change things. It can be further inferred that the process of making art and interpreting art adds to our understanding as new ideas are presented that help us see in new ways. These creative insights have the potential to transform our understanding and as a consequence inform and extend the various descriptive, interpretive, and explanatory systems of knowledge that frame individual and sociocultural awareness. In creating new knowledge and contributing to new understanding, artists, art writers, and art teachers construct theories of artistic knowing and develop theories about learning and teaching art. Although these theories do not carry the explanatory signature of causality, they are grounded in the praxis of human engagement and yield outcomes that can be seen to be individually liberating and culturally enlightening.

Central to my argument is the premise that to better appreciate how visual arts can contribute to human understanding, there is a need to ground visual arts research within the theories and practices that surround art making. It is from this central site of investigation that other derivative practices emerge, such as critical and philosophical analysis, historical and cultural commentary, and educational experiences. This notion is a far cry from the stereotype that sees visual arts as a warm, fuzzy, and essentially private experience. Rather, it acknowledges the cognitive capacities that inform artistic making and thinking, and this claim is taken up in more detail in Chapter 4.

Furthermore, this assumption acknowledges the crucial role visual arts can play in cultural critique, historical inquiry, and educational development. It is the centrality of visual arts to human engagement that warrants the development of a theoretically robust foundation for research in order to extend the important role of art in institutional, political, and cultural settings.

THEORIZING IN PRACTICE ●

The role of theory in research and practice is mostly unquestioned. The process of seeking explanations of phenomena that can be captured in elegant yet powerful abstractions carries high status as a goal of inquiry. Equally valued is the acceptance that theories are provisional and are subject to continual change as more well-researched accounts and well-argued positions supplant less-convincing views. There is agreement that there are "big" theories that deal with the larger issues of life and the universe, as well as practical theories that service our need to explain and understand everyday occurrences. In addition to grand theoretical proposals and commonplace practical reasoning, we construct theories that help to rationalize the structures put in place to plan and implement all sorts of institutional policies, programs, and practices. Within a traditional research regime, inquiry practices are mostly theory-driven so that studies are designed in accordance with existing knowledge and results are seen to help fill in the gaps. In practice, the outcomes can be much more surprising and consequently challenge existing theories and take a field in new directions. The promise of new insights and the possibility of more compelling theories is why people do research, because this holds the prospect of improving the structures and actions we put in place to conduct our lives.

A similar kind of compulsion impels people to make art. It is believed that there is benefit to be had for individuals, communities, and cultures from the imaginative insights offered and the potential changes made possible. As with other disciplines with long traditions, there has been much theorizing done that seeks to explain what the visual arts are, why artworks are made, how they are viewed, what the cultural impact is, why and how art might be taught, and so on. In the minds of aestheticians the issues discussed generally sit within the scope of philosophy so that theories of art can in most instances be directly linked to broader genealogies of ideas, issues, and debates. The rules regarding the fashioning of statements and the specification of argument and logical reasoning remain the same whether talking about life or the visual arts. Consequently, theories of visual arts wrestle with varying conceptions of art and yield different kinds of theoretical descriptions. These can include analytical claims about concepts, content, and distinctive relationships among visual arts practices, empirical statements about visual arts based on information that can be collated and confirmed, and normative arguments about the value of the visual arts in various contexts and circumstances (Efland, 1995).

Instrumental Theorizing: Means and Ends

Within institutional settings the kind of theorizing that is most common is the use of formal strategies that help direct reasoning and apply criteria for assessing the credibility of evidence and arguments. This is what Dennis Mithaug (2000) calls "constructive theorizing" because it helps to construct explanations about what, why, and how problems arise, and how discrepancies between what is believed and what is encountered are resolved. This is a generic process that describes theorizing as a form of problem solving and is evident in related practices such as the scientific method, logical and rational thinking, moral reasoning, and the like. As Mithaug notes, "the scientist searches for reasons to explain circumstances, the philosopher searches for reasons to judge their moral significance, and the policy maker prescribes adjustments to those circumstances" (p. 119).

Within scientific research, constructing theories using this problem-solving strategy is based on the premise that an inconsistency exists between what is observed and the lack of adequate explanatory theory. To find a more robust theoretical account the researcher follows the well-traveled path described in Robert Pirsig's (1974/1999) motorcycle analogy for the scientific method I quoted in Chapter 2. A similar practice, of course, is well known in visual arts circles as the "design process"—and here I refer to the problem solving, product-based, market-driven design process of modernism, not the hybrid, high-tech morphed practices of contemporary design research (Laurel, 2003). The Bauhaus-inspired design process of modernism amounts to a procedural algorithm that begins as a design problem, proceeds through phases of experimentation and testing, and results in elegant solutions; this tradition of problem solving by design encourages a pluralistic aesthetic where there can be any number of "correct" design solutions. The cycle of inquiry involves the identification of a design problem that includes criteria for its resolution; the compilation of relevant background research about what has already been done; devising a plan of action; producing an object or prototype; and concludes with an evaluative stage where the product is tested against the problem conditions. If the result is unsatisfactory, then the cycle begins again.

The use of problem solving as an academic strategy has been given a new lease of life with the advent of doctoral research in art and design programs, particularly in England, Australia, and Canada, and I will consider these approaches in general later in this chapter in the section, "Art Practice as a Construction Site." In situating problem solving as the central research practice used in satisfying higher education degree requirements at the doctoral level, Stephen Scrivener (2000) lists several criteria for assessing whether a student has "arrived at the problem and its solution in a self-conscious and reasoned way." For Scrivener, a research student needs to have

> demonstrated that there is a problem to be solved; shown that the solution to the problem will result in a new or improved artefact; shown that the problem is one that the World would like to see solved; demonstrated the usefulness of the solution; demonstrated that the knowledge exemplified in the solution can be abstracted (i.e., described and/or formalized); considered the general applicability and transferability of this knowledge; proved this knowledge (i.e., demonstrated that the problem has been eradicated or ameliorated by the solution). (p. 4)

The influence of means-ends theorizing using problem-solving protocols has, over the years, won high educational status in many fields. This is partly a reaction to a perceived emphasis on content coverage that, it is argued, remains unrelated to real-life applications. More commonly known these days as "problem-based learning," the principle of learning how to access and apply information in response to authentic demands makes efficient use of existing knowledge, locates the process of learning within professional practice, and allows for relatively easy accountability.[1] More specifically, the strategy of problem solving requires an organized and rational approach to learning, for once a problem is encountered, the task is to retrieve all of the relevant data available, and access to information technology means that this is close at hand. This emphasis on knowledge acquisition assumes that the outcomes provide tangible, practical evidence of learning that requires a range of conceptualizing, analyzing, synthesizing, and generalizing skills. The emphasis on praxis and process learning is at the heart of problem-solving approaches to theorizing and these characteristics, of course, feature strongly in the conceptualization of participatory action research models of inquiry (Brown & Jones, 2001; Kemmis & McTaggert, 1988) and critical approaches to teaching and learning (Apple, 1999; Giroux & McLaren, 1989). Overall, theorizing as problem solving and its variations asserts that the learner is a practitioner and a researcher and is therefore responsible for goal setting in the form of problem-identification and capable of self-assessment as a consequence of the cyclical process followed.

Irrespective of the particular protocol used for means-ends theorizing, be it problem-solving, practical reasoning, or inquiry-based teaching, the procedures for articulating the relationship between theory and practice generally remain constant. The analytical principle is based on logical reasoning and conceptual adequacy is framed by the consistency in the way the parts match with the whole so that there is an easy translation between means and ends, practice and theory, and vice versa. The heuristic value of means-ends theorizing, however, is more tangibly directed toward educational consequences as the components of theory and practice can be readily broken down into elements that can be developed as curriculum structures, teaching approaches, and learning protocols. Therefore, the benefit of means-ends theorizing is best seen as a way to translate conceptions into applied structures such as curriculum frameworks. This theory-*driven* approach leaves little room for theory *construction,* yet maintains a consistent interplay between low-level theorizing and implications for practice.

How versatile and robust is this kind of theorizing as a basis for claiming that visual arts practice has the power to construct knowledge that is plausible and trustworthy? Although we can be reasonably confident that structures and strategies can be used to theorize how visual arts practice might inform teaching and learning in educational settings, how might we conceptualize what we do in the studio or the classroom as a form of inquiry that has explanatory power and contributes to human understanding? To theorize about the visual arts in this way, one needs to consider the general domain of practice pursued by those involved. This description helps draw a sharper focus around art as a place where philosophies and practices can be located and investigated, developed and applied. Although the more formal kinds of visual arts practice might be seen in the work of artists and art writers, and in artworks and visual culture, Michael Leunig reminds us that these roles are incomplete descriptions of where we find art.

Domains of Visual Arts Practice

The domains of visual arts practice I identify describe the work of the artist, art writer, and the study of the artwork and visual culture. These areas reflect the different constituencies involved in the process of making art, studying art, and teaching art and the kind of research approaches that might be used. I briefly address each area of practice, beginning with the artist. The artist is the key figure in the creation of new knowledge that has the potential to change the way we see and think. Therefore the studio experience is a form of intellectual and imaginative inquiry and is a site where research can be undertaken that is sufficiently robust to yield knowledge and understanding

Michael Leunig, *Is this the Art Gallery?* (2000). Pen and ink on paper 15 × 20 cm. Reproduced courtesy of the artist.

that is well grounded and socially and culturally relevant. The main research interest is to investigate how knowledge is created *in* the process of making art. Research in the visual arts therefore asks questions about the processes and products of artistic knowing. To do this the artist is both the researcher and the *object* of study. Many of the self-study protocols available can be deployed if the desire is to formally investigate and subsequently communicate the outcomes of an inquiry to a wider constituency (Bullough & Pinnegar, 2001; Feldman, 2003; Reed-Danahay, 1997). Alternatively, the artist can be the *subject* of a case study (Cole & Knowles, 2001; Denzin, 1989).

Art writers respond to the visual arts they see and offer insights that take the art experience to new levels of engagement and understanding.[2] As producers of new knowledge *about* the visual arts, critics, historians, and philosophers give insights into why and how art is made and interpreted, and ways it functions in society. The main research interest is to study forms, methods, and meanings by making interpretations about art. To do this the art writer makes use of the many idiosyncratic, theoretical, and methodological approaches available to study the visual arts. These studies are shaped not only by the purpose of the inquiry but like all areas of human engagement they are subject to individual, ideological, and institutional influences. Yet like any researcher, the task of the art writer is to produce work that is grounded in evidence that justifies the questions raised and supports the claims made.

The artwork carries its own status as a form of knowledge. Research *of* art subsequently communicates new insights into how objects carry meaning about ideas, themes, and issues. As an object of study an artwork is an individually and culturally constructed form that can be used to represent ideas and thus can be examined as a source of knowledge.[3] Historical research provides an array of ways that images can carry meaning whether by means of description, representation, expression, or in symbolic form. More recent cultural discourse disrupts the relationship among the artwork, the artist, and the viewer and provides much more scope in the potential for meaning making that might result from encounters with works of art. This ensemble of influence factors allows the researcher to adopt many perspectives where the focus of study might be on the work of art itself, or other surrounding contexts that shape the way artworks take on cultural meaning. This is magnified by the expanding range of nondiscursive forms the art object assumes as artists craft new technologies into service.

Researchers who study the way that art practice might function to assist us to better understand the contexts surrounding the visual arts will be interested in the communicative and political role of art. Here the approach is to seek understanding by conducting research *through* the visual arts so as to determine the many functions and purposes to which art can be put. Using visual forms as agencies to advance various social, cultural, and political ends has a long history and the pervasive impact of visual culture that surrounds us warrants critical study. The analysis of artworks, artifacts, and other mediated texts, and the circumstances surrounding their production and presentation, means that both the forms themselves, and the viewing public, are subjects of study. But to move beyond the realm of critique there is a need for researchers to produce knowledge that can be acted upon. This educational role requires the use of a range of critical processes that are not constrained by discipline boundaries, nor restricted to particular textual forms, but draw on a broad visual and verbal image base.

This framework for theorizing visual arts practice incorporates several of the dimensions of inquiry covered in the art education literature, especially debates about the importance of interpretation, the study of artworks, and the advocacy for visual culture.[4] What is not so apparent in the field is the study of the studio setting as a place of inquiry and as a site for sustained research that has the potential to yield significant knowledge. For some art educators, the studio is a unique place for problem finding and problem solving, media exploration, and giving form to ideas of personal and social relevance. Understanding the studio art experience by doing studies of artists that reveal insights into the creative mind as an individual and cultural construct is a common approach used to model artistic learning processes.[5] For others, it is the educational consequences of the studio experiences that offer tangible outcomes, and these tend to change in relation to different sociocultural circumstances and political interests (Brown & Korzenik, 1993; Zurmuehlen, 1990).

The basic description of the research practices of artists in art, and research by art writers about art, and the domains of inquiry of the artwork, and through visual culture, helps to get a sense of how practices in the field can be conceptualized. Furthermore, by positioning the way the visual arts are created and studied in individual, historical, and cultural contexts, discrete and comparative approaches to inquiry can be proposed.[6] However, while the practices are extensive in carrying out inquiry "in" the visual arts, "about" the visual arts, "of" the visual arts, and "through" the visual arts, the premise presented here is that the studio experience is the core around which research centers. Within this context, the studio is seen as a site of inquiry that is not bounded by walls, nor removed from the daily grind of everyday social activity. Furthermore, studio art experiences are inclusive of the full range of ideas and images that inform individual, social, and cultural actions. These may spark inquiries into issues that subsequently take place within the orbit of the artworld or at the institutional level and these can investigate quite different areas and directions. These are some of the potential conditions that inform studio-based art practice and need to be seen as part of broader theoretical systems. Graham Blondel's *Seeing Through Redfern Man* (2002) gives a visual hint of the kind of research that might be undertaken in his studio as he explores his mixed images *in* his streetwise cultural snippets and touches of serious humor. It is not difficult to consider how this studio search might be taken further as an inquiry *of* Redfern Man, or *about* the work as it might be interpreted in relation to various views, or seen *through* the context of particular ideological positions. Only when these kinds of issues are examined and the arguments are sufficiently viable to withstand scrutiny might it be possible to appreciate the phenomena that we see in studios where individuals are transformed by the knowledge and understanding gained through art making. Before examining this proposition in more depth, I would like to turn to another forum of discussion where others in higher education are addressing the question about the evolving relationship between visual arts practice and research.

A chance find of a batch of commercial woven Mao fabric images, a visit to a high kitsch Mao/Cultural Revolution–bedecked restaurant in Singapore, a general interest in chinoiserie, and a 2002 residency as part of Beijing's Redgate Gallery international studio program all make for a paradoxically humorous but often quite serious commentary on both Chinese and Western cultures. Blondel believes that the not so "sleeping giant" of Asia is to have a pivotal role in shaping this century's history. Blondel's mixed images are a synthesis of collected material found on recent field trips to Paris, New York, and Tokyo. Along with paraphernalia gleaned from the streets of Sydney, be it reproductions of footpath chalk drawings done by dispossessed street people or that of supermarket derived detritus, are all blended together with his newfound Chinese images into very 21st century, near schizophrenic compilations.

Graham Blondel, *Seeing Through Redfern Man* (2002). Acrylic on woven fabric. 71 × 45 cm. Private collection. Reproduced courtesy of the artist.

● THEORIZING VISUAL ARTS AS
PRACTICE-BASED RESEARCH

The genesis of the debate about the status of visual arts practice within the university setting can be tracked back to the early 1970s and 1980s in the United Kingdom when questions were raised about the status of arts programs in higher education within the context of microeconomic reform.[7] Within the wake of the global economic rationalist agenda this discussion soon spread to other countries. However, so did opportunities to reconfigure how the visual arts and design might become more directly connected to cultural production. There are three factors that shape the debates. Two of these are causal: One involves legislated change to institutional structures,[8] and the other surrounds the provision of government funding support, especially in the U.K., Canada, and Australia.[9] The other feature is something of an unintended consequence with vigorous questions being raised about the theory and practice of the visual arts as an academic discipline and ways of conceptualizing studio inquiry as a form of research.

The changing circumstances that thrust art schools, art teacher education programs, and other studio-based professional courses into unified university systems occurred in most of the countries mentioned above, which caused something of an identity crisis. There was a curious clash of confidence as relationships were forged, structures reframed, and, in some cases, control relinquished to others. But there was an enthusiasm that jolted free past complacency that had caricatured the visual arts in higher education. Student learning could no longer be believed to result from the mere presence of an artist in the room. Art programs needed to be more than a private rite of passage of personal discovery. The possibility of new academic career paths within the university setting opened up for visual artists. They became eligible for professional support through research funding because those in universities teach and do research. Artists who work in art schools *in* universities also teach. But do they research? At issue was a critical question: *Can visual arts practice be accepted as a form of research?*

At the moment this discourse mostly involves a coalition of theorists and practitioners from Europe, the United Kingdom, Australia, Canada, and New Zealand, although there are representatives from some universities in the United States whose concerns center on particular discipline interests such as design, or in interdisciplinary research that spans the arts, humanities, and sciences. Although this body of literature is framed by a set of institutional conditions that are unlike those that currently confront theorists, artists, and art teachers in the United States, the content covered is very relevant. As described earlier, the role and status of the artist in higher education has been the topic of much debate, and the changing demands of professionalization indicate that this remains so. The College Art Association (CAA) seems comfortable that the discipline interests of art history and theory, and related visual studies programs continue to contribute to the production of cultural knowledge that advances credibility for the field. The position of the recalcitrant artist within higher education, however, remains less certain despite overtures that the lack of credentialed faculty at the doctoral level limits the full academic acceptance of the visual arts in higher education.[10] The enduring concern about institutional status is yet to be supported by a profound debate in the United States about the way the visual arts can contribute to broader cultural discourse and understanding that is the outcome of *what artists do.*

What artists do, of course, is to make art, and as an object and subject of study art has been well picked over by aestheticians, historians, psychologists, sociologists, critics, and cultural commentators for a long time. But what artists do in the *practice* of creating artworks, and the processes, products, proclivities, and contexts that support this activity is less-well-studied from the perspective of the artist. As an "insider" the artist has mostly been content to remain a silent participant, even if the inquiring eye of interested others has given plenty of insights into artistic experiences and activities. When circumstances require a more clearly articulated account of *what* visual art experiences, objects and outcomes are, and *how* they might contribute to the stock of human knowledge and understanding, the arguments often retreat to essentialist claims that are hard to defend, or offer well-meaning instrumental reasons that are easy to dismiss.

Art Making as a Construction Site

Practice-based research is the term used in current discussions to describe the profile of "making" disciplines in higher education and is used in debates about the status of research in the visual arts, design, and, to a lesser extent, architecture, in higher education. The U.K. Council for Graduate Education report (Frayling, 1997) describes the characteristics of practice-based research thus:

> [T]he *practice-based doctorate* advances knowledge partly *by means of practice*. An original/creative piece of work is included in the submission for examination. It is distinct in that significant aspects of the claim for doctoral characteristics of originality, mastery and contribution to the field are held to be demonstrated through the original creative work.
>
> Practice-based doctoral submissions must include a substantial *contextualization of the creative work*. This critical appraisal or analysis not only clarifies the basis of the claim for the originality and location of the original work, it also provides the basis for a judgment as to whether *general scholarly requirements* are met. This could be defined as judgment of the submission as a contribution to knowledge in the field, showing doctoral level powers of analysis and mastery of existing contextual knowledge, in a form which is accessible to and auditable by knowledgeable peers. (Emphasis in original, p. 14)

Arguments continue within and around the field of visual arts regarding the status of studio practice as a form of research and focus on two main issues. The first centers on questions of theory and practice and debates about what constitutes visual arts knowledge as seen within institutional structures (Brown, 2000; Frayling, 1997; Green, 2001). The second issue concerns methodologies of visual arts research (Candlin, 2000; Gray, 1998; Gray & Pirie, 1995). Let me discuss the first of these issues.

Examining the theory and practice of the visual arts can involve a retreat to dualistic thinking that is similar to the focus on means and ends mentioned earlier. When considered this way, theory and practice are easily seen to support rationalist perspectives, where hierarchies of knowledge, discipline distinctions, and objective methods are favored. For Jenny Wolmark and Eleanor Gates-Stuart (2002), the trap of binary logic limits the potential of what visual arts research is, and they see the need to consider research as a cultural practice rather than a codified form of academic inquiry.

> One way forward in this debate is to think about research as a cultural practice that is generated by and through the intersection with other cultural practices, and that knowledge can therefore be understood as "situated." . . . Situated knowledge is no longer decontextualized and removed from the social and cultural relations in which it is embedded. (p. 2)

The notion that research is a cultural practice does not mean that there is any loss of specificity in establishing the relationship between theory and practice, nor the methodological demands of conducting research that is focused, rigorous, and trustworthy. Rather, the view that similarities rather than distinctions between theory and practice open up possibilities of how knowing in the visual arts can be conceptualized (Reilly, 2002).

In dealing with issues of epistemology, choices need to be made and argued about how knowledge is viewed. For instance, if the decision is made to adopt criteria for defining *the* knowledge—in a similar way to finding *the* truth—then this singular conception assumes that knowledge is based on true and justified beliefs and therefore equivalent instances need to be identified in visual arts. This objectivist position sits comfortably within a rationalist world but has a hard time accounting for the breadth and depth of knowing that is disclosed within hermeneutic and artistic traditions of inquiry. As is argued throughout this book, the tendency to refashion the foundations of a field according to conditions set in place by other disciplines offers false hope. Alternatively, if the claim is made that knowledge in the visual arts comprises different ways of knowing, this requires conceptual clarification to distinguish types of knowledge. Many theorists in the arts and education present arguments in support of this view and offer variations of Gilbert Ryle's distinctions between *knowing-that*—or propositional knowledge (facts)—and *knowing-how*—or performative knowing (skills). For instance, Bennett Reimer's (1992) educational argument for the arts is based on the distinctive cognitive character of the processes and products of aesthetic understanding that he defines as knowing *of (within); knowing how;* knowing *about* or *that;* and knowing *why.* For Reimer, addressing the epistemological argument is only part of the issue, for arts learning also has to be seen as a normative process that is central to claims about what it is to be human. To date, however, arguments that claim artistic ways of knowing to be a distinctive modality of human engagement that is set in opposition to other forms of knowledge construction run the risk of denying the complexity of what it is to know, to see, and to understand.

A question for those advocating practice-based research is not so much a concern for analyzing types of visual arts knowing and their effects, but the significance of art making as a site for knowledge construction and meaning making itself. For instance, some practitioner-theorists with a particular interest in design have an affinity with the early work of Donald Schön (1983, 1987) whose constructivist thesis of "knowing-in-action," "reflection-in-action," and "reflection-on-art practice" firmly centers the inquiry process on the practice of designing (Gray & Pirie, 1995; Scrivener, 2000). Others draw on contextualist approaches that are more directly informed by the physical and material properties of the object and the social conditions that occur "in a shared cognitive environment with common rules, which is also a physical environment, organized and transformed around artefact systems and the actions which produce and reproduce them" (Maffei & Zurlo, 2000, p. 2).

The search for a theory of practice has been less of a concern for artists, although there is a rich history of explanatory efforts to locate the essence or pretense of the imagination. The enduring tendency to partition Western thought into thinking and feeling dualisms relegated some artists in past centuries to the role of visual tricksters or sensory romantics. The more recent legacy of the modernist mantra that "form is all" rode roughshod over any theoretical attempts to suggest that there might be something more than meets the eye. For many artists, there is no need to talk about their work because no words can ever substitute for what the image can do. Another reason artists remain silent is because they are mostly content knowing that practical knowledge and the intelligence of creativity has been drastically underestimated by those outside the field of practice. Where others may talk of reflective action as a procedure or a protocol, artists' practice, with less concern for functionalism, can be seen as a metacognitive and reflexive response to the impulse of creativity. Perceptions about artistic practice are therefore shaped as much by what others say as artists themselves readily mythologize it. This makes it easier for artists to pass on the job of defining and defending what they do to aestheticians and historians. But to delegate authority to others is no longer an option as the nature of artistic practice has changed the responsibilities of artists as cultural theorists and practitioners. Greta Refsum (2002) describes these conditions.

> Artists and the field of visual arts deal primarily with that which happens before artworks are made, this is their specialist arena, what comes afterwards is the arena of the humanistic disciplines. If the field of visual arts wants to establish itself as a profession with a theoretical framework it must, in my opinion, build its theory production on that which happens before art is produced, that is, the processes that lead to the finished objects of art. (p. 7)

The status of knowledge production in the visual arts remains a vexed question for many. A typical distinction asks whether knowledge is found in the art object, or whether it is made in the mind of the viewer. This debate is ongoing, and insightful accounts are beginning to appear that seek a more profound philosophical basis for situating art practice as a form of research within institutional settings. Neil Brown (2000, 2003), for instance, presents a realist perspective whereby artworks as institutional artifacts are seen to exhibit properties that are primarily objective, theory dependent, and knowable, which gives access to insights that can be intuitive, mindful, and discoverable. When seen in relation to the demands of research, Brown (2003) maps an extensive set of "symptoms of practice" that highlight different areas of shared emphasis between art making and research practice. Other positions take a broad look at knowledge that seeks to keep in dynamic tension the various constituent interests that surround art practice and research. If taken from the perspective of the artist, both knowledge production and the functions to which knowledge is put are best seen to be a dynamic structure that integrates theory and practice and contributes to our personal, social, and artifactual systems of understanding. For Mike King (2002), scientists and artists who are actually involved in the intense inquiry and engagement of practice within their different domains reveal how the theoretical edges between these practices easily soften in reality. For Stephen Awoniyi (2002), it is the polymorphism, or multiplicity of knowledge construction and the many forms of representation that it can take that reflects the integrated nature of theory and practice in art and design. A good example of the interdependent relationship among the artwork, the viewer, and the setting can be seen in conceptualizing studio-based visual arts research within higher education, as all these forms interact within an interpretive community. In this instance, knowledge embedded in practice, knowledge argued in a thesis, and knowledge constructed as discourse within the institutional setting all contribute to new understanding.

The Academic *Artworld*

Another condition that influences how visual arts practice can be understood as an agency of cultural production within the academy is the mediating role played by institutional practices. Past research strategies that sought to identify generic artistic processes such as the psychological basis of creativity, or the structural foundations of visual symbol use, were mostly immune to the impact of social relations and regimes. As a framework for considering the way that visual arts is construed as an academic practice, Neil Brown (2003) describes the different identifying roles it has assumed.

Making art is variously represented in university postgraduate programs as a method of research, as the outcome of research, or as a research equivalent. As a method of research the visual arts are employed with increasing confidence as a mode of ethnographic inquiry into cultural objects and events. Considered as the outcome of research, artworks are represented as the product of poetic, technical, and other measures of cultural investigation. As a research equivalent artworks are accorded the status of research but only insofar as an imprecise analogy can be drawn between the value of innovation in art and science. (p. 2)

Although Brown sees these art practices as minor components of a larger claim visual arts can make as an institutional practice, they represent the various ways that research programs in art and design are structured and inquiries directed. Furthermore, these practices provide a perspective from which to review the way institutional arguments have been mounted to defend the position of visual arts research in the academy. For instance, the strategy used to determine what it is that artists do is to consider the kind of work undertaken in studios in university settings in light of prevailing views about research. For many, trying to understand what visual arts is about means comparing art practice with scientific research. Although plenty of games around definitions and outcomes are played out in various reports (Harris, 1996; Strand, 1998), all the while the edifice of what is described as "traditional" research looms large to shadow artistic research activity.

Two main strategies characterize the quest to confirm the academic status of studio-based research. The first involves assessing "equivalency" whereby the features of visual arts practice are set on a scale that is comparable to levels of scholarship associated with more traditional disciplines. For instance, a one-person exhibition might be assessed as equivalent to the publication of an article in a refereed journal. Yet there is an inherent folly in assuming that practices from different fields can be validly compared if criteria are drawn from the disciplines of authority. In the case of the applied sciences, a prevailing emphasis on marketplace research mostly assesses outcomes in terms of product yield and economic return. This utilitarian focus, however, can be questioned as a basis against which to assess the outcomes of visual arts research.

The second institutional criteria used to assess the relative position of visual arts research in the academy is "benchmarking" or moderating. This is an evaluative process for identifying practices of merit based on the principle of peer assessment. The procedure involves the nomination of benchmarks that are local interpretations of what constitutes high-quality performance. Although this approach acknowledges diversity, it is labor intensive and requires considerable documentation to support assessments and to offset perceived problems of lack of objectivity and comparability. Research in university settings is also characterized by its dissemination to a growing audience of professionals who are in a position to evaluate the outcomes against agreed upon, if often unstated, performance indicators. In some cases, the criteria applied will be external to the discipline, such as the amount of competitive research funding secured or other similar institutional measures. Benchmarking, however, with its obvious similarity to the refereeing procedures used in the humanities and the sciences comes close to the peer review processes that are part of artworld practices. Like all forms of public adjudication, the criteria for assessment centers on the assumed congruence between the evidence presented and the interpretive decisions made.

There are two problems with this kind of reckoning. First, trying to expand a set of existing institutional categories to include a renegade membership (such as the visual arts) has little merit as ownership is always invested in the authority of someone else. What happens is that inherent values are transferred into a new realm and this denies the circumstances that granted status in the first place. What we cherish others may not. The second concern is the way the naïve notion of equivalence can be easily usurped. In the final analysis, equivalence is a concept that can readily be seen to endorse imitation, and mimicry or pastiche should not be part of the process. Yet the caution is clear: Conditional entry to the research academy is given to the visual arts as a domain of inquiry that promises a platform, but not necessarily a voice. Under these conditions we may construct our exclusion by playing a game according to rules that can only be changed by those who make them. It seems far better to publicly proclaim and profile outstanding examples of contemporary art that confound narrow prescriptions and exemplify the breadth and depth of visual arts research practice. For instance, the statements about the art of Maurizio Pellegrin highlight how his installation is at once an historical archaeology, a poetic and profound cultural investigation, and a lyrical disturbance of time.

Reflections and Intentions: The Art of Maurizio Pellegrin

The Italian artist Maurizio Pellegrin has been exhibiting his installations and site-specific works throughout Europe, Asia, and North America since the mid-1980s. He lives in Venice and New York. The statements below are a sample of responses to his installations (Pellegrin, 1999).

Essentially, his picture of reality is decoupled from the clarity of structure that is one of the chief virtues of language. The fragmented nature of Pellegrin's carefully staged compositions echoes the frustratingly fragmentary nature of contemporary consciousness, where discrete experiences and events seem to coexist in a close but stubbornly detached proximity that makes any coherent overview difficult. In this sense, the artist's private cosmology is a solution that allows him to combine many elements into an identity that becomes a multiplicity of one. Terrie Sultan, Curator, 1992.

The objects which make up Pellegrin's work are always displayed in confrontation to contradictory images. This accentuates the development and transformation of the original meaning of each object. It does not imply that the meaning of things changes, but rather, that Pellegrin stretches the horizon beyond its earlier limits. The artist's constant reference to Venice, a place where he grew up surrounded by artistic masterpieces, becomes a familiar, common image. He places the spectator at the crossroads of perception: history and art on the one hand, and the object's individual history on the other, in combination with how this object conditions the art in its presence. Francesco Bonami, Director, 2003 Venice Biennale, 1994.

Maurizio Pellegrin's work focuses on new methods of communication. Each object in his installations has its own accent and dialect. On the wall, he mounts rigorously selected series of similar objects—leather belts, rubber stamps, balls, coils of rope—in combination with other items totally unrelated in terms of style, material and size . . . Pellegrin uses a number of methods to disrupt the simple reading of his poetic themes. A blindfold is a device used to mask the viewer, but Maurizio Pellegrin blindfolds his artworks instead. He wraps his found objects in black cloth to alter their contours and "also to contain their energy." Jonathan Turner, Curator, 1994.

What is that swordfish doing in a typical Venetian courtyard? Where do those Chinese chopsticks come from? Are those figures on the floor really African totems? Our few indisputable, Cartesian certainties, which regard the material world, made of familiar objects and landscapes, suddenly vanish, leaving behind only doubt, disorientation, puzzlement. Art is not anymore an element of comforting illumination, but of an ironic bewilderment which leave us defeated, inanimate. Diogo Mainardi, Writer, 1999, pp. 16–17.

Pellegrin, on the concrete level of making art, does not try to reconstruct a context, as a historian would do, but he constructs its form starting from the materials of memory. What come out is a score, not an execution; to do this belongs to the viewers, each one with his own individuality. In fact, the elements of the artist's composition appear like signs within the warp of staves: though they are graphically isolated, they interweave tensional relationships among one another thanks to their connotative energy inherent to each of them. Igino Schraffl, Linguist, 1999, p. 21.

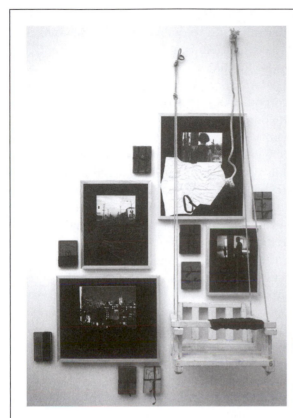

Maurizio Pellegrin, *The Green Swing* (1994). 83 × 58 × 16 inches. N. 13 Elements: Fabric, Tempera, Photograph, Wooden Objects. New York, private collection. Reproduced courtesy of the artist.

Thesis and Exegesis

So what do practice-based doctoral research projects look like? Part of the discussion about their structure and format revolves around the changing place of theory in higher education. Rather than occupy the high ground in a theory-driven enterprise, philosophers of practice have in recent decades moved amid the empirical underbrush to reinvigorate the nexus between theory and practice (Denzin & Lincoln, 1998; May, 2002). Typologies of research indicate that the approaches tend to be either practice-centered, culture-based, or more formal kinds of research that have links to established discipline methods in areas of art history and theory, or in related areas of science and technology (Douglas, 2000). Within this range it is the various ways that art making is interpreted that is the most contentious, as the effort to align art practice with more codified research methods mentioned in the discussion of equivalency indicates.

Old claims about where visual arts knowledge resides is at the heart of these concerns. Part of this translates to questions about how practice-based research might be conceptualized as a dissertation argument, and where this theorizing might be located: within the realm of the artwork produced, within a contextual form such as a related "exegesis," or in some combination of the two (MacLeod, 2000). The formal designation of an exegesis as a required research component has raised the ire and support of many. For some, an explanatory exegesis is seen as redundant because it fails to acknowledge that art making can *be* research because it maintains a distinction between academic research and visual arts practice. For others, the inclusion of an exegesis that contextualizes the research is necessary because it acknowledges that visual arts theorizing is a diverse practice that can be articulated in many visual and verbal forms (Candlin, 2000; Webb, 2000). Nancy de Freitas (2002) argues that this form of "active documentation" helps to critique, confirm, and reconfigure theoretical positions and research directions, yet "in a practice-based research project it should not be seen as the research itself, but the method through which ideas can be developed" (p. 4). An example of institutional concerns and a flexible response to the issue of the "written component" of practice-based research is described in the following extract from the Green (2001) report on Research Training in the Creative and Performing Arts and Design.

> It was broadly agreed that the written element should be more than a factual report, that it should define some critical and intellectual perspective and that it should not merely "justify" the practice. This debate on the purpose of the written component linked closely to that on contextualization. The group agreed that a definition of the research or creative context was a necessary aspect of the degree. Here, though, the group offered a range of interpretations. (pp. 16–17)

This review of practice-based research highlights current issues and debates among international theorists and practitioners seeking to reinstate the "artist-theorist" as a critical figure in higher education research. The circumstances surrounding institutional change and the potential to develop viable and visionary research practices are at hand. Grounding visual arts research within the practice of art making offers the possibility of advancing understanding of how research in the arts and the human sciences can be conceptualized. But pathways remain to be sketched in greater detail.

THEORIZING ART PRACTICE ●
AS TRANSFORMATIVE RESEARCH

As we have seen, theorizing visual arts practice embraces a diversity of positions and perspectives. However, to propose a viable way to conceptualize art practice as research requires the construction of a robust and defensible framework for considering the relationship between the theories and practices that inform how art is made, and how it can be studied and taught. Such a structure would be expected to cater to different theories of inquiry and practices of visual arts in order to accommodate the range of content interests. A broad set of outlines would also serve as a reference for theory construction that is part of the research process as experiences, observations, and reflexive understandings are analyzed and interpreted. Consequently there are several good reasons for constructing a framework for theorizing visual arts practice that describes this interdependency of interests, issues, and approaches.

- First, the identification of a range of theories and practices underscores the notion that the visual arts is an eclectic and hybrid discipline that is firmly centered on art making, and also involves the constituent practices of art writing.
- Second, a flexible framework that can be adapted to suit different purposes, emphases, and scales, yet retain a dynamic relationship between the parts and the whole, will guard against the tendency to codify visual arts research practices.
- Third, such a framework serves as a forum that helps position debates in the field and related areas that inform visual arts research practices.
- Fourth, as new visual arts research is undertaken, it can be located and critiqued within dimensions of theory and domains of inquiry so as to ascertain how practice informs theory and theory informs practice.
- Fifth, as new research strategies emerge in other areas such as the use of visual methods, transdisciplinary projects, and computer-assisted research technologies, they can be assessed in relation to research practices in the visual arts.

Finally, a framework for theorizing offers the possibility that visual arts practice can be readily translated into other forms of research language if the purpose demands it. In this way the research culture remains grounded in the theories and practices of the visual arts, yet the outcomes can be communicated across disciplines.

A Visual Framework

Figure 3.1 shows the theoretical framework for arguing that art practice is a form of research. I describe its visual and conceptual features here and explore more detailed interpretations in later chapters as the focus changes to visual knowing and strategies of practice. It is important at this point, however, to emphasize that this conception of visual arts research should be read in an analogical way, as there is no intention to try and prescribe any theory, model, or method. On the contrary, the position argued in this chapter is that the quest for theory as it is currently understood in research can restrict rather than release the potential for carrying out inquiry that is not only timely and well grounded, but also innovative in purpose and design. The intent, then, is to offer a set of heuristic devices in visual and verbal form that present ideas about research. This comes from a critical analysis of visual arts research practices and related areas in the social sciences and humanities, as well as information drawn from research projects in which I have participated.

A further caveat is also relevant. There is a need to be cautious about describing any analytical framework that brings together related elements for the purpose of examining the relationship between theory and practice. Any systematic structure has the potential to usher in a new orthodoxy as preferred interests and methods function to normalize practices. To this end the boxed boundaries shown in the diagrams are presented in the spirit of bridges rather than barriers. Rather than borders and boundaries, the edges in the diagrams should be seen to more closely resemble the "folds" of postmodernism as described by Stronach and MacLure (1997) in Chapter 2. What is difficult to portray is the idea that although conceptual borders help to define areas of interest, they are permeable barriers that allow ideas to flow back and forth. This flexible condition is especially relevant to perceiving Figure 3.1, Framework of Visual Arts Research, as the components are shown neatly nested in a set of relationships. This association is also shown from a different perspective in Figure 3.4, Transformative Visual Arts Research: A Braided Relationship, a side elevation, with an exploded sectional view shown in Figure 3.5, Braided Framework (Expanded View). It needs to be remembered, however, that the forms shown in Figure 3.1 can be viewed as components that are bound together as a braided set of connected strands, or teased apart as separate threads.

Figure 3.1 shows four interconnected areas of visual arts inquiry. The center strand is *Art Practice,* which is the site where research problems, issues, and contexts originate. This placement is not meant to be self-serving. Rather, it captures the reality that the visual arts are grounded in the studio experience, yet practitioners move eclectically across boundaries in their intellectual and imaginative quests. Although this is the core from which research is undertaken, when seen in relation to the surrounding areas, different

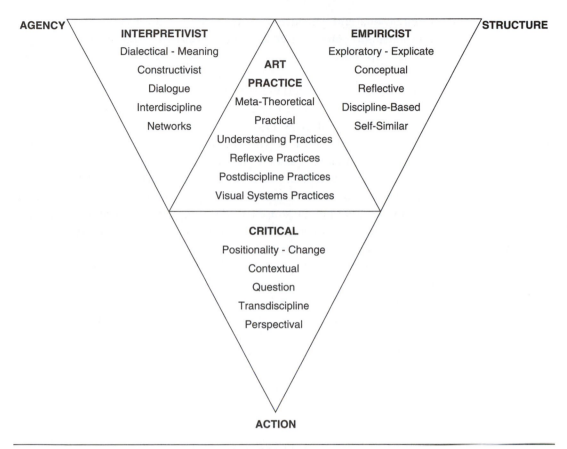

Figure 3.1   Framework of Visual Arts Research

perspectives and practices may emerge as inquiry twists into new positions and turns toward different sources. The border areas labeled *Empiricist, Interpretivist,* and *Critical,* are *domains of inquiry* and describe different research traditions and methods. These paradigms are well documented in the research methods literature (Alvesson & Sköldberg; 2000; Denzin & Lincoln, 1998; May, 2002). The empiricist, interpretivist, and critical perspectives owe a debt to Jürgen Habermas (1971). He expressed his pragmatic interest in arguing that inquiry is socially grounded and drew attention to the need to broaden the scope of knowledge structures to include technical, contextual, and critical understanding. Raymond Morrow (1994) paraphrases Habermas's three-tier knowledge schema as follows:

We seek to know in order to control social and natural realities (the empirical-analytic interest), to qualitatively interpret and understand such realities (the hermeneutic-historical interest), and to transform our individual and collective consciousness of reality in order to maximize the human potential for freedom and equality (the critical-emancipatory interest). (p. 146)

In Chapter 2, I discussed the mixed heritage of empiricism as a paradigm and its pervasive impact in regimes of research in the social and human sciences. Following Morrow (1994, p. 32), I make a distinction between "empiricist" and "empirical" in that the latter term is often mistakenly used to describe quantitative research only, as if areas of qualitative research are somehow not involved in empirical discovery and verification. Although best represented in quantitative systems of analysis, the rapid growth of qualitative offshoots that open up sense-based strategies to practical reasoning give a sense of the methodological utility of empiricism. So I use *empiricist* to reflect a general focus on research that is mostly data-driven, where evidence is derived from experience of social reality and is collected in many forms and analyzed using a range of related methods and techniques.[11]

Another border strand is *Interpretivist.* In Chapter 2, I discussed some research conceptions that persist where perspectives and practices are seen in dualistic terms—objective and subjective realities being a case in point— and I want to restate my rejection of this binary thinking. My use of interpretivist is within the hermeneutic[12] tradition of Habermas (1971) and Paul Ricoeur (1981), and the constructivist perspective of Egon Guba and Yvonna Lincoln (1998) who fashion a form of inquiry that helps understand the uniquely human process of making meaning. Here the central role is experience as it is lived, felt, reconstructed, reinterpreted, and understood. Consequently, meanings are made rather than found as human knowing is transacted, mediated, and constructed in social contexts. These views indicate that research practice itself is a site for creating and constructing interpretations as meaning is made during the inquiry process.

From Ricoeur's notion of textual interpretation comes the idea that when a written text is read it takes on a level of autonomy and "what the text signifies no longer coincides with what the author means" (p. 139). This serves the visual arts well as it opens up the interpretive space among the artist, artwork, and the setting as relevant interests and perspectives may reveal multiple methods and meanings that are enlivened by exposure to interpretive communities of art writers and theorists. As Arthur Danto (1981) notes, "in art, every new interpretation is a Copernican revolution, in the sense that each interpretation constitutes a new work" (p. 125). However, he reminds us, "you can call a painting anything you choose, but you cannot interpret it any way you choose, not if the argument holds that the limits of knowledge are the limits of interpretation" (p. 131). Alvesson and Sköldberg (2000) provide an account of the hermeneutic-constructivist notion of understanding referred to in Figure 3.1.

Understanding constitutes a creative, re-productive act, in which the researcher appropriates the meaning of the object, rather than mechanically mirroring it. The researchers carry around their own frames of reference, and inevitably make their interpretations in accordance with these. This is also the reason why interpretation always possesses only a *relative* autonomy, never an absolute one. (Emphasis in original, p. 68)

The final boundary component shown in Figure 3.1 is labeled *Critical*. This is a global term that draws its conceptual direction from the discussion of Doubting Doctrines given in Chapter 2. The broad purpose of critical forms of inquiry is the enactment of social change. Under the glare of a critical eye that breaks apart social structures that privilege those in control, the situation of groups marginalized by cultural characteristics such as their race, gender, economics, or ethnic identity is examined. Using methods such as deconstruction, the narratives and perspectives of groups mostly omitted from formally documented historical accounts, or who are denied access and voice within social structures, are revealed and re-presented. Opening up a dialectic aims to enlighten and empower individuals to challenge the circumstances that deny their entry so that "change is facilitated as individuals develop greater insight into the existing state of affairs (the nature and extent of their exploitation) and are stimulated to act on it" (Guba & Lincoln, 1998, p. 215). Critical traditions of inquiry are, of course, a prominent feature of visual arts theory and practice, having been given a considerable boost by the revisionist perspectives of recent decades. In particular, the feminist critiques of art history and the critical analyses of gendered practices in contemporary cultural politics undertaken by artists as well as critics are especially revealing. These offer content direction and methodological cues for an expanded domain for visual arts research that looks to integrate critically engaged visual and verbal languages within the kind of framework shown in Figure 3.1.

VISUAL ARTS RESEARCH PRACTICES ●

The regions of Empiricist, Interpretivist, and Critical that surround Art Practice describe research paradigms suitable for adaptation in inquiry in the visual arts. There are also several kinds of practices described in Figure 3.1, and each offers a different perspective for designing and undertaking visual arts research. These elements are *meta-theoretical practical, understanding practices, reflexive practices, postdiscipline practices,* and *visual systems practices.* A brief summary of each of these is given below, along with references to the diagrams.

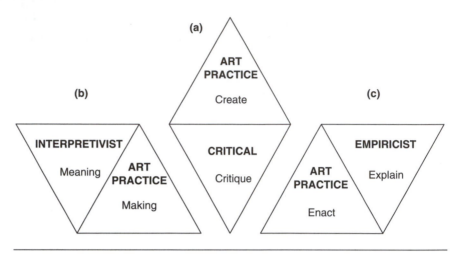

Figure 3.2   (a) Dimensions of Theory: Create-Critique
(b) Dimensions of Theory: Making-Meaning
(c) Dimensions of Theory: Enact-Explain

Practices in Theory and Inquiry

A feature of the visual framework (see Figure 3.1) is that there are various *dimensions of theory* embedded within the structure that help to further articulate how studio art practice can be integrated as part of the research process. Theories serve as important points of reference in research as they embrace conceptual systems, explanatory structures, methodologies, and practical pursuits that offer insights into issues that shape fields of inquiry. For art practice to be considered research, artist-theorists need to engage directly with theoretical concerns that can be investigated in studio contexts as well as through other mediated forms and methods. Figure 3.2 isolates dimensions of theory that are related areas although each shows a different theoretical focus. When these dimensions are seen in relationship to each other, it is possible to get a sense of how art practice can relate to theory in other disciplines. Three such relationships are shown. Figure 3.2a, Dimensions of Theory: Create-Critique, links Art Practice and Critical, as theoretical interests are investigated through a cycle of processes involving creating and critiquing. Theoretical issues surrounding Art Practice and Interpretivist dimensions can be explored by means of making and meaning processes (see Figure 3.2b, Dimensions of Theory: Making-Meaning). On the other hand, the dimensions of theory that can be analyzed in the relationship between Art Practice and Empiricist (see Figure 3.2c, Dimensions of Theory: Enact-Explain) involve enacting and explaining strategies. The theorizing processes and practices described in Figure 3.2, Dimensions of Theory, are mere guidelines because different dimensions of

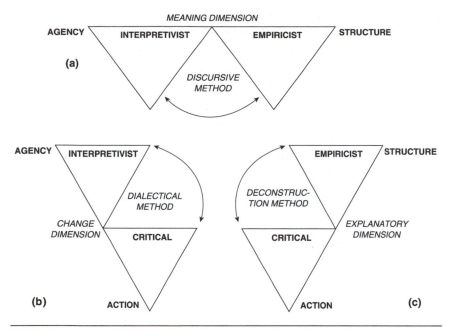

Figure 3.3   (a) Domains of Inquiry: Discursive
                    (b) Domains of Inquiry: Dialectical
                    (c) Domains of Inquiry: Deconstruction

theory can be related in different ways to discipline areas depending on the purpose of an inquiry.

There are also inquiry practices that describe methodological approaches contained in Figure 3.1. These are *domains of inquiry* and the general characteristics of these are outlined in the discussion of the regions titled Empiricist, Interpretivist, and Critical. There are, however, more direct methodological implications that can be drawn out when these are seen in relation to each other. Figure 3.3, Domains of Inquiry, describes approaches to inquiry that are informed by dimensions of theory (shown as a continuum along the base joining the two edge shapes) that bring together two discipline domains by means of a method of inquiry. These wedges of inquiry and content areas are brought to bear on issues of art practice in the process of undertaking research. For instance, Figure 3.3a, Domains of Inquiry: Discursive, investigates the theoretical dimension of *meaning* as the empiricist focus on structure and the interpretivist emphasis on agency are reviewed through *discursive* methods. Similarly, Figure 3.3b, Domains of Inquiry: Dialectical, explores the theoretical interest in *change* as the interpretivist sense of agency, and the critical perspective of action, is analyzed using *dialectical* methods. The third example, Figure 3.3c, Domains of

Inquiry: Deconstruction, examines explanatory dimensions of theory as the critical element of *action,* and the empiricist focus on *structure* are engaged using methods of *deconstruction.* Taking into account the diversity of content and methods within each of the domains of inquiry, it is easier to understand how identifying research problems in visual arts and exploring them in related disciplines is a matter of clarifying purposes and practices.

Figure 3.1 describes four other kinds of visual arts research practices: *understanding practices, reflexive practices, postdiscipline practices,* and *visual systems practices.* These practices are additional means by which visual arts practitioners can respond to issues of theory and practice through research.

Understanding Practices

An understanding practice describes the way visual arts knowledge is framed, encountered, critiqued, and created during the research process as insight is achieved and communicated. There are at least four kinds of understanding practices that can be considered to be part of a theoretical framework for conceptualizing art practice as research. First, visual arts knowledge is *transformative.* This means that knowledge creation in visual arts is recursive and constantly undergoes change as new experiences "talk back" through the process and progress of making art. Second, visual arts knowledge is *constructivist.* This means that knowledge is produced as a consequence of integrating theory and practice and this praxis results in descriptive awareness, explanatory insight, and powerful understanding. Third, visual arts knowledge is *conceptual.* This means that knowledge is grounded in the practice of making that uses knowledge that is available through personal cognitive systems and culturally accessible domains. Fourth, visual arts knowledge is *contextual.* This means that knowledge that is produced by artists enters into communities of users whose interests apply new understandings from different personal, educational, social, and cultural perspectives. These features of visual arts knowledge are by no means definitive, and each aspect owes a legacy to paradigms of theory and practice that, under certain circumstances, may be used as explanatory systems, interpretive frameworks, or imaginative forms.

Reflexive Practices

Reflexive practice is a kind of research activity that uses different methods to "work against" existing theories and practices and offers the possibility of seeing phenomena in new ways. Four reflexive practices are identified here. First, within the visual arts a *self-reflexive practice* describes an inquiry process that is directed by personal interest and creative insight, yet is informed by discipline knowledge and research expertise. This requires a transparent understanding of the field, which means that an individual can "see through" existing data, texts, and contexts so as to be open to alternative conceptions and imaginative options. Second, in responding to empirical understandings, a visual arts researcher will *reflect* on information gathered so as to review conceptual strategies used and consider other approaches. This reflexive practice is meta-analytic in focus and reveals the plurality of new views, much in the same way a gallery curator does when reassembling a collection so as to present a different reading of artworks. Third, the plausibility of an interpretation of research findings will be determined in part by the capacity of the reflexive researcher to openly *dialogue* with the information. This means that significance of meanings derived from a process of inquiry is subject to debate and discussion as a dialectic between the researcher and the researched takes place. Fourth, a reflexive practitioner will *question* content and contexts as problematic situations are revealed within particular settings. Issues-driven inquiry of this kind not only identifies problems, but also opens up areas whereby participants become responsive to potential change. This emancipatory interest offers opportunities for those most directly involved in a common cause to enact artistic, social, political, educational, or cultural change. These versions of reflexive practice in visual arts draw on the notion of "reflexive interpretation" proposed by Mats Alvesson and Kaj Sköldberg (2000).

> Reflexivity arises when the different elements or levels are played off against each other. It is in these relations and in the interfaces that reflexivity occurs. This approach is based upon an assumption—and implies—that no element is totalized; that is, they are all taken with a degree of seriousness, but there is no suggestion that any one of them is the bearer of the Right or Most Important Insight. (p. 249)

Figure 3.1 shows the interaction among different reflexive practices that Alvesson and Sköldberg discuss. The prospect of conducting inquiry that is *self-reflexive, reflective, dialogic,* and *questioning* so that each informs the other has considerable appeal for visual arts researchers whose practice, in general, is investigative, multilayered, and eclectic.

Postdiscipline Practices

Postdiscipline practice describes the way visual arts research takes place within and beyond existing discipline boundaries as dimensions of theory are explored and domains of inquiry adapted. The discipline perspectives that surround art making reflect ways of engaging with relevant theoretical issues and how appropriate methods might be deployed to meet research interests and needs. They also represent the major inquiry practices and cover the prominent empiricist, interpretivist, and critical traditions. In completing projects within the academic setting, the methods deployed by a studio-based researcher will center on art making and be surrounded by different discipline perspectives and practices. As shown in Figure 3.1, there is a *discipline-based* position that is embedded within the empiricist tradition of research. Within the interpretivist paradigm, it is through an *interdisciplinary* investigation of cultural texts that theories and practices are teased apart and meanings disclosed. Inquiry from the critical perspective, on the other hand, is more of an incursion as existing systems, structures, and practices are interrogated and changes enacted—this approach can be described as *transdisciplinary*.

When planning and undertaking research, artists also make informed choices about imaginative and intellectual approaches, just as they do when they create and respond to art. The process of making insightful decisions when carrying out research in art is not predicated on the assumption that there is a prescribed body of knowledge one learns and then applies. Notwithstanding the benefit of prior knowledge, at the outset there is little in the way of prevailing explanatory systems of knowledge within which new advances might be framed. Various theories of human processes, communal practices, and cultural agencies obviously abound, and these serve as both a grounded set of conditions and an interpretive framework around which inquiry is referenced. This is as basic to creative inquiry as it is to scholarly research. However, making informed choices about creative purposes involves selecting, adapting, and constructing ways of working and ways of seeing, and to do this one has to construct the tools of inquiry from an array of practices. When working from a base in contemporary art, the conceptions of the discipline are uncertain and the informing parameters are open-ended, yet the opportunity for inventive inquiry is at hand. In these circumstances, the artist-theorist is seen to be participating in a postdiscipline practice. There is little reliance on a prescribed content base; rather it is the deployment of a suitable methodological base that supports the questions being asked, which may take the researcher beyond content boundaries.

Although the university setting exerts its own institutional authority, the challenge is how to not only satisfy these demands, but also to maintain a degree of integrity about what constitutes visual arts research. It is in the area of research where these distinctions come into sharp contrast. A research problem will be broad yet also personally relevant. There is also a public consideration as the creation and communication of research outcomes becomes an educational act that can have an impact on others. Even if an artist eschews public commentary or critical response, the artwork occupies a public space for others to encounter. As the artwork is subject to public discourse, it enters into a set of institutional relations and as such becomes part of an interpretive regime. Once the personal is made public, an exchange that involves others is underway.

Visual Systems Practices: A Braided Metaphor

To appreciate the comprehensive yet flexible perspectives and methods involved in visual arts research, several approaches have been described. Each approach is identified in relation to its particular emphasis on theory or inquiry and in relation to content conceptions and discipline connections. There is, however, another research practice I want to present that is more holistic and encircles all the areas shown in the diagrams. *Visual systems practices* describe ways of visualizing and conceptualizing, and are presented as a metaphor for thinking about expansive relationships such as theory and practice connections, or concrete concerns such as the representation of visual knowledge.[13]

The overarching metaphor that best captures the idea pursued here—that visual arts research is both a complex and a simple practice—is the image of the "braid" (Sullivan, 2002). This notion draws from several sources, but the principal reference comes from Murray Gell-Mann's (1994, 1995, 2003) conception of "plectics."

> My name for that subject [simplicity and complexity] is *plectics,* derived from the Greek word *plektós* for "twisted" or "braided," cognate with– *plexus* in Latin *complexus,* originally "braided together," from which the English word complexity is derived. The word *plektós* is also related, more distantly, to *plex* in Latin *simplex,* originally "once folded," which gave rise to the English word *simplicity.* The name *plectics* thus reflects the fact that we are dealing with both simplicity and complexity. (Emphasis in original, p. 47)

The idea that contrasts such as simplicity and complexity could exist in useful tandem echoes the organic learning metaphors used by educators such as Froebel in the 19th century who saw great merit in the concept of the "unity of opposites." Similarly, of course, is the prevalence of the idea of oppositional balance in 20th-century formalist aesthetics. Another indirect reference is the connection the braided metaphor makes with the "field of metaphors" surrounding a clothes/body association of fabric and folds that Ian Stronach and Maggie MacLure (1997, pp. 27–30) use to describe limited images of postmodernism. Jean Dubuffet (1988) also uses the notion of a braided relationship to describe cultural responses to art. In his writings he is critical of the cultural elite and antagonistic toward art critics. He thinks art criticism is like strands of unraveling rope where meaning and the work are intertwined or disconnected so the same image can mean different things depending on the perspective of the viewer (or which part of the rope you are holding). Although Dubuffet sees this practice as a liability, it is also possible to see it as a context-dependent account that opens up the possibility of considering many perspectives.

There are four features of visual systems practices that can be connected to the metaphor of the braid: *complex and dynamic systems, self-similar structures, scale-free networks,* and *perspectivalism.* Viewing visual arts practice as a complex, interactive system that is distributed throughout the various media, languages, situations, and cultural contexts is a plausible account and is at the heart of the arguments in this book. Similarly, if research, like art making, involves asking "big" questions, then inquiries will invariably deal with structures, phenomena, networks of relationships, passions, and perspectives, and all manner of theories and practices that are part of our dynamic learning life. The belief that creative processes are complex associations of skill and agency that offers important insights into human understanding suggests that the research procedures used to investigate this potential need to be equally inventive yet suitably grounded in rigorous practices. But what are complex systems and how might they offer some metaphoric appeal to this quest?

Anyone interested in human engagement in a changing social, cultural, and global world brought into sharper focus by the critical cuts of postmodernism and the pervasive possibilities of technologies can't help but be excited. Amid this uncertainty and creativity there are dilemmas as past convictions come under challenge. For instance, the reductive paradigm that served art and science so well for so long no longer reveals the elusive truths thought to reside within matter and motion. Scientists and artists who are *really* interested in finding order within chaos and who see the micro and macro world around us as the lab or the studio are looking deep into material processes and organizing patterns with surprising outcomes. And these investigations often get carried out in the spaces between disciplines and without the safety net of codified practices. For instance, from the study of complex systems scientists are obtaining robust insights to suggest a need to rethink established canons as they are unable to explain what is now known to be happening. Although an agreement of what "complexity theory" is

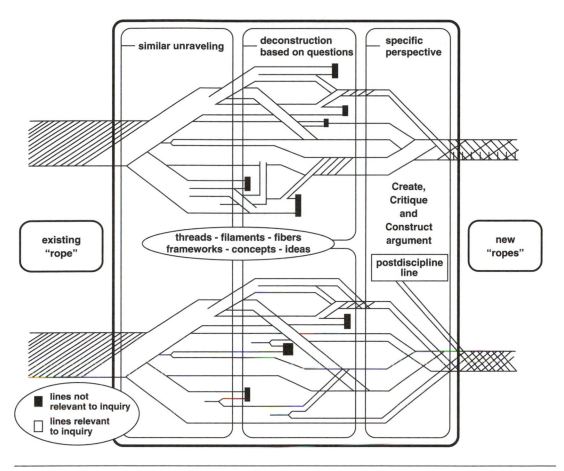

Figure 3.4   Transformative Visual Arts Research: A Braided Relationship

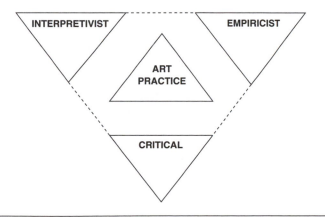

Figure 3.5   Braided Framework (Expanded View)

remains elusive, Peter Coveney and Roger Highfield (1995) offer a rousing rendition.

> Within science, complexity is a watchword for a new way of thinking about the *collective* behavior of many basic but interacting units, be they atoms, molecules, neurons, or bits within a computer. To be more precise, our definition is that *complexity is the study of the behavior of macroscopic collections of such units that are endowed with the potential to evolve in time.* Their interactions lead to coherent collective phenomena, so-called emergent properties that can be described only at higher levels than those of the individual units. In this sense, the whole is more than the sum of its components, just as a van Gogh painting is so much more than a collection of bold brushstrokes. This is as true for a human society as it is for a raging sea or the electrochemical firing patterns of neurons in a human brain. (Emphasis in the original, p. 7)

There are many artists who share the enthusiasm of Coveney and Highfield (Casti & Karlqvist, 2003). If we accept their definition as an exploration of changing relations among humans and their life worlds that is beguiling because small changes can bring unexpected outcomes in unusual ways, then we have a description of artistic inquiry into the human condition. Even more intriguing, however, is the prospect that an examination of these complex patterns and structures might not only reveal insights into the 20th-century theme of the human condition, but the 21st-century prospect of human design.[14]

Self-similarity is another feature associated with science that has conceptual appeal in the visual arts as new ideas, structures, and relationships are considered as part of the task of defining frameworks for inquiry. Let me explain what I mean by *self-similarity*. Reductionism and Euclidean notions of space are powerful systems that guide inquiry in both the sciences and the arts. The assumption is that a change in scale brings about new kinds of information so that the more things can be reduced to their basic essence, the better the chance of figuring out how they work. But nature and humans resist such simplistic design. It is not so much an evolutionary move from simple to complex that holds promise, but rather it is the capacity to embrace both the simple and the complex at the same time. Self-similarity is a concept that has its origin in Chaos Theory and describes iterative patterns that appear both simple and complex, but generally look irregular. James Gleick (1988) explains:

> Self-similarity is symmetry across scale. It implies recursion, pattern inside of pattern . . . self-similarity is an easily recognizable quality. Its

images are everywhere in the culture: in the infinitely deep reflection of a person standing between two mirrors, or in the cartoon notion of a fish eating a smaller fish eating a smaller fish eating a smaller fish. (p. 103)

Therefore if one ponders Chartres Cathedral in France, Antonio Gaudi's Sagrada Familia in Barcelona, or Frank Gehry's Guggenheim Museum in Bilboa, it is hard to identify a dominant structural form because the scale of these buildings is found in the smallest shape as well as the largest space. As Gleick would say, these buildings have "no scale" because they have "every scale" whereby "an observer seeing the building from any distance finds some detail that draws the eye [and] the composition changes as one approaches and new elements of the structure come into play" (p. 117). There is a self-similarity that is symmetrical across scale because when viewed close up or from afar, there are details that seem to draw the eye in ways simple shapes cannot. And for me, this similarity exists in all its simplicity and complexity at the micro level in the meeting of minds, and at a macro level in the meeting of cultures.

The concept of self-similarity shown in Figure 3.6 nicely captures the capacity of transformative visual arts to deal with issues and concerns at all

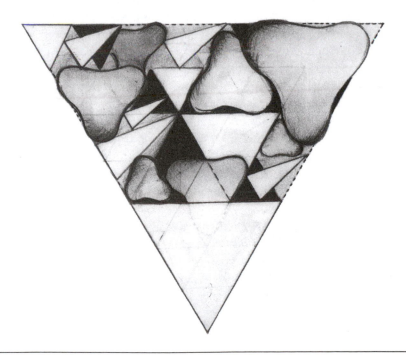

Figure 3.6   Concept of Self-Similarity

levels of theory and practice.[15] This characteristics means that visual arts research practice is independent of scale, which suggests it has a similar structure if undertaken in the studio, in the community, or within the culture. The basic triangular unit within this structure exhibits the properties of self-similarity because there is no underlying structure upon which more detailed systems are built. Instead, no matter whether viewed at the micro or macro level, the structure has similar properties and characteristics—it is both simple and complex at the same time. The claim I make here is that knowledge, ideas, beliefs, and values are aspects of human knowing that are independent of scale. Even though their inculcation within social structures conforms in general to hierarchical models, there is merit in thinking about these conditions as nonlinear and nonfoundational, but capable of new, emergent possibilities. As such, opportunities for research can be seen to be both informed by existing knowledge structures, but not to be a slave to them.

The other two visual system practices can be dealt with briefly. These are *perspectivalism* and *scale-free networks*. The first, perspectivalism, is readily understood in its various guises that alert us to the position of the "other" and is a widespread concept found in most contemporary domains of inquiry. In feminist studies, for instance, positionality has been instrumental in the critique of essentialism, and helpful in multicultural critiques in locating ideological leanings that "reveals the importance of identifying the positions and frames of reference from which scholars and writers present their data, interpretations, analyses, and instruction" (Banks, 1996, p. 6). Knowing that perspective frames our interpretations is also central to cultural discourse. Whether at the individual level, where our cognitive scripts shape how we understand things, or the mechanisms put in place in society that mediate what we encounter, we constantly confront positions that more than likely privilege certain perspectives. But to be able to critique and thereby control these circumstances is part of perceiving perspectives and being able to move beyond them as limiting structures. This is what Alvesson and Sköldberg (2000) paraphrase as a cumbersome term they call "perspectivization."

> This involves seeing familiar phenomena as strange, trying to differentiate one's understanding of empirical fragments (conversations, body motions, artefacts) from the primary impressions acquired from participant observation, trying to see different kinds of pattern, switching between levels of thought, and trying to think in similes (metaphor). (p. 184)

Finally, the visual systems practices of *scale-free networks* describes a way of thinking about how phenomena are related that adds to our understanding of existing structural forms such as hierarchies, taxonomies, matrices, distributions, and the like. As conceptual organizers these structures serve as reductive devices that allow us to represent information to assist with easy interpretation. Most methods of representing large-scale phenomena subscribe to a hierarchical principle whereby parts of a system are indexed under broader categories. Yet not all phenomena easily conform to such a structure; therefore it is profitable to consider other forms of representation. As has been revealed from complexity theory (Eve, Horsfall, & Lee, 1997), complex systems do exhibit particular organizing principles yet offer more extensive ways of configuring relationships among things. What is particularly attractive to visual arts researchers is the concept of "scale-free" networks in the sense that complex phenomena, no matter how big or how small, have some elements that have both unique and universal characteristics. This is quite different from normal distributions that reflect random occurrences and probability characteristics that are so much a part of traditional quantitative research. It is not that any radical theoretical insights from complexity theory or chaos theory (which is anything but "chaotic") will drastically change our conception of all the possible ways of investigating phenomena. However, the prospect that there are alternative conceptions that allow us to see things differently as we further our understanding of relationships and networks of connections, influences, and changes is intriguing for visual arts researchers to ponder.

CONCLUSION ●

This chapter argues that understanding is a viable goal of educational research and that explanatory theories of human learning need to be supplemented with transformative theories of individual and social action. It is further contended that these theories can be found within the thoughts, ideas, and actions that result from making art, for it is from a base in studio experience where the capacity to create in order to critique is given form. This posits the view that art practice can be claimed to be a legitimate form of research and that approaches to inquiry can be located within the studio experience. Therefore art practice needs to be seen as a valuable site for raising theoretically profound questions and exploring them using robust research methods. Furthermore, there is an extensive range of modalities and methods that can be used to yield critically grounded and individually transforming outcomes. From this perspective, artistic practice can be seen to comprise a critical coalition of practices that involve an ongoing dialogue between, within, and around the artist, artwork, and context where each has a role to play in the pursuit of understanding. But to appreciate the possibility of art practice being presented as a form of research in this way there is a need to accept that the visual image is replete with potential evidence of knowledge. This is a plausible claim if we consider how images operate as texts, artifacts, and events that embody cultural meanings. And within this layering of image structures there are mediated processes and systems of production and exchange that further complicate and intensify the status of images as information sites and cultural codes.

Within this cultural regime the artist-as-theorist takes on a larger responsibility. Old traditions that render the visual arts as emblems of privilege and privy to a select few are no longer tenable as access and ownership of the creation and communication of images of all sorts is in the hands of the many. But it is not this pervasive presence of a visual currency that demands the attention of artists; rather, it is a necessity to lead the way. The circumstances are such that there are new vistas among the visions because ideas these days are less constrained by discipline rigidities. Additionally, the complement of surrounding theories continues to open up new possibilities for locating links among areas such as the sciences, the visual arts, and newer technologies. Consequently, it is no longer plausible to accept empty rhetoric such as the claim that the visual image is merely a way of saying what cannot effectively be said in words or numbers. Rather, based on the concepts and conditions covered in this chapter, it can be argued that a new era of visual arts research is possible for those who see studio art as a site for conducting transformative research that has individual and cultural relevance. Furthermore, there is a degree of flexibility in how visual arts research might be formalized to meet the credibility demands of institutional practice, be it the goal of "good research" in the academy, or the quest for "good art" in the artworld.

● NOTES

1. Medical schools pioneered problem-based learning using the case method as a simulated learning protocol. Here the problems posed were incomplete or purposefully vague and required research, discussion, and consultation in order to arrive at a well-reasoned diagnosis. For an example of problem-based learning in the teaching of aesthetics in the elementary school, see Costantino (2002).

2. David Carrier (1987) defines *artwriting* as the process of studying the approaches to art criticism used by contemporary critics and philosophers who write about art, and he has written extensively about the artwriting of many of his contemporaries. His more recent work (2003) examines the use of narrative as an explanatory form used by art writers and fiction writers in their reading of artistic images. I find this term useful in a more global sense because it encompasses the loose group of critics, aestheticians, historians, and cultural critics whose job it is to

draw our attention to the visual arts. Not only does this serve as a generic term, but also it reminds me that art writers are like artists and come to encounters with art with their own perspectives, proclivities, and passions.

3. See, for example, Young (2001), who argues that the function of art is to provide either pleasure or knowledge. See also *Working Papers in Art & Design*, Vol. 2 (2002), a special issue devoted to knowledge claims in the visual arts within the context of practice-based research. Retrieved September 14, 2003 from http://www.herts .ac.uk/artdes/research/papers/wpades/vol2/intro02.html.

4. The list of sources that deal specifically with interpretation as a realm of art criticism is extensive and can be grouped into many typologies, depending on the aesthetic interest, sociocultural perspective, or political bent. For particular positions see Berger (1972); Danto (1986b); hooks (1995); and Pollock (2001). For explorations of interpretation and criticism in art education see Barrett (1994, 1996) and Lankford (1992). There is extensive literature on visual culture in the field of art education. See, for example, Duncum and Bracy (2001) and Freedman (2003). Several of the art education journals have published theme issues dealing with visual culture; see, for example, *Studies in Art Education,* 2003, *44*(3), *Visual Arts Research,* 2002, *28*(2), and *Art Education,* 2003, *56*(2).

5. See, for example, the writing of Kenneth Beittel (1979), who advocated a phenomenological approach to the study of art practice. Although there is no distinctive genre of art education research dealing with contemporary artists' practice, there are accounts that address particular perspectives. See, for example, Irwin and Miller (1997), Krug (1992/1993), LaChapelle (1991), Nadaner (1998), Sullivan (1996, 2002), and Taylor (1989).

6. The strategy of means-ends theorizing is quite common across disciplines in the arts and humanities. For instance, in citing Christopher Frayling's use of ideas adapted from Sir Herbert Read, Darren Newbury (1996) identifies a research framework that involves research *into* art and design, research *through* art and design, and research *for* art and design.

7. For a synopsis of practice-based research across several generations of researchers, see Bird (2000), Candlin (2001), and Gray (1998).

8. There are several government-sponsored reports and professional association responses and conference papers that track the political changes and legislated frameworks put in place during the 1980s and 1990s as the visual arts came under close scrutiny in higher education. For example, in the United Kingdom, see the *Harris Report* (Harris, 1996), Frayling (1997), and Green (2001). Within the Australian context see Rowley (1994) and Strand (1998).

9. In countries such as the United Kingdom and Australia, government funding of research undertaken in higher education is linked to prevailing policies and national assessment measures are periodically undertaken to determine the ranking of research activity in the disciplines across institutions. In the U.K. the institutional research ranking is known as the Research Assessment Exercise (RAE). See http://www.hero.ac.uk/rae (last accessed on March 18, 2004). A similar scheme in Australia is called the Institutional Grants Scheme (IGS). See www.dest.gov.au/ highered/research/igs.htm (last accessed on March 20, 2004). These policies set in

place a "dual" model of funding whereby research support (grants, research students enrolled, etc.) produced by universities becomes part of a cycle of accountability that is further supported by government funds. Although there is access to private funding sources, by far the most prominent are government-supported agencies such as the Arts and Humanities Research Board (AHRB) in the U.K., and the Australian Research Council (ARC) in Australia. In recent years, the definition of research has been modified to accommodate the needs of disciplines such as art and design. For instance the AHRB states that it "supports work that seeks to enhance or develop creativity, insights, knowledge and understanding in the artistic and creative activities, history, languages, literature, and systems of thought and belief, both past and present." See http://www.ahrb.ac.uk/ahrb/website (last accessed on March 18, 2004). In 2004, the Canadian government awarded the first of the series of Research/Creation Grants that are designed to support innovative research about "real-life issues" in the humanities and the social sciences being undertaken in higher education. Sponsored by the Social Sciences and Humanities Research Council of Canada (SSHRC), a base budget of $195 million (Canadian) was approved for 2003–2004. Recipients of these inaugural grants included many projects being undertaken by Canadian arts-based researchers. See http://www.sshrc.ca/web/apply/program_descriptions/fine_arts_ e.asp (last accessed on May 12, 2004).

What is apparent is that as the expectation to carry out research in higher education increases within the orbit of government policy and institutional priorities, there is a need to ensure that disciplines such as the visual arts are able to describe a research practice that satisfies, and hopefully extends, any institutional or government definition.

10. A challenge for CAA is to define studio-based teaching and art learning practices not only as a form of professional training, but also as scholarly inquiry. There are moves afoot to expand the range of academic opportunities open to studio faculty in the visual arts being promoted by the CAA as the master of fine arts (MFA) is seen to be an inadequate exit credential for university-level teaching.

11. For debates and discussions about the nature of qualitative evidence within different research perspectives see, for example, Clifford and Marcus (1986), Coffey and Atkinson (1996), Jaeger (1997), May (2002), Reichardt and Rallis (1994), Silverman (2001), and Strauss and Corbin (1990).

12. The original purpose of *hermeneutics* was to critically examine obscure or contradictory texts from religious sources in order to achieve an authoritative interpretation. This was also known as an *exegesis* or an interpretation of a text (usually biblical). Nowadays, hermeneutics is situated at the very heart of individual meaning making, and as is discussed earlier in the chapter, *exegesis* is the term used in practice-based research in reference to the textual interpretation that is part of doctoral study.

13. Suggestions for visualizing, conceptualizing, and designing visual arts research that originates in studio practice are given in Chapter 6.

14. Reconceptualizing and visualizing the physical and emotional structures of what it is to be human was a common theme in the 2003 Venice Biennale where genetic revision, human-animal mutation, and environmental surveillance were all part of the human remix. See the work of Daniel Lee (*108 Windows*), András Gálik

and Bálint Havas (*Little Warsaw*), Patricia Piccinini (*We are Family*), and Hannah Greely (*Silencer*) in Francesco Bonami and Maria Luisa Frisa (Eds.). (2003). *50th International Art Exhibition: Dreams and Conflicts—The Dictatorship of the Viewer* (pp. 506–507). Ca' Giustinian, San Marco: La Biennale di Venezia.

15. The notion of self-similarity shown in Figure 3.6 is a self-similar structure based on the *Koch Snowflake* used to construct a Koch curve first described by the Swedish mathematician Helge von Koch in 1904. Self-similar structures of this kind define areas that are less than that of the original yet require lines that are progressively longer; therefore an "infinitely long line surrounds a finite area" (Gleick, 1988, p. 99). In other words, the structure of a shape can appear to get infinitely smaller yet retain the same form, although it will require more and more detail to document it.

CHAPTER 4

VISUAL KNOWING

Maxine Greene says that art can't change things, but it can change people, who can change things. She talks of the imagination as the place where the possible can happen; a place of "resisting fixities, seeking the openings," where "we relish incompleteness, because that signifies that something still lies ahead" (2003, p. 22–23). The promise of change that comes from wonder takes shape in the things we create, through what we make and experience, or from what we come to see and know through the experience of someone else. Using the visual arts to turn questions into understanding that give rise to more questions not only describes an aesthetic process of self-realization but also describes a research process. If we believe that the outcome of inquiry is the creation of new knowledge, then "knowing," or the capacity to use our understanding in new ways, will always be incomplete. Although this sense of unknowing propels the imagination as Maxine reminds us, there is always an element of completion as our new knowledge helps us understand things we did not know before.

It is from this sense of knowing and unknowing, and how we deal with it, that visual arts practice can be described as a form of research. This is why the previous chapter argues that understanding is as significant *as* explanation as a goal of research, for understanding requires knowledge to be created from which explanations can be extracted: To create, the researcher has to enter into the realm of imagination, to take on the possible, as well as the plausible, and probable. This practice is well known to artists and art writers. For instance, David Hockney's (2001) controversial claim that some of the European masters may have used lenses to help draft many of their paintings, or parts of them, arose when he recognized a similarity in the linework of the 19th century European artist Jean-Auguste-Dominique Ingres, and the 20th century American artist Andy Warhol. For Hockney, the assured clarity and representational accuracy of Ingres's quick sketches of people reminded him of the bold but deft portrait tracings Andy Warhol made with the help of overhead projector transparencies. Hockney saw a resemblance in the line of Ingres and Warhol. His subsequent inquiries and analyses convinced Hockney that the use of lenses and other devices for reproducing images was a common if secret practice among many European masters and that the evidence was in the paintings themselves. It comes as no surprise that Hockney's claims have been ridiculed by many, in particular historians who have their own less-secret knowledge base on which to draw. A common dismissive response is that an artist with less skill than the European masters might have good reason to suggest that such accuracy could only be obtained with the use of a visual trick.[1] But what is not mentioned in the debates is that it took an *artist* to be able to see an unlikely connection: a fellow observer skilled at making marks and expert at figuring out how to solve visual problems.[2] That art historians did not notice what Hockney did may be because they did not know what to look for, as practical-theoretical knowledge is not normally part of a connoisseur's toolkit. But Hockney's thesis remains moot unless there is independent corroboration. However, the importance he draws to visual evidence, and then going public with his display of the artist's compulsive need to know, is an instance of how art practice can lead to a different route of inquiry that reveals fresh perspectives.

An example of how art writers *create* knowledge that is used to better understand what might be already known is the invented dialogues of Giorgio Vasari in *Lives of the Artists* (1568/1993). In his biographies Vasari re-creates scenes and encounters. His account of Michelangelo Buonarroti (vol. 3, pp. 111–234) features several instances of invented dialogue that give a glimpse of events and circumstances and what might have transpired between the artist and his teachers, fellow artists, and patrons. Rather than rejecting Vasari's inventions as fictional history, we can trust his capacity to present plausible accounts as he established one of the first art academies, the *Accademia del Disegno* in 1562, that included more than 30 distinguished artist-members, so he had insider knowledge. The consequence is that we are transported into the lives of the artists in a way that helps us to understand things. From this position we are more easily able to add flesh to the facts that are more formally documented so that any historical explanation is more fully enriched by this appreciation of the times. This approach is similar to that taken by the historian Simon Schama who seeks out connections between events, as they are known, and narrative accounts enhanced by scenarios and simulations he creates, and this forces the reader or viewer into an active participation in an historical moment.[3] Schama draws on a broader knowledge base than Hockney does, although the demand for corroborative support remains the same for both. Yet it can be argued that it is possible to create knowledge from which new understanding arises because it allows us to see things in a new light, particularly when compared to what is already known. In other words, to *create* and *critique* is at the heart of visual knowing.

The purpose of this chapter is to explore in more detail the conditions that influence how artists work to create the things they do. This builds on the research framework proposed in Chapter 3 and strengthens the argument that art practice can be seen to be research activity. In the next chapter we will look at how others, such as art writers and art teachers, create and use different kinds of visual arts knowledge through their critical research and studio-classroom inquiry. But for now, in order to propose visual arts practice as a type of research uniquely equipped to deal with issues of individual and cultural significance, there is a need to be clear about some of the structures and strategies artists use. This also needs to be examined in relation to how artists respond to content interests and methods from other disciplines, contexts, and perspectives and adapt them in inquiry. The first section examines visual cognition as a domain within cognitive science that is building a more complete picture of visual information processing and giving a clearer understanding of the relationships among seeing, sensing, and knowing. Visual cognitive processing is then positioned within debates about the role of context on knowing. From this foundation the thinking practices in the visual arts are reviewed by tracking traditions where cognitive conceptions moved through phases I describe as *thinking in a medium, thinking in a language,* and *thinking in a setting.* This analysis is used to describe a framework for visual arts knowing that can be located within the braided structure for research presented in the previous chapter. Research projects and artist profiles that present examples of visual arts knowing within a research framework of art practice conclude the chapter.

VISUAL COGNITION ●

The cognitive sciences attract considerable interest across different disciplines today as the simplicity and complexity of our visual information processing system is further unraveled. A somewhat simple realization is that there is no such thing as pure perception, for what we see is shaped by what we know. This belies the immensely complex architecture through which images are tracked and treated as meanings are made. There is by no means complete agreement about how images are processed in the brain, although it is obvious that visualization is a mindful activity. What is also apparent to many is that how we make sense of visual images is both a private and public activity. Here, personal proclivities may serve as cognitive frames, but the cultural filters constructed around us also shape these interpretations. These two conceptions of visual knowing, mentalism and contextualism, warrant further discussion and I examine them in the sections called *Sensing and Knowing* and *Visual Context*.

Sensing and Knowing

The study of visual perception and information processing and its relation to brain functioning has long been a topic of interest to cognitive scientists and those interested in the creative capacities of the human mind. The use of diverse visual thinking processes is, of course, a well-documented strategy used as much by scientists as by artists (Austin, 2003; Perkins, 2000; Wallace & Gruber, 1989). As shown in Chapter 1, there were times when science and art were indistinguishable. When studying a painting in 15th-century Florence, it would have been difficult to tell the difference between geometry, draftsmanship, and illusion. These days the structure and functions of the visual system is well documented in introductory science texts. It is mostly shown as a causal structure that explains how things are perceived by the eye and interpreted by the brain. Although the mechanics of the process are clear-cut, there is still conjecture about how we make meaning from what we see. Empiricists see sensory perception as the basis of knowledge, and philosophers see it as the site of experience. The reliability of the senses has, of course, been questioned since classical times, and concerns take many forms. For instance, philosophers are more interested in errors of logic in what is perceived, and scientists focus on errors in observations caused by the tricks perceptions play. But perception is not mindless sensation. Although it may be immediate and intense, perception does not just provide data picked up by the senses; it also plays an active role in conceptualization. This relationship between perception and conception has been debated for a long time and it is somewhat similar to questions posed earlier about where knowledge resides: Is it in the artwork (objective), or in the mind of the viewer (subjective)? But such questions have rhetorical (or historical) appeal only, for it is readily accepted that conceptions of mind and perceptions of matter are inextricably linked (Bechtel & Abrahamsen, 1991; Newell & Simon, 1981). But how?

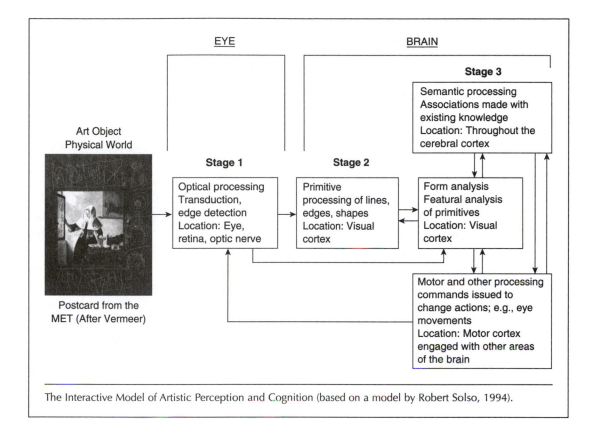

The Interactive Model of Artistic Perception and Cognition (based on a model by Robert Solso, 1994).

The mechanics of the visual system are often shown as cross-linked pathways that track an image as it is seen and absorbed as patterns of light, and passed from the retina at the back of the eye through neural flips and onto the brain—and all in a split second. The senses serve as transducers that take in energy from the external world (such as light through the eyes) and change it into channels of stimuli that form neural messages, which are decoded by the brain. We don't really see with our eyes, they merely take in the sights and send them on their way via the optic nerve to the brain where they become insights. So it is in the brain where we see representations of the world around us—in the mind's eye. As Robert Solso (1994) states, "[W]e 'think' art as much as, no, even more than, we 'see' art" (p. 147). These images are made from visual bits drawn from different regions of the brain that we construct as conceptions, schemata, cognitive scripts, and so on. They may exist in many forms of representation and in many areas tucked within the labyrinthine layers of the brain. Solso reminds us that the process of seeing and understanding is a meeting of the minds in the sense that initial perceptual processes are *bottom-up* in that these stimulus activities perceive information in basic structural forms that are subject to *top-down* processing where cognitive operations give meaning to what we see (p. 110).

If we identify key concepts that contemporary scientists are currently investigating, these can be seen to focus on the usual areas of language, memory, and mental representation, but also on realms of emotion, surprise, feelings, flexibility, multiple representations, alternative paths to meaning making, and the like. Many of the scientists who study the complexity of thinking are researching topics that comfortably sit within the content interests of artists and art educators. If we analyze the theoretical issues directing research in cognitive science, we see an emphasis on computational modes of cognition (Chomsky, 1980; Newell & Simon, 1981) and connectionist theories (Bechtel & Abrahamsen, 1991; Rumelhart, 1998), along with recent speculations about more dynamic models (Thelen & Smith, 1994).

Those advocating a *computational* model of the mind explain cognition in terms of the unique human capacity to use symbolic structures, problem-solving capacities, and rule-governed processes as we hone our adaptive behavior. Building on early research in computer simulation, the brain is seen to make use of rules and operating principles (the hardware) that organizes how we process information (the software). This structure is generally believed to be a genetically constrained adaptive system, and the most prominent examples are seen in linguistics, an early example being Noam Chomsky's theory of syntax (1980), or more recently Steven Pinker's language "instinct" (1994). These days this quest to devise ways to explain and represent human cognition relies less on the digital computer as the model of the mind, and problem solving as the computational device, for the cognitive demands are taking the research across discipline boundaries. This is attractive to those in the visual arts who support the view that art is a form of symbolic functioning.

Another approach to the study of cognition is *connectionism*. This draws together metaphors about the brain and computers and models an architecture of the mind that consists of an enormous array of parallel neural networks that describe learning as a means of "connecting." To this extent, information is *in* the connections and "it means that almost all knowledge is *implicit* in the structure of the device that carries out the task rather than *explicit* in the states of units themselves" (Rumelhart, 1998, p. 210, emphasis in the original). What Rumelhart is saying is that there is no index of ready-made symbolic meanings in the brain from which we draw. Rather, the meaning is in the making, and content connections could come from anywhere. Based on an associationist model, the neural architecture is seen to be a system of interconnected hubs and units that are activated simultaneously in many areas as information is accessed. As a parallel rather than a serial process, connectionism is not governed by any executive function or central processor. Rather, cognitive processing activates links strengthened by previous learning, but is also open to intuitive and opportunistic connections. Many visual artists would have little difficulty endorsing a view that favors this kind of intuitive integration of prior knowledge and the possibility of new associations.

There is, however, a third orientation that offers intriguing insights about cognitive functioning. This is a *dynamicist* theory that sees cognition as a systemslike model that is continually changing as a consequence of the interactions between a thinker and the surrounding environment. Activities in dynamic systems have a self-organizing capacity which means that the parts are able to relate or connect to any other in multiple, nonlinear ways. When seen within the context of cognitive functioning, this amounts to new possible ways of thinking as different structures can emerge from chaotic and complex states. Whether such complex systems will ultimately lend themselves to robust modeling remains to be seen. The acknowledgment, however, that cognition can be seen as a dynamic mix of individual action amid environmental constraints will be attractive to artists who favor a contextualist view of thinking and learning.

Visual Context

In the minds of many cognitive scientists, the somewhat traditional distinction between basic research and applied research remains the criteria for determining how to study cognition. Consequently, it is mainly those behaviors believed to be essential to human functioning and adaptation that are investigated, while other aspects of mental activity are dismissed as frivolous, or are seen to deal with qualities that do not lend themselves to scientific inspection and explanation. For example, in the mind of Steven Pinker (1997), if the "psychology of status" is taken out of the "psychology of the arts" not much remains that is relevant to study (p. 523). This curious response maintains a reductive hierarchy of content and method that constricts rather than creates opportunities to see things anew. Yet there is a realization among many cognitive scientists that, for instance, pursuing a computational model of the mind, where a theory gets operationalized as a computer program, is limiting. Although the computational metaphor was prominent during the early genesis of the cognitive movement, it is less evident in recent years where a more embodied notion of cognition is preferred. In some cases, a computational model makes for relatively clean and clinical experimentation, but to embrace the interconnections between human systems of mind and matter requires a view from up close and from afar—and scientists know this as much as artists. Therefore, unless research traditions continue to expand in scope and method the arts and the sciences will remain caricatured in their own way, with both the scientist and the art enthusiast seen as experts that continue to know more and more about less and less.

Researchers interested in human knowing in all its forms not only consider the immediate situational factors that might impinge on understanding, but broader contexts as well. We know that the mind is a complex adaptive system because it learns. Therefore it is reasonable to assume that those faculties of the mind and the features of our surroundings that help us learn warrant investigation. There are at least three kinds of connections that offer the chance to consider how relationships between mental processing and contextual framing influence how meanings are made. First, in thinking about thinking in its broadest sense, it is through interdisciplinary discourse that promising conversations are to be had. In looking at how various discipline traditions consider the relationship between theory and practice, common concerns can be identified, as well as limitations that may hinder exchange. Second, interest in the developing mind as a valued social goal means that institutional and community support become structures to consider that mediate cognitive functioning. Finally, there are situated events where encounters among individuals and specific circumstances set up opportunities for grounding cognitive learning within the practice of real-life settings.

An example of the first kind of cognitive context is given by Ronald Schleifer, Robert Con Davis, and Nancy Mergler (1992) in their account of conceptual links they establish between cognition and culture. Their approach is to situate cognition across the discipline boundaries of science and literature in order to move beyond the epistemological limitations of each. The aim is to show how the rational critique that characterizes continental semiotic theory, and the empirically grounded conception of Anglo-American cognition, both offer insight into cognitive activity. In other words, the semiotic process of examining the signifier-signified relationship of meaning and understanding, reason and rationality, subjectivity and objectivity, is used to critique the structure and mechanism of cognition. The underlying principle is that during cognition we come to understand things as a consequence of apprehending relationships that exist empirically in the world. Therefore Schleifer and his colleagues assert that matters of fact supported by empiricism are governed by the same reasoning that the mind uses in the process of cognitive functioning.

> We are arguing that Continental semiotics, growing out of a rationalist tradition, emphasizes the *simplicity* of understanding—its parsimonious logical coherence—whereas Anglo-American empiricism emphasizes the attempt of understanding to account for matters of fact as *exhaustively* as possible. (p. 5, emphasis in the original)

By undertaking a critique of the semiotics of cognition that go beyond the dominant models from cognitive psychology, the intention of Schleifer et al. is to better understand the intersections between culture and cognition. Culture in this sense refers to the broad characteristics of phenomena much in the way that paradigms represent distinct positions, and therefore the quest is to get a better sense of the particular and general features of cognition. This strategy is similar to that discussed in Chapter 3 and described in Figure 3.1 that aligns the Empiricist, Interpretivist and Critical domains as different theories and practices that can be integrated through purpose-driven inquiry. The art of Tracey Moffatt slips seamlessly among this framework. The brooding, painterly photographs are experienced empirically as disarming memories or childhood nightmares. And the emotional burden is readily referenced to other interpretive texts that broaden the scope of the critical overtones of gender and race. To discuss the other kinds of relationships that connect cognitive processing and contextual influences, I turn to a discussion of cognitive practices in the visual arts, because these describe a basis of visual arts knowing.

Tracey Moffatt, *Invocations #5* (*left*) and *Invocations #10* (*right*) (2000). Photo silkscreen. 58 × 48 inches. Series of 13 images, edition of 60. Reproduced courtesy of the artist and Roslyn Oxley9 Gallery.

● THINKING PRACTICES IN THE VISUAL ARTS

To describe a framework for visual arts knowing there is a need to provide a brief historical account of changing conceptions about artistic thinking practices. Many theories seek to explain the workings of the creative mind and what constitutes artistic knowing (Gardner, 1982; Wallace & Gruber, 1989; West, 1997). Once seen as a human capacity contained within the inventive headspace of the gifted but socially mute individual, more recent conceptions acknowledge creativity as a social construct (Csikszentmihalyi, 1988; Goodman, 1984). Yet describing the cognitive foundations of artistic thinking remains an elusive goal for researchers. Of the theories and practices we proclaim, there are, however, some enduring principles at play. Some things stand out: The visual arts involve thinking, and imaginative thinking, as Maxine Greene (1995) reminds us, is never fixed as it embraces what is known and unknown. The importance of thoughts becomes apparent when they are enacted in some form. Although the value of artistic thinking has long been championed, the mechanism by which thoughts are generated may be more clearly understood as an interactive cognitive process, but how mental images are given creative form remains delightfully obscure. Artists are versatile in using insights and intuitions to bring ideas to fruition in ways that might initially appear strange or novel but in retrospect can seem entirely appropriate once the contextual implications are absorbed. For many artists, imaginative thoughts may arise in planning, during the process of making, as a consequence of critical reflection, or through meanings made by others. These significant others can include art writers, cultural critics, and art teachers, because when artworks are made and displayed, they open up an opportunity to think and learn, not only about the visual arts, but also about other relevant issues of personal concern and public importance.

At various times in the history of aesthetics and art education a prevailing belief was that visual arts knowing should emphasize the *process,* and at other times, the *product.* This brings to mind the discussion in the previous chapter about the site where art knowledge is believed to reside: Is it in the process of making art, in the artwork itself, or in the mind of the viewer? As I describe, one of the outcomes of postmodernism is the rejection of binary thinking as a conceptual strategy that limits how we might think about the interdependencies among phenomena. The process-product dichotomy is one such characterization that benefits from a critical review as a way to reconceptualize the cognitive structures and contexts that comprise visual arts knowing. To do this, I explore three perspectives below that I describe as *thinking in a medium, thinking in a language,* and *thinking in a context.*

From this analysis, I then propose an integrated approach to visual arts knowing I label *transcognition.*

Thinking in a Medium

This perspective describes artistic thinking as primarily being the consequence of thought and action that is given form in a creative product. Drawing as it does from areas of psychology as the defining paradigm, *thinking in a medium* is a useful description of this orientation. In general, we associate this view with Anglo-American traditions in cognitive psychology. In art education, this position is well represented in the "visual thinking" research of Rudolf Arnheim (1969, 1974) and Claire Golomb (1974, 1992), and in the art-media studies of Judith Burton (2001; Burton, Horowitz, & Abeles, 2000) and Nancy Smith (1993). Other approaches take a more systemslike approach and see cognitive functioning as a form of symbolic processing (Gardner, 1973, 1983), and in some cases, different cognitive functions are associated with different media (Hirschfeld & Gelman, 1994) that emphasize the domain specificity of knowing. The extrapolation of these ideas relative to the creative processes used by adults (Gardner, 1993) further emphasizes that some artists think in a medium, even as the medium moves to embrace structural and cultural constraints.

In working within this perspective an assumption is made that the art product is an outcome of artistic thinking and therefore is a site for answering questions about how art knowledge is acquired and represented. Inquiries make use of empirical traditions where the quest is for self-evident truths found within an objective world of reality. Thoughts are the structural bits of cognition that help grasp the meaning of relationships and these exist empirically in the world so that mental phenomena are understood within an economy of behavior. The goal is to present a view of understanding that is simple, exhaustive, and generalizable, and based on information collected that is observable, confirmable, and therefore knowable. Within this tradition of inquiry into human cognition, it is generally assumed that the mind *finds* nature.

When translated into inquiries in the visual arts, the expectation is that the study of perceptual processes is the best way to understand visual thinking. Visual arts knowing, as such, is a form of symbolic functioning that may be associated with the visual properties of different media where physiognomic qualities lend themselves to expressive potential in the hands and minds of artists and children. In this sense, artists think in a medium, and particular dispositions and habits of mind help individuals give form to meaning during the process of making. Paul Bowen, a sculptor from Provincetown,

Massachusetts, provides an example of thinking in a medium. For Bowen, the material he uses becomes a site for ideas rather than a carrier of any other notions such as romantic references to place, or visible traces of history. In describing the way images can be recovered from materials during the sculptural process Bowen likes to let forms emerge from the activity of working, rather than attempting to impose ideas. He explains, "[F]requently I'll screw wood just flat to the wall and look for some kind of form that may in some sense already exist there and try to . . . pull something out of it" (cited in Sullivan, 2001, p. 4). Artists like Bowen think in a medium.

Thinking in a Language

Artistic thinking is also seen as a process whereby cognition is a socially mediated process. This view has its genesis within the traditions of hermeneutics and semiotics (Barthes, 1968; Ricoeur, 1981). Rather than focusing on behavioral outcomes to study cognition, we try to make sense out of the intrinsic way language is used to construct stories and meanings through art talk or discourse that is sparked by encounters with art (Barrett, 1994; Parsons, 1992). In visual arts, this cognitive orientation emphasizes the process and is best described as *thinking in a language.* In this view, knowledge of cognition is built on the basis of the way linguistic signs function and understanding emerges as a process mediated by social and cultural conventions. Therefore, thinking in art, and thinking about art, is language dependent.

This perspective draws on European interpretive traditions where understanding what an image might mean can be grasped through rational discourse and critique. The focus is on language and narrative construction with images and objects seen as texts that carry forms of cultural coding that require analysis and deconstruction to reveal readings. Therefore meanings are not found, but are *made* within the conditions that mediate responses where art talk is grounded in the sociocultural conventions of language. In a similar way, understanding in art is mediated by the life world of the individual as the mind remakes nature. An example of cognition as process is provided by Maria Magdalena Campos-Pons, who is a Cuban-born installation artist working in the United States. The reflective thinking that shapes Campos-Pons's art practice is grounded in her deep cultural affiliation. The realization that she could explore complex issues by making art that documented personal paths convinced her that private passions and cultural concerns were inextricably linked. Narrative is a primary means used by Maria Magdalena Campos-Pons to critique the cultural dislocations observed in her Afro-Cuban heritage and serves as a framework for dialogue with viewers.

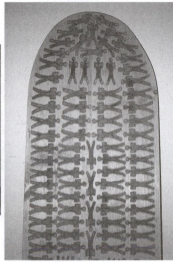

As a Cuban born artist, the reflective thinking that shapes the art practice of Maria Magdalena Campos-Pons is grounded in a deep cultural affiliation. For Pons, inquiry into cultural histories involves dealing with the way her black heritage is represented and the realization that "the history that I have access to is the history that is told through a voice that is not necessarily of the black people." In investigating these historical dislocations Pons uses the body as a window through which to explore autobiographical aspects of the past. The human form in this sense can be considered to be a body of information that includes formal details, memories, feelings, and the rich repertoire of culturally grounded knowledge. On the other hand, the body can also record the physical and symbolic ruptures inflicted on individuals throughout history.

Maria Magdalena Campos-Pons, *The Seven Powers Coming by the Sea* (section) (1992). Timber, soil, metal, photographs. Variable dimensions. Reproduced courtesy of the artist. Photograph by Graeme Sullivan.

Campos-Pons uses story to explore and reassert histories about her race and culture as a way of reviving traditional techniques such as low relief carving, and as a metaphor around which she shapes her working processes. Artists like Campos-Pons think in a language of ideas and interpretations.

Thinking in a Context

The importance of context as an informing agency in learning and understanding is central to many recent arguments about cognition (Lave & Wenger, 1991; Light & Butterworth, 1993; Sternberg & Wagner, 1994). In considering the role of context, it is important to acknowledge that this includes human involvement as well as situational factors, physical features, and other environmental and cultural cues. This includes related descriptions, such as situated cognition and distributed cognition, which David Perkins (1992) describe as the ways in which thinking occurs within an interactive system that includes the self, others, and the artifacts we use. Situated cognition is sometimes called sociocultural cognition whereby reality is a social construct and understanding emerges as a consequence of commonsense transactions in language and other forms of communication (Rogoff & Lave, 1984). Inquiries into the informing role of factors such as discipline characteristics and individual constraints offer important insights into the cognitive contexts of art learning (Efland, 2002). This process is ongoing in a constructivist way, and strategic in nature, as meaning is encompassed and negotiated. Activities that take place in the studio constitute a form of inquiry that is responsive, reflective, and strategic and yields actions that construct and create new relationships in form and meaning.

Arguing that cognition is a mental and physical activity that takes place within a range of sociocultural contexts suggests that the binary-bound idea that art is a process or a product needs to be abandoned. Viewing art practice as displaying cognitive processes that are distributed throughout the various media, languages, situations, and cultural texts offers the possibility of a more plausible argument. The belief that process and product inform each other does not mean that we reduce things to their common elements in the manner of viewing two overlapping circles or a Venn diagram. Rather, there is the expectation that both represent complex systems of skills and understanding, and instances of interaction and overlap are strategic rather than all-encompassing or reductive. Thus it is from an understanding that comprehensive cognitive practice in the visual arts involves thinking in a setting that requires further discussion.

● VISUAL ARTS KNOWING: A FRAMEWORK

Figure 4.1 shows the perspectives and practices that capture the various ways visual arts thinking has been described. This configuration reflects many things. A historical perspective is evident. Trends in how we conceptualize and conduct research are shown to move *around* the central core of art practice as we look to locate the essence of visual arts knowing within the artwork, within the viewer, or as a consequence of the encounter. If we refer to the framework for visual arts research shown in Chapter 3 (Figure 3.1), it becomes clear that these inquiries conform to the general domains of research associated with the empiricist, interpretivist, and critical paradigms.

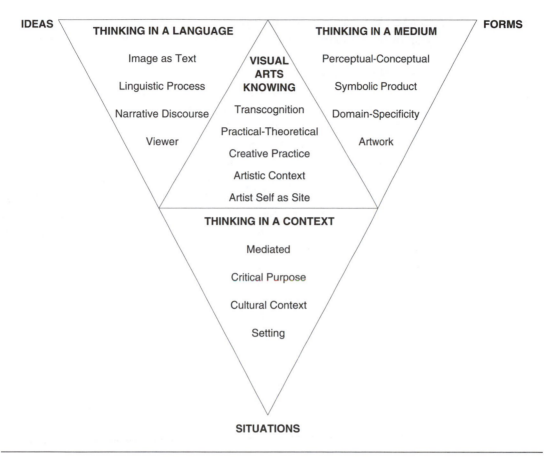

IDEAS

FORMS

THINKING IN A LANGUAGE

Image as Text

Linguistic Process

Narrative Discourse

Viewer

VISUAL ARTS KNOWING

Transcognition

Practical-Theoretical

Creative Practice

Artistic Context

Artist Self as Site

THINKING IN A MEDIUM

Perceptual-Conceptual

Symbolic Product

Domain-Specificity

Artwork

THINKING IN A CONTEXT

Mediated

Critical Purpose

Cultural Context

Setting

SITUATIONS

Figure 4.1   Framework of Visual Arts Knowing

There is good comfort in appreciating the historical significance of the patterns of practice that researchers have followed in asking questions about what it is to know in the visual arts. A theme often discussed in the educational literature deals with the possibilities and problems for a field in looking to establish research agendas and methods of practice modeled on other disciplines (Sacca, 1989). Positioning practice within the theoretical structures of the dominant ideology is part of the heritage of emerging disciplines and how we have conducted our inquiries in the visual arts conforms to this strategy. For instance, traditions of inquiry in fine arts in higher education align with practices that at various times have been grounded in anthropology, hermeneutics, critical theory, and the like. Similarly, in art education the dominant framing discipline has been psychology, and more recently the social sciences and critical studies.

Yet the various perspectives and practices shown in Figure 4.1, Framework of Visual Arts Knowing, have more than historical appeal as the framework reassigns the centrality of visual arts knowing within the orbit of artists' practice. Furthermore, in taking on broad aspects of research modeled on the metaphor of the *braid* described in Chapter 3, the dynamic and changing quality of visual arts knowing can be appreciated. Consequently, approaches to conceptualizing cognitive structures in the visual arts, when viewed from the position of artists, are seen to be instances of alignment and emphasis, rather than distant and discrete domains. This cognitive coalition involves an ongoing dialogue between, within, and around the artist, artwork, viewer, and setting, where each has a role in co-constructing meaning. Therefore the process of coming to know is recursive and purposeful in nature as meaning is created and critiqued. I describe this as *transcognition* because it captures the movement of the artistic mind. Transcognition is a process of visual arts knowing where the forms, ideas, and situations are informing agents of mind that surround the artistic self during visual arts practice. These strategic interactions occur over time and involve iteration and negotiation as individual purpose is mediated by situational factors.

If we consider this framework of visual arts knowing in relation to research practices, then some traditional dichotomous distinctions do not hold up. For instance, if visual arts practice is considered to be a form of research, then issues and ideas get recontextualized as concerns and interests change focus. For example, concerns about

theory and practice become interests in *structure, agency,* and *action;*

knowing what and how become interests in *creating, critiquing,* and *constructing;*

form and content become interests in *images, ideas,* and *contexts;*

process and product become interests in *purpose, practice,* and *progress.*

This reflexive process is characteristic of research in general and indicative of visual arts practice in particular. For instance the perspective of the "other," be they other artists, viewers, art writers, or theorists, provide an interpretive lens through which critical inquiry is referenced but not constrained. This is a review process that necessarily involves both an interrogation of existing theories and practices and a reinterpretation or review in light of personal proclivities and research interests. This focus is at the heart of transcognitive practice as it privileges the intent of research much like visual arts practice is fueled by creative desire. From this central premise the design and structure of purposeful inquiry emerges as ideas and issues are investigated and enacted in research practices. A case study follows.

VISUAL ARTS AS TRANSCOGNITIVE PRACTICE ●

The last section in this chapter describes a project, Critical Influence, undertaken with two artists whose creative practice is reviewed and critiqued in light of the framework for visual arts knowing (Figure 4.1) and the research framework described in Chapter 3 (Figure 3.1). The purpose of the example is to add some flesh to these bones, and perhaps a little heart. However, there are a couple of caveats that need emphasis. The first concerns what the frameworks are *not:* They are not *theories* that explain neither art practice nor visual arts knowing. There is no rational way to "falsify" these systems, therefore much more focused inquiry is needed to tease out the explanatory constructs that might be lurking amid these artistic practices and sociocultural processes; and if it is theory that is sought, then the range of constructs and variables considered would need to draw from this scale-free system of micro and macro experience. However, with that proviso in mind, what can be claimed is that the frameworks presented are *descriptive* structures that help us to understand the dimensions of theory, domains of inquiry, and perspectives on knowing that inform art practice. The other qualifying condition to be kept in mind is that the project that follows is not an example of visual arts research that is *artist based*; rather it is artist centered. Therefore this is a study *of* visual arts practice as research, not an inquiry *in* visual arts practice as research. The task here is to better understand the frameworks of inquiry that surround, inhere, and interact with visual arts practice.

A CASE STUDY: CRITICAL INFLUENCE ●

To examine the contextual factors that influence visual cognition, a study was undertaken where two artists were invited to participate in a 12-month research project that culminated in an exhibition, Critical Influence (Sullivan, 1998), held at the Ivan Dougherty Gallery,[4] a contemporary art space in Sydney, Australia. The aim of the project was to investigate approaches to contemporary visual arts practice so as to be able to better understand how artists think, act, and create. The project documented the studio practice of two artists as they prepared work for a two-person exhibition. As well, the role of other artworld agents including the exhibition context, a gallery director, a critic, and a curator-researcher were all considered to be active elements in the artistic enterprise. The participating artists were Jayne Dyer and Nikki McCarthy. Both are midcareer artists living in Sydney, Australia. As well as producing artworks for exhibition, each artist participated in a study that tracked the influences on their art practice. Information was collected in the form of interviews with each artist, along with studio observations recorded in written, photographic, and video formats. Interviews were also conducted with those involved in the exhibition process, including the gallery director Nick Waterlow[5] and art critic Joanna Mendelssohn,[6] both of whom wrote catalogue essays. The interviews were transcribed, and along with the observations, all the data were analyzed using the NUD●IST computer software (Gahan & Hannibal, 1998).[7]

Critical Influence culminated in an exhibition that presented the work of both artists, along with documentation from the curator-researcher, the gallery director, and the critic, both of whom wrote about the artists' work. Given the opportunity to participate in a two-person show at a highly regarded gallery, both artists produced work that built on their oeuvre with the context of this professional challenge. Jayne Dyer's contribution to the exhibition was to produce an enormous work titled *Site,* which stretched from floor to ceiling over several walls of the gallery. It was almost overpowering in its scale and impact. *Site* created a brooding mood that took the viewer across surfaces that were scratched, scutched, rubbed, and layered with paints and chalks that traced a journey of pasts and places. Nikki McCarthy is an indigenous installation artist. She describes herself as an artist who is both Aboriginal and Australian with an obligation to locate links through her art. Whether using neon, glass, light, industrial enamels, or colored sand, her artworks are evocative explorations of her Aboriginality. Her art practice is grounded in a persistent search for clues of connection. These contain messages and meanings that often imply connections across time and space where a sphere can be a dot on the landscape, or the entire globe at the same time.

The documentation associated with Critical Influence was presented in two forms. A series of six broadsheets served as an exhibition catalogue. Each of these presented a different perspective on the practices investigated. A more detailed account was contained on a CD-ROM that was on view for the duration of the exhibition and formally completed afterward as additional material was added. What follows are accounts of the various practices explored during the project. The first two are profiles of the participating artists, Jayne Dyer and Nikki McCarthy. The next explores curatorial practice as a form of collaborative inquiry. An essay written by the gallery director, Nick Waterlow, presents an artworld perspective. A critical response by Joanna Mendelssohn provides an example of the art critic's role. And, finally, a concluding essay summarizes the research issues that arose from the project and how these can be considered in relation to the frameworks of inquiry and visual arts knowing presented in this section of the book.

Artist Practice: Jayne Dyer

Jayne Dyer's artworks serve as sites for mapping meanings. As someone who seeks to engage that which is transient and mutable, her art is as much about figments of thought as fragments of a material presence. The manner of working against the surface pits allusion against form on a scale that opens the eye and catches the mind. The influences that inform Dyer's work cannot be traced to easily identified seminal sources. Rather, they exist as momentary encounters of places and things, appear in spaces located by tangents drawn by others, and all the while are evident as traces held in the work on the floor and walls of her studio. The power of the visual form remains central in the store of image influences Dyer collects. The fragmentary references to memories and histories embedded in Dyer's work get caught in the mind's eye. Image snippets may spark the past and sense the future for the "before" and the "beyond" is relatively easy to position. But it is the present that defies capture. These moments are always on the move. The traces of other times and places serve multiple ends that deny any possibility of a singular truth in the way that a morning mist cloaks yet clarifies our awareness of the landscape. Jayne explains:

> I saw the rubbings in 1996 at the China Art Gallery in Beijing. The paper was rectangular or square but the images were irregular. These rubbings were evidences of architectural and cultural history, a history that was disintegrating—the corner of a building, or the edge of a doorway, or whatever. The fragment, the remnant, that part of a history that cannot be entirely known.

A basic principle that defines what it is to be human is the need to be located within contexts that confirm our identity. The art of Jayne Dyer suggests that this place and identity may occupy a space that is caught between the physical and temporal. Like a foreign language, or marks on an X-ray, or bumps on Braille, certain forms remain as hidden information unless revealed through experience. Making meaning becomes a negotiation between what is known and felt as the concrete becomes the critical. Any site, therefore, is shaped by insight. As an avid traveler, Dyer collects maps much in the manner others take photographs. While these record sites that grid the

Jayne Dyer, *Site* (1998). Variable dimensions. Drawing installation in the Critical Influence exhibition, Ivan Dougherty Gallery, Sydney. Reproduced courtesy of the artist.

landscape, they negate the existences of those who live within their borders. Drawing on Gaston Bachelard's notion of the "poetics of space," Dyer's art suggests that where and how we locate ourselves requires an acceptance that our relationship with place is neither stable nor able to be coded. Rather, it constantly shifts in the space between the tangible and the transient.

Material Difference

Jayne Dyer says she is "attracted to opposites, the mirroring of notions such as intimacy and immensity; the fixed or permanent against that which is mutable and temporal; and the relationship between exterior and interior space." The notion that difference can explain both the material presence and the visual sense is at the heart of her artwork. Materiality in these terms can be described as that which is found chalked beneath the fingernails and embedded in the psyche. It is also seen when black fades to white as the forms shimmer and shift and felt when light is used as both a source and a surface. These extremes in essence and embodiment allow the surfaces of Dyer's work to be charged with intensity. Black is as much about absorption as it is about absence that allows the vague to become vivid in the way that shadows profile things. Similarly, in her work, white can be read as both a vessel and a void as it embraces everything and nothing and thereby qualifies what it is to be different in kind rather than to be different by degree. Dyer takes liberties with conventions of building up surfaces so as to layer materials and meanings. She prefers to work against the surface to scutch, scratch, spread, and skim. The ambiguity in the way the materiality may be read further disarms as the scale of her work takes hold. "I intend the work to be sensed, felt, not literally interpreted. I want the scale of the work to force the viewer to engage physically as well as visually."

Citing Sites

To situate one's practice within broader fields of experience is to signal to others what is reflective yet distinctive about art practice. Dyer resists the current practice of appropriating the experience of "the other." Rather, there is a curious twist in the way the ideas of others serve to influence her art. Direct sources are referenced indirectly, and indirect influences are embraced more openly. Let me explain. To discuss her work, Dyer chooses to make considerable use of what others say as quotes are collected to draw attention to a community of ideas and issues. But the intention is only to reveal part of the picture. Like stage lights that freeze-frame momentary actions, it is not what is captured in the spotlight that is of interest, but often what happens on the fringes. Dyer deliberately makes "evidences" ambiguous. While she draws on direct sources, these circumscribe ideas that help focus on what is left unsaid, and it is within these shifting seams that her work can be located. It is the indirect influences that result when histories are revealed, languages stumbled upon, and images captured that selectively inform her work. While the information is ephemeral, the tracking process is quite rational and intentional. The critical sources that inform Jayne Dyer's art deny ready access, yet influence is both seen and felt, and as it passes through, it leaves traces and connections. She acknowledges that she is "not interested in concrete information or proven data. These provide poor insights into the nature of our temporality."

Artist Practice: Nikki McCarthy

Nikki McCarthy's art practice is grounded on a persistent search for clues of connection. This elusive reality is embodied in the technological breadth of the media she uses and the cultural depth of the messages she imbues. McCarthy's artworks meld disparate themes and influences as sculptural forms take on many meanings. A mysterious arc is as much a dome and a universe as it is a dot on a painted landscape. A neon outline becomes an archetype of a past and future existence. The influences that inform

McCarthy's artistic thinking cluster around spiritual, practical, and physical concerns. Within each of these domains there is a conscious attempt to bridge what she sees as a disruptive divide. Underlying this is a belief in the educative power of art to instruct and reveal what is new and possible. She says, "to me art has to touch you emotionally some way or another. And it doesn't matter whether it hurts or it upsets, or it brings you to the point of ecstasy, you've got to have some emotion."

Tribal Metaphysics

The spiritual dimension of Nikki McCarthy's art practice is centered on her notion of *Tribal Metaphysics*. This concept highlights distinctions and similarities between indigenous beliefs and unexplained phenomena. Being native to a land and culture is a generic description of indigenousness and many cultural groups share common bonds and beliefs. For McCarthy, a central connection to the land, for instance, offers strong synchronicities across cultures. She also believes indigenousness is mostly perceived as belonging to the past. Yet the belief structure of many indigenous cultures is part of a living tradition that transcends the past. McCarthy argues that the many mysteries related to the metaphysical and mythical content of indigenous artworks are still to be disclosed or adequately explained. "*Truth* takes the image and connections into a technological interpretation that represents the very essence of indigenous spiritual and metaphysical beliefs and the unexplained." Part of the quest Nikki McCarthy sets for herself is to create artworks that symbolize the past, present, and future tense of Aboriginal culture and explore its continuation and survival. As with the concept of indigenousness, she believes the media and technology used by non-Western cultures is often assumed to include only age-old methods and techniques. Her use of new technologies does not exclude older, more traditional mediums, but simply leaves room for a broader understanding of what has been known and taught by indigenous people throughout time. Within the artistic brief McCarthy sets herself, the use of new technologies also has the capacity to bring together indigenous and nonindigenous people and allow for a clearer perception of what it is to be different. At various times McCarthy's art includes the use of media as diverse as feathers, earth, sand, clay, beeswax, wood, leather, shells, ochers, string, twine, and other materials mostly seen as traditional to indigenous art making. At other times she uses media generally associated with scientific and industrial methods, such as glass fusion, neon lighting, polymer, plasma light, and bronze casting. McCarthy's purpose is to extend the context of her art and its connection to ritual, progress, and survival, in a technological world that is as diverse as the indigenousness it strives to maintain.

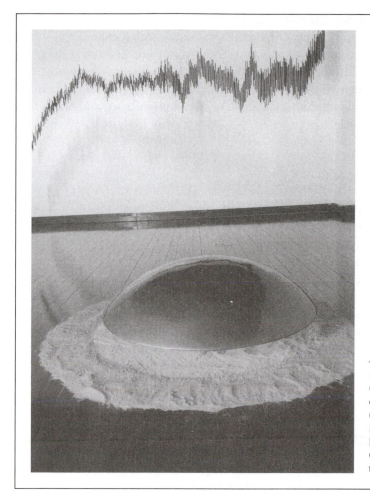

Nikki McCarthy, *Arrival (foreground)* (1998). Plaster, titanium baked enamel, light, sand. *Black Lightening (background)* (1998). Scientific glass. Nylon thread. Installation in Critical Influence exhibition, Ivan Dougherty Gallery, Sydney. Reproduced courtesy of the artist.

Intuition and Object

The power of Nikki McCarthy's artworks relies in large part on the visual impact of the object. This is enhanced by content drawn from many origins. She asserts that "when you're doing an artwork that has a lot of meaning and you're really serious about it, you have respect for the source that's giving you the information." Despite the acknowledged sources that influence her work, the process McCarthy follows is curiously indeterminate as meaning is slowly revealed. Intuition, uncertainty, and a sensing intellect reveal for McCarthy certain symbolic properties she sees embedded in objects and materials she finds around her. While McCarthy places great faith in her intuitive thought processes, it is the way she deploys her critical and reflective skills that clarify her artistic intentions. This is both a strategic and a spiritual conversation McCarthy has with herself that begins with a visualizing process that happens within herself and finds form in her art. There is a deep felt need to communicate that surrounds Nikki McCarthy's art practice. The diversity of influences that source her work, and the issues she raises about received histories and traditions, serve to question, instruct, and reveal new possibilities.

Curatorial Practice

Curatorial practice involves research about the visual arts. As a process that searches out new insights, there is an obvious artistry to the curator's quest. This is shaped by an equally rigorous attention to scholarship. Curatorial practice also has an educational intent that seeks to challenge and inform an audience. Embedded in these somewhat lofty goals are other human characteristics that put fire in the curator's eyes. There is an imaginative tenacity that moves beliefs beyond blind faith and into thoughtful actions. There is an acceptance that knowledge is partly drawn from authority yet always moves by intuitive possibility with the direct experience of art. A curator's effort is given form in exhibitions that invariably include a collaboration with artists and others who share a common goal in search of a new view. Critical Influence is an example of such a collaboration.

Artists' Explorations

The participating artists in Critical Influence were Jayne Dyer and Nikki McCarthy. Jayne's recent work involves investigations of the transitory nature of sites and surfaces on a scale that engages the viewer visually and physically. She says, "If I think about what I want people to take from my work, it's not really specific, logical bits of information, as such. It's much more about inference." Nikki's installations are explorations of tribal metaphysics and technology and alter the perspective about what it means to be an urban indigenous Australian artist. Nikki comments that "there's constantly different sources that information is coming from, all those connections, little bits here and there will come through to make a specific work." An initial response is to see the work of these artists as distinctly different. The contrasts in form and content are obvious. What is not so apparent, however, is an underlying imaginative quest that may be elusive to source but is manifest in substance. Trying to capture these realities is difficult but not impossible and the result extends our understanding. By documenting each artist's imaginative response to

Critical Influence, the viewer can engage with the artworks produced as well as explore the interpretive readings provided by others.

Presenting Ideas

The Ivan Dougherty Gallery occupies an intriguing position with the art world. Ideas are explored that otherwise might not be shown and the institutional links to the University of New South Wales advocate a spirit of inquiry and research. This charter formed the backdrop for Critical Influence. The director of the gallery, Nick Waterlow, expresses a commitment to not only the exposition of artists' work but to the investigation and "dissemination of ideas that underpin the full meaning and interpretation of a visual language." Nick adds:

> I see my role [gallery director] as partly interpretive, but quite largely concerned with original research. . . . I prefer to work to create exhibitions, large or small, that bring forward information that hasn't been revealed before. And one of the great joys of working in the curatorial field is that there are always those possibilities. There are always artists whose work hasn't been revealed in a particular way. And there are always ideas that haven't been revealed through the work in a particular way.

Artworks are an important source of new knowledge, personal meaning, and cultural appreciation. Not only are artworks studied but the context in which they are produced and presented influences the kind of meanings made by viewers. Art writers provide an interpretive lens that reveals new insights about what it is to understand art. Joanna Mendelssohn describes art criticism as a process similar to pulling an old clock to pieces. In taking things apart for a closer look, there are always surprising results, because expectations are often blunted, new insights emerge, and different things often happen when the clock is put back together again.

In Critical Influence, Joanna Mendelssohn responds to the art produced by Jayne Dyer and Nikki McCarthy. Joanna identifies traces of commonality that track through their work, yet in experiencing the pieces on display, she reveals even more by highlighting their differences. Critical Influence is also an inquiry into the relationship between visual arts practice and research. The project investigates and documents the art practice of two artists and art world agents such as the exhibition context, gallery director, critic, and the curator-researcher, all of whom are considered to be active participants. The rich mix of personal, cultural, and contextual influences evident in the artists' practice, the use of various qualitative research methods, and the institutional setting provide a basis for more clearly articulating visual arts research processes.

Artworld Practice by Nick Waterlow[8]

The Ivan Dougherty Gallery is committed to the principles of research, as it is committed to the exposition of artistic practice and to the dissemination of ideas that underpin the full meaning and interpretation of a visual language. It was for these reasons that the Critical Influence exhibition was agreed upon. The work of both Jayne Dyer and Nikki McCarthy, created for this exhibition, which also exerts the demands of a watching, though not voyeuristic, and measuring, yet not judgmental, action in the viewer, shares some fascinating and eternal, though differently sourced, links. Dyer, in relation to space, location, and the self, states that ". . . you get this sense of information about what the land is. And in fact how we locate ourselves. But not in any sense of the way we expect space to work. So it becomes again that fragment, but particularly another way of seeing how we position and locate ourselves in space. So that we become these dots or notes. Almost like the mathematical point in that location." McCarthy, on the subjects of belief and conviction in her work, says,

> You can take that as a very strong religious belief because it is coming from a spiritual [source], but you can't sort of say it's a specific religion. It's more of a universal belief in a greater power that is watching over you and telling you that you've gotta do this because if you don't, something bad will happen down the track from you not expressing it. And if enough people express it, and are hearing those messages, especially artists, well then, maybe that's what art's about. Maybe that's the only connection that you've got that is a pure connection.

Researching and Exhibiting Visual Language

Graeme Sullivan's methodical inquiry into the relationship between art practice, as it is understood by professional artists, and as a form of research, had, as he has written, in part arisen from the example of three previous Ivan Dougherty Gallery exhibitions. Drawing on Inspiration invited a wide range of artists to show a drawing that had inspired them beside one of their own; Asia and Oceania Influence revealed recent work by artists alongside a selection from their own collection focusing on the exhibition's title; and In Process explored the idea base of artists working within the college faculty. Each project asked questions about the source of ideas in a considerable variety of art practices, and by implication, provided invaluable research into a wide range of methodologies that transform disparate experience, analysis, and observation into coherent visual statements, albeit in an enormous variety of formats. Complexities of cultural difference were revealed, as were the presence and absence of tradition and technical excellence, as well as of new technology, and also the function of works of art as well as questions of their delineation. Critical Influence examines not only the practice of Nikki McCarthy and Jayne Dyer, it asks them to articulate and dissect the very nature, the true essence of that practice from a variety of angles. It should, therefore, provide the viewer with keys to an understanding of the work that are not always necessarily available. A heightened perception may result.

Research is too often seen as either an esoteric or product- and profit-driven pursuit, but in this instance, in Graeme Sullivan's words, "These studies seek to develop appropriate research methods, which help explore and reveal the complex cognitive processes that inform and shape art practice." It may be a tall order, but it is nonetheless a particularly important one within a university and, indeed, in a global culture that increasingly demands quantification, effectiveness, tangibility, and measurability. In architectural parlance there used to be an understanding of the need for a "folly," but nowadays cost-effectiveness governs what can and cannot be built and follies abound but not of the original and true kind. There also exists a disturbing belief that art must be easily comprehensible and commercially viable.

Artistic practice is being forced to reestablish its credentials in this somewhat unaccommodating climate, and it is projects such as Critical Influence that provide the possibility for the dissemination of ideas that might otherwise remain obscure. Jayne Dyer hints at the nub, "I actually think it gets down to a few quite simple things that we try to make complex, but that simplicity is incredibly complex. . . . It gets down to something that's reasonably clean, I suppose is the word . . . clean, it's just there, it's this seam line of need that [you] want to explore or deal with." Dyer's works, in a sense fragments of her cosmos, constantly collide memory, place, and vision; they are immediately accessible as enigmatic icons yet also possess the possibility of transporting one's understanding toward previously inaccessible territory.

Nikki McCarthy's work generally manages to provide you with its location, whether using traditional materials such as feathers or new technologies for casting domes. She says, "I have a moral obligation to my race of people to keep that [culture] going. But it doesn't mean I have to overlook new technology. So what I'm trying to do in, say, *Tribal Metaphysics* [a work in Critical Influence], is a bonding of the two cultures together. I'm always aware I'm Aboriginal and I'm always aware that I'm also an Australian. So I've got the double thing happening with the double obligation." Critical Influence provides a rich mix of two very different art practices that share more common ground than immediately meets the eye. A revealing of the background, motivation and inspiration that provides the impetus for the professional lives of Jayne Dyer and Nikki McCarthy will help all of us better comprehend the creation of visual language.

Art Writer Practice by Joanna Mendelssohn[8]

I first became aware of Nikki McCarthy's work about 5 years ago when she entered the NSW Traveling Scholarship exhibition. I remember the way she integrated traditional Aboriginal forms and understandings into a more personal vision. There were ethereal shapes and forms using feathers. One year, in the graduating exhibition at the College of Fine Arts, there was a large and elaborate net, all studded with feathers. It seemed to float in air. In terms of time-honored skills of craftsmanship, it was exquisite; as a work of art, a piece of sculpture, it posed questions about ancient forms and changing notions. I didn't get the opportunity to write about her work at the time. Despite what people may think about the total freedom of critics, there are constraints on what and who we may write on and conflicts of interest loom large. When I saw Nikki's work, it was either in a scholarship exhibition that I had judged or a graduating exhibition at an art college where I was a staff member. So I kept my appreciation of her delicate tracery out of print, but it still remained very much at the forefront of my mind.

And now her sculpture has changed again, developed further. There is still the same awareness of her Aboriginality, she continues to honor past traditions of seeing, past ways of thinking about shape and form. But her years of study within the Western tradition have also shaped her art. Nikki McCarthy can now be seen as one of the new generation of Aboriginal artists who pays homage to the cultures of the past while working in the technologies of the present. Her most recent work has moved away from feathers and nets. The links with Aboriginal cultures are still there, but rather than reworking ancient themes, there now is a visual questioning into the whole nature of Aboriginality.

Images of Change

In *Arrival,* McCarthy creates an object of artificial smoothness, and places it onto sand. She has said that this is a work about change and new technology, as well as the status of the "dot," that traditional painting technique which now for many defines art as "Aboriginal." There is of course the other reference, identified in some of her other statements; the quotation from images of science fiction. Her technique, combining as it does appropriation of building technology (a plaster cast made from a Plexiglas skylight), craftsmanship (rubbing back the cast by hand to make it slightly uneven), and then adding metallic baked enamel, emphasizes the strangeness and other worldly nature of her craft. And what is *Arrival?* Is it the arrival of Aboriginal people into the world of modern technology, or are we seeing a prototype of *Independence Day*–type space invasion? *Tribal Metaphysics* asks the same questions as it uses light, shadows, and glass to create an image of change, an unstable space in a world in flux, another hint at a world of future shock as well as past knowledge, and the sense that there is continual flux.

Exploring Limits

Changing layers of meaning are also integral to Jayne Dyer's work. She paints her giant strips, her fragments of black, and then she rubs them down, scrapes them, reworks them, until they are aged, imperfect, and right for her purpose. But then they may be pasted over by new layers, changed again. In Jayne Dyer's world there is no constant, there is no objective eternal truth. She quotes Gaston Bachelard's *The Poetics of Space:* "Memory . . . does not record concrete duration." Perhaps the object becomes real only when it is used as an aide-mémoir, only when it has an association with another time and place. And so she creates her walls, which are not walls but fragments of dreams of pasts which may have happened. There is a roughness about this work which I find especially satisfying, a determination to look at the hand-made, not the high tech. And she has limited herself to one color—black— and its infinite variations.

Together these artists create harmony. There is the deliberate rough of Dyer's work and the sensual smooth of McCarthy's. There is the questioning of the nature of reality that characterizes Dyer's sensibility contrasted with the adventurous metaphysics of McCarthy. Both are women of the same generation, both have a similar background in formal art education. If they share any common characteristics, it is a desire to explore the limits of their chosen materials and to limit their tonal range, but their objectives and the subsequent appearance of their work could be from different worlds.

Reframing Research Practice

The outcomes of the Critical Influence project indicate that mapping the cognitive character of practices surrounding the production and exhibition of visual arts requires the boundaries to be moved to take in the breadth and depth needed to conduct comprehensive inquiry. The two artists participating in the Critical Influence project exemplify transcognitive art practice. The influences that inform Jayne Dyer's work cannot be traced to easily identified seminal sources or discrete periods of her life. The ensemble of thoughts and actions that inform her art practice are fluid and dynamic. There is a strategic character to her thinking that exploits the mutability of cognition. For Jayne, the transcognitive character of her art practice is seen in the way she embraces change and uncertainty as compatible cognitive capacities. The influences that source the work of Nikki McCarthy and the issues she raises about received histories and cultural traditions serve to question, instruct, and reveal new possibilities. Her indigenous understanding that the metaphysics of change and identity are dimensions that coexist across time and space is at the heart of her art practice. There is an intuitive character to Nikki McCarthy's thinking that is identified within her spiritual connections and located in the external physical forms she creates. Intuition in this way taps into a wellspring of knowledge that cannot be anticipated or denied. For McCarthy, the transcognitive process is one of recognition.

But what can we learn from this visual arts research project, remembering that this was an artist-centered rather than an artist-based inquiry? Initially it can be appreciated that it is difficult to "freeze-frame" the reality of the visual arts and any inquiry needs to take into account its variable character. Once it is agreed that not all phenomena are related in a linear way, then it can be accepted that research *in* the visual arts, and research *about* the visual arts, is a complex process. An aspect that is clearly documented in this project is the reflexive role played by the curator-researcher. Whether doing research in the visual arts, or making inquiries about the visual arts, the researcher's viewpoint is critical. After all, interpretations will always be filtered through an individual lens, for this is the way we see and understand things. Suitable strategies, however, need to be used to ensure personal information is able to be challenged as much as confirmed. The researcher's perspective is also critical in the interrogative sense of the word.

The research process used in Critical Influence draws from elements described in the framework of visual arts inquiry (Chapter 3, Figure 3.1) and focuses on interests identified in the framework of visual arts knowing (see Figure 4.1). Generally, in the visual arts, artists and artworks are the two main subjects of study. In Critical Influence, Jayne Dyer and Nikki McCarthy and their art were primary sources of new information. As a knowledge source, artists provide a perspective from *within,* and this helps reveal information about their practices. On the other hand, research *about* the visual arts might focus on the artist as the subject of a profile or a case study. The artwork has always been an important source that can be investigated for meaning. Not only are artworks studied, but the context in which they are

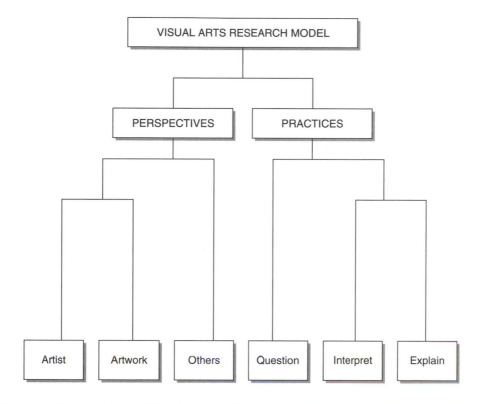

The Visual Arts Research Model is a visual description of the process used to analyze the information collected during the research process. It mirrors the "tree" index structure that emerges when the NUD•IST computer assisted qualitative data analysis software is used (Gahan & Hannibal, 1998). In terms of the deconstruction and reconstruction of the index trees, the process is like removing branches from an emerging tree structure and repositioning them in places that are more theoretically stable. A useful image that helps conceptualize the dynamic nature of this qualitative process of analysis is to conceive of the tree structures as mobiles that rotate through three dimensions and allow all categories to be aligned in proximity to others. Therefore the components can be seen to move like an Alexander Calder mobile whereby the proximity or sequence of the components can be changed to suit different questions or situations.

Figure 4.2   Visual Arts Research Model

produced and presented is taken into account, for these circumstances influence the kind of meanings made. In Critical Influence this involved the sustained documentation of the art of Jayne and Nikki in the period leading up to the exhibition. The perspective of others is also a source and a context for interpreting information. This is an important database and brings into focus the interpretive power of those whose interests may influence readings of the research. As well, establishing an interpretive framework that positions the research in relation to other relevant work provides important comparative textual information.

Visual arts research practice describes a basic process of inquiry. In general terms this means interpretations are subject to challenge and change in light of other views. In practitioner research, a range of methods are used whereby divergent views are identified, compared, and synthesized so as to shed light on complex phenomena. In the visual arts, insight emerges from a process of feeling and critical reflection as experience is encountered and acted on, either by making art or by critically responding to it. Visual arts research practice therefore progressively contests information for its meanings as questions and ideas are explored, interpretations made, and explanations sought. Questions emerge from inquiries undertaken in all the settings where visual arts practice takes place, including the studio, on-site, in the gallery, on the Internet, or wherever. As a reflexive practice, questioning can serve many purposes as issues are explored, concepts challenged, and ideas clarified. A critical art practice not only considers what is apparent and assumed, but addresses that which may be neglected, contrived, and contested.

● CONCLUSION

Although the status of the visual arts remains shadowed by science, they share the spotlight as vital human activities that make us think. In a simplistic sense, scientists think about how progress leads to change, and artists think about how change leads to progress. A useful example that blurs these distinctions is given by Angelo Caranfa (2001) who contrasts the paths pursued toward truth and understanding followed by Charles Darwin and Paul Gauguin. These two South Seas travelers achieved a kind of harmony in their respective jaunts. Darwin found that the explanatory utility of science relied in part on the use of analogy and metaphor as he pieced together his puzzle; Gauguin's rapture with nature was guided by a deductive reasoning that drew its form and content from imagined experience that made visual what otherwise "cannot be seen by the physical eyes" (p. 157).

In pursuing these kinds of quests, artists cast their minds to issues, ideas, and experiences that reveal imaginative insights, yet the process resists capture by the freeze-frame of clinical analysis. Art practice cannot be reduced to standardized dichotomies of cause and effect, input and outcome, or process and product. To come to better understand these visual arts practices we need to invest more time and energy in investigating what it is we do by documenting and disseminating this to wide audiences. This is important, for the experiences we have in our studios, communities, and cultures are the kind where mind and matter merge. Making art and responding to art remains an iterative and strategic encounter that comprises a creative coalition of individuals, ideas, and actions. It is messy, mindful, and magical. But it is not mysterious. Rather, it is a resistant practice that requires us to work against those theoretical, social, and political boundaries imposed on the visual arts that keep it bordered beyond the mainstream of research and inquiry. It seems appropriate to conclude with reference to Maxine Greene (1995) who introduced this chapter and whose enthusiasm for opening the imagined possibility always occurs in tenacious response to constraints and controls. Maxine reminds us that "to resist such tendencies is to become aware of the ways in which certain dominant social practices enclose us in molds or frames, define us in accord with extrinsic demands, discourage us from going beyond ourselves, from acting on possibility" (p. 112).

NOTES ●

1. Paul Lieberman reported in the *New York Times* that Susan Sontag mocked David Hockney's assertions that his theory did not lessen the quality or importance of the European masters. Sontag is reported as saying, "[I]f David Hockney's thesis is correct, it would be a bit like finding out that all the great lovers of history have been using Viagra" (p. 2). Retrieved on January 18, 2004, from http://www.koopfilms.com/hockney/articles.html.

2. The intensity of artists as they attend to technical problems is captured in the following quote from the late Elwyn Lynn, the Australian artist and critic. He is commenting on the painting, *Portrait of Elwyn Lynn* by Bryan Westwood, that was awarded the 1989 Archibald Prize. "When he told me he went to the Prado in Madrid and looked at Velázquez through a pair of binoculars to see how the lips were painted I was amazed. He showed me how he did the lips in this portrait, and because my lips were a bit supercilious and a bit snarly he had to work hard with under painting and over painting. The observation was so intense. A critic has to be alert to these things" (cited in Sullivan, 1994, p. 111).

3. Simon Schama's historical narratives do, however, draw criticism about what some see as his creation of fictional histories—a view I do not share. For me, the strategy of creating knowledge as a means to better understand what we know and don't know is a particular capacity that the arts and humanities do extremely well. For a debate between Schama and Will Hutton over the BBC television series, *A History of Britain*, see *The Observer* at http://observer.guardian.co.uk/comment/story/0,6903,738290,00.html (last accessed on October 26, 2003).

4. The Ivan Dougherty Gallery is located at the College of Fine Arts, University of New South Wales, Sydney, Australia. See http://www.cofa.unsw.edu.au/galleries/idg (last accessed on January 19, 2004).

5. Nick Waterlow is the director of the Ivan Dougherty Gallery and a senior lecturer in the School of Art History and Theory at the College of Fine Arts, University of NSW, Sydney, Australia. He was director of the Biennale of Sydney in 1979, 1986, and 1988, and Chair International Selection in 2000. He has curated many exhibitions in Australia and other parts of the world and is currently working on curatorial projects on the Australian presence in London in the 1960s. He is also an art writer and has published in *Art and Australia*, *Art Monthly*, *Art & Text,* and *Studio International.*

6. Joanna Mendelssohn is an author, an art critic, and a professor in the School of Art History and Theory at the College of Fine Arts, University of NSW, Sydney, Australia. She is the author of several books on aspects of early 20th century Australian art. Her art writing has appeared in many art journals, magazines, exhibition catalogues, and the mainstream press, where she has served as the art critic for *The Bulletin, The Australian, Independent Monthly,* is the Australian correspondent for *Terra Celeste*, and contributing editor for *Artlink.*

7. NUD●IST is an acronym for Non-numerical Unstructured Data, Indexing, Searching and Theorizing, a software package used for computer-based qualitative data analysis. See http://www.qsr.com.au (last accessed on December 21, 2003).

8. Extract from Critical Influence exhibition catalogue, *Artwriter Practice*, January 1998, Ivan Dougherty Gallery, College of Fine Arts, University of New South Wales.

CHAPTER 5

ARTIST AS THEORIST

I n an interview in 1979, Christo was asked by C. Y. Chang (1982) about the relative importance given to the *process* of planning large-scale, site-specific art projects, and the final product. His reflective response was that the emphasis was not so much on process and product, but on "process and the *progress*" (emphasis added, p. 200). The long period from the initial conception of the idea, through the endless negotiation among many agencies and individuals and the final realization of site-specific projects is a creative and educational enterprise that has, according to Christo and Jeanne-Claude, many outcomes. For the many persons involved, either as participants or observers, the process can indeed lead to progress as attitudes change, views broaden, and awareness is awakened. This pattern of planning, reviewing, adapting, managing, analyzing, and revealing is characteristic of the transformative nature of visual arts research. This attitude and practice is also reflected in the art of the late Chen Zhen, the prominent contemporary Chinese artist whose work is characteristic of those who move between and among cultures as their art reveals connections and opens ruptures in how we think about who we are. Melissa Chiu describes the art of Chen Zhen this way:

> Although Chen left a great legacy in his artwork when he died in 2000, another legacy was his concept of "transexperience," a notion he developed for his own art practice, but one that can be applied to a more general consideration of diaspora. According to Chen, transexperience "summarizes vividly and profoundly the complex life experiences of leaving one's native place and going from one place to another in one's

life." This condition, characterized by in-betweenness, has similarities to many other descriptions of the diaspora, but the departure from convention lies in the way that Chen considered transexperience as a creative catalyst. On an individual level, transexperience allowed Chen to incorporate his Chinese training and experience into his work without resorting to a dichotomous relationship between China and the West. On a broader level, Chen's concept facilitates a more sophisticated conception of the diaspora that accounts for the present and future as much as the past embodied in the homeland. (2003, p. 33)

The expanding landscape of imaginative and critical inquiry pursued by artists, cultural commentators, and teachers is purpose driven, where the need to explore new domains for creating and critiquing knowledge is being taken up by the challenge of personal belief and public need. This process is being shaped in part by artists who see structures that define traditional discipline areas not as boundaries or barriers, but as potential pathways that can link ideas and actions in new braided ways. To examine these practices in more detail, this chapter examines changing patterns and sites of visual arts inquiry and the rich tableau of issues and ideas that is often held within the complexity and simplicity of visual images.

What is apparent is the reemergence of artist-theorists as important sources of vision and voice within the cultural politics of these times, and the approaches they use that require different ways of thinking about artistic inquiry. Three themes capture this dynamic move within the visual arts. In keeping with the strategy used in previous chapters, the breadth and depth of artistic practices is shown to extend from a focus on the artist-as-theorist to encompass constituent practices more clearly identified with empiricist, interpretive, and critical traditions. I argue that the inherent eclectic nature of the visual arts means that constituent theories and practices are regularly embraced and reworked toward all manner of different purposes as artists explore creative practices that I identify as *Making in Systems, Making in Communities,* and *Making in Cultures.* Practices that might be defined within the area of *Making in Systems* are complex and exploratory in nature as artists open up new visual forms and structures that are both grounded within discipline knowledge and skills, but also transcend these boundaries to intersect with other domains of inquiry. *Making in Communities* is "reinterpretive" in character and mobilizes the communicative capacity of visual arts to make new connections among individual ideas, public issues, and broader histories. Artists working within the domain of *Making in Cultures* capitalize on the immediacy of a critical art practice and investigate ways of challenging perceptions through visual encounters. These three frameworks

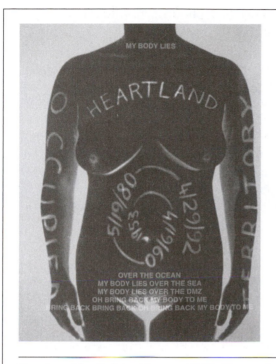

Yong Soon Min, *Defining Moments* (1992). Six-part photographic installation. Body image (*left*) 1/6, Gwangju image (*right*) 4/6. 20 × 16 inches. Reproduced courtesy of the artist.

of practices are the kind of inquiries that are helping to change the way we think about the visual arts as a site for research and I examine them in more detail later.

To understand the role of the artist as a creator of visual images with the potential to conduct research "in" art in the context of studio practice, there is a need to consider the different functions of the artist and the image as a data source. The idea of the artist as social recluse or a cultural lamplighter of genius is an inadequate representation in this day and age. Nor is it reasonable to accept the image of the artist-teacher as someone whose creative expertise is merely a model to emulate. Contemporary artists adopt many practices that dislodge discipline boundaries, media conventions, and political interests, yet still do so within a realm of aesthetic experience, cultural commentary, and educational relevance. The image of the artist as creator, critic, theorist, teacher, activist, and archivist partly captures the range of art practice today. Many contemporary artists move easily over the terrain of other disciplines as they absorb, adapt, and co-opt a research language. To support her artistic vision, a sense of historical and cultural critique is achieved by Yong Soon Min in her 1992 photographic installation, *Defining Moments*. Yong Soon Min describes the work this way:

> All of the images and dates of *Defining Moments* refer to dates with personal significance that have uncanny connections to important events in Korean and Korean American history. The year 1953 was the year of my birth as well as the year that the Korean War ended. The next date is known in Korean as "Sa-il-gu" or 4/19, the date of the popular uprising in South Korea that overthrew the Syngman Rhee government which I witnessed as a child. This event allowed our family to leave Korea. 5/19/80 refers to the Gwangju uprising and massacre, an important turning point in Korean history that served as a catalyst in my growing interest in current Korean history. The last date, "sa-i-gu" or 4/29 refers to the LA riots, which also happens to be my birthday. (Cited in Hwa Young Choi Caruso, 2004, p. 201)

● SITES OF PRACTICE

Three areas of visual arts practice are described in this section: *Making in Systems, Making in Communities,* and *Making in Cultures* (see Figure 5.1). New settings and situations such as those opened up by digital environments, community spaces, and cultural collaborations are creating new places for creative and critical inquiry that require alternative forms of research and scholarship. Research about contemporary art practice that includes direct contact with artists and their work reveals how artworks can be seen as "sites of possibility" for making art, thinking about art, and teaching art. Artists and others explore these spaces and places in ways that disrupt assumed boundaries. By investigating the potential for knowledge creation that exists *between* theory and practice, and *beyond* assumed discipline boundaries, artists pursue issues and ideas that have personal and public relevance. In examining the components of these practices, I use examples drawn from contemporary art that help reflect the breadth and depth of what artists do.

For artists working within the general area designated *Making in Systems* there is a desire to move beyond discipline boundaries and into areas of inquiry that interact and intersect and require new ways to conceptualize forms and structures. For instance, artist-theorists working at the interface of art and science within the digital environment are finding that past notions of theory and practice no longer serve as adequate systems around which to define plans and actions. As such, concepts of collaboration are grounded less on notions of expert systems that divide up roles in terms

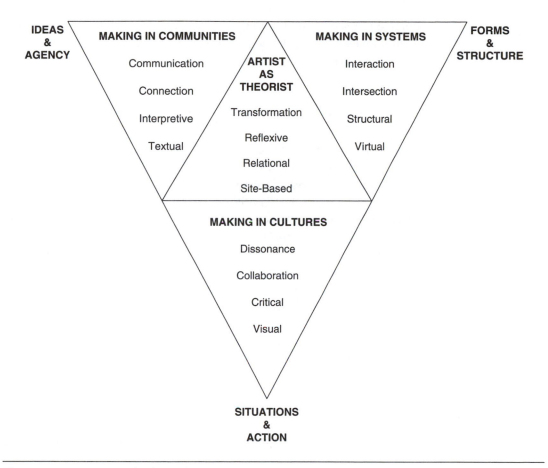

Figure 5.1   Framework of Visual Arts Practice

of ends and means, or design and delivery, but more like a shared wonder that requires new ways of thinking about visual and virtual systems of inquiry.[1] *Making in Communities* might be seen to incorporate the visual arts practice of those artists working within the orbit of community-based art practice who look to dislodge restrictive paradigms of thought. For instance, indigenous art practice can be considered in this way, as Western conceptions of the art object or the scientific method of inquiry cannot be expected to accommodate the interlacing nature of experience and understanding that is at the heart of indigenous knowing.[2] On the other hand, those contemporary artists whose practice might be seen to encompass the broad area of *Making in Cultures* use their hybrid experiences growing up and working across countries and cultures as a basis for their imaginative and intellectual experiences. Examples might be artist-theorists working from a cultural reference located within Asia and the Middle East who provide insightful images that "talk back" within the cultural diaspora in ways that open up new dialogue and dislodge old myths.[3]

Making in Systems

The underlying premise here is that art making is a systemslike practice because it exists within a broad set of private and public relationships. This does not deny the intensely personal function of the visual arts, or the wider corpus of social processes and purposes. In thinking about systems, I describe two main types because this suits my purpose here. There are *static* or *closed* systems, and there are *dynamic* or *open* systems. The difference is in the relationship with the environment where static systems are independent of external influence, while dynamic systems are constantly changed by interactions with the surroundings. Static systems are somewhat mechanical, have useful heuristic value, and may be used to describe what something is (e.g., a system for printing photograms); they may be prescriptive structures that designate causes and effects (e.g., making clay pots and firing them in a kiln); or they may be predictive systems that are explanations and theories about how and why something is likely to work (e.g., using the conventions of perspective to show the illusion of space). Dynamic systems, on the other hand, are transformative. By this I mean that as a consequence of continual interactions among the elements in a system and among features of the environment, things change. And in this exchange, the feedback from both the surrounding influences, and the features of the system, produce effects that are new and different.[4] These outcomes are more than merely a result of the "sum of the parts" because from these transactions new phenomena are realized—much in the way that J. M. W. Turner's scientific knowledge of the properties of paint pigments became something quite different when this was transformed by his understanding of the aesthetic qualities of what oil paint could do.

This is known as "emergence" and describes how new features emerge from an interaction that is independent of any of the parts themselves. This also highlights the nonlinear character of dynamic systems. By nonlinear I refer to the way that simple cause-and-effect relationships are *not* involved because there is no direct connection between the input and the outcome. A linear relationship is different; it indicates that there is a proportional association between a cause and an effect (e.g., if you increase the amount of water added to watercolor pigment you get a related increase in transparency). Because dynamic systems are nonlinear, a small influence or action can cause myriad outcomes on any scale. Dynamic systems and emergence are components of complex adaptive systems (CAS) that are in a continual state of interactive change. And CAS are found at all levels of our natural and human worlds. In a way, a CAS can be seen to provide a braided frame within which artists create ordered forms from chaotic schemata in a transcognitive encounter with their surroundings. Murray Gell-Mann (2003) sees the interactions among the artist, artwork, viewer, and historical context as being a meeting of the minds and circumstances in a complex adaptive process of exchange and development.

> In the case of the individual work, the regularities can be described by embedding it in a conceptual ensemble. For the oeuvre or the work of the school, we may describe the regularities by embedding the whole series of pieces in a conceptual ensemble of series. Throughout, we are considering the artist as a CAS, the school or movement as a loose aggregation of complex adaptive systems functioning more or less as a CAS, and the viewer as a CAS learning about the art in question. (p. 57)

What is crucial about the dynamic systems described by Gell-Mann and others (Coveney & Highfield, 1995; Eve, Horsfall, & Lee, 1997) is the interactive nature of these artistic components and processes. The area of visual arts practice where this kind of complexity is most apparent is at the intersection of art, science, and technology, where artists are exploring the digital world. After all, as a site, the Internet is like installation art and only "comes alive" when someone interacts with it. Valovic (2000) describes cyberspace as "part technology, part human interaction" that is shaped by the mutual interaction of digital systems and human systems whereby the Internet "does not do anything in the absence of the human mind—in fact, the human mind is the sole source of its viability" (p. 39). This element of interactivity changes the relationship between the artist-creator of digital forms and the viewer-participant because there is no longer a direct line from the image to its public reception; in fact, the artwork, as a physical object need no longer exist. And just as there are many choices the artist can make in forming and presenting a digitally encoded image, the viewer can also determine how, where, and when to engage with it. Margot Lovejoy (1997) describes interactivity as a primary feature of digitally based visual arts that "is a flexible, nonlinear interactive system or structure, one designed and coded with linking capabilities which allow the viewer to make choices in moving along different paths through the work" (p. 165). She adds that

> with interactivity, readers, viewers, listeners can pass through the boundaries of the work to enter it. This puts them in a position to gain

direct access to an aspect of authoring and shaping the final outcome of a work in a way that never before existed before the advent of the computer. The artist gives up total control in favor of a new kind of viewer communication and experience, one which offers a less passive position for the viewer, one which also celebrates the inherent creative capacities of all individuals. Interactivity offers important new avenues for cognition to take place, where works can begin to flow with the more psychological internal associations of the individual viewer's make-up and identity in mind. (p. 166)

This new form of representation created in the digital setting is no longer a mechanical reproduction copied from an original in the manner described by Walter Benjamin (1968). Rather, it is a simulation that exists as a codified program of numbers that in many circumstances can be re-created in any version or form desired. In addition, the digital image often may include sound and text, thereby increasing the capacity to embody experience, carry information, and offer up new understanding in a dynamic, interactive way. This is somewhat different from an art object produced within the tradition of studio-practice, which can be "surrounded" by relevant contextual details such as biographical data, evidence of production, related research, and the like, for this is static testament that supports the artwork. Therefore artist-researchers working within the digital domain are opening up more varied opportunities to explore the capacity of visual images to be created and critiqued as sources of new knowledge and understanding.

Artistic practice undertaken in a digital environment is giving rise to research that is no longer challenged by questions about the human condition but is challenged by the need to revise what it is to be human. Information is more than an "object" from which knowledge is gleaned; it is a space where meaning is negotiated within the dynamics of changing contexts. This changes the way we think about inquiry and takes into account the point of view of the researcher and the researched. Cyberspace is radically altering these notions of individuality as modernist conceptions of identity grounded in traditional psychological perspectives are being replaced by a reflexive and decentered sense of self. Sherry Turkle (1995) refers to the many windows we use on the computer screen as a metaphor that reflects our capacity to seamlessly operate within several contexts at the same time. She adds that "as a user, you are attentive to only one of the windows on your screen at any given moment, but in a sense you are a presence in all of them at all times . . . your identity on the computer is the sum of your distributed presence" (p. 13).

The response of artists to the social implications raised by these questions about human engagement with new technologies is yielding innovative inquiries and adventurous projects. A comprehensive account is given by Stephen Wilson (2002) who presents a detailed review of more than 250 international artists working in various collaborations with scientists on technologies connected to areas of biology, the physical sciences, mathematics, telecommunications, digital systems, and other emergent fields of research. It is the development of newer technologies sparked by the digital revolution that is forging links between the arts and the sciences. According to Wilson, common interests and distinctive methods are bringing artists and scientists together within technological settings where they are able to exercise initiative and maintain independent responsibility. Within this context, Wilson describes research as a cultural activity where outcomes are seen in terms of human exchange and development and as such are not the province of particular domains, or privileged methods of inquiry. For artists, the conceptual cues come from discourse in critical theory and cultural studies because it is debates about society, visual culture, and technology that raise important issues, and investigating these often requires a collaborative response. For scientists, established parameters and methods of inquiry are proving inadequate in dealing conceptually and imaginatively with the possibilities opening up with the new technologies, and in doing so, they are having to address questions being raised by cultural theorists. What Wilson does in his opus is to organize his survey of the many research initiatives being undertaken by highlighting the uneasy but fruitful convergence of methods and practices within a divergent framework of issues and ideas. For Wilson, the arts are crucial to this enterprise because they "can fill a critical role as an independent zone of research, in which artists integrate critical commentary with high-level knowledge and participation in the worlds of science and technology" (p. 35).

The challenge of participating in innovative research that draws its imaginative focus from the visual arts, and its intellectual locus from intersections of science and technology, requires the artist to take on a more clearly identified public role. This is true also for other kinds of visual arts practice that might be described under the generic banner of making in systems. Even a radical historical incursion such as Dadaist performance can be seen to rely on a kind of systemic, critical vision that was enacted within a small, but nonetheless public, network. Threads of this form of arts infusion can be tracked to present-day performance art that quite readily places itself amidst literary, visual, and theatrical technologies where conditions of the private and public self are probed, processed, and repositioned. Mostly occurring in public spaces, the compression of content into a performed text disrupts any stable meaning and relocates it within the language of the production, the dynamics of the action, or the minds of the audience. Installation artists seek a somewhat similar dynamic where the artistic intent tilts toward the viewer as environments, sites, situations, and events become interactive spaces and systems of reference, inference, and meaning (Reiss, 1999).

Just as visual artists today feel more open to locating their practice within systems of inquiry and collaborative structures, so, too, do art historians and cultural theorists who see the image as less of a form yoked to mainstream histories, and more of a case or a genre in a broader class of visual information. James Elkins (1999), for instance, reconfigures the history of images as an inclusive system that considers fine art images and nonart pictorial forms as carriers of informative, as well as expressive, content, and therefore of interest to all. His proposal creates a sort of braided history of images that cannot be categorized within the formal traditions of art history, yet creates its own system of connections, dislocations, and legacies of expressive meanings.

> Instead of preserving the differences between the histories of art, science, and mathematics and studying the "science of art" or the "art of science," we should perhaps acknowledge that in the end many divisions between kinds of images are untenable, and that it is possible to begin writing the history of images rather than that of art. Images are found in the history of art but also in the histories of writing, mathematics, biology, engineering, physics, chemistry, and art history itself. (p. 46)

Arguing for a similar rehabilitation of the image as a visual source of knowledge with its own rich history, Stafford (1994, 1996) presents a rationale for the "*intelligence* of sight" based on the notion that "imaging, ranging from high art to popular illusions, remains the richest, most fascinating modality for configuring and conveying ideas" (emphasis in the original, p. 4).

The renewed interest in the role of art making and the studying of images within collaborative systems of research, cultural inquiry, and historical critique is also opening up new ways of thinking about teaching the visual arts. Although visual arts teaching in higher education has an ambivalent heritage as a practice, it requires the capacity of personal vision and the conviction of a public voice. As a process, teaching gains from both institutional system support and the distinctive character of the discipline. So it is not difficult to consider how pedagogical practice might be configured around fresh ideas that align with the emerging innovations underway as artists and cultural theorists look to forge new relationships across domains of inquiry.[5] Although the status of teaching as a practice within the visual arts has been caricatured in the past as intrusive or irrelevant, artists taking on pedagogical roles as a natural part of their art practice characterize some of the most radical and innovative periods of art history.

Despite the ambivalent climate surrounding the research and teaching practice of artists today, the opportunity to reconstruct an image of the "artist-as-researcher-teacher" is at hand. Today, contemporary artists work in

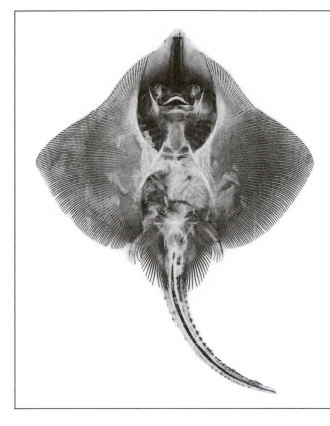

Brandon Ballengée's fascination with biological data and studio art practice saw him collaborate with a biologist to collect specimens and data to make his artworks. The relationships with scientists grew over time as did his interest in doing field environmental research. He now breeds indigenous species in a studio in Flushing, Queens, New York, where he hosts a variety of dead and live samples of artistic inspiration and flies frogs to an LA gallery for an exhibition while teaching as a BioArtist-in-residence at Hartwick College. (Sherry Mayo, 2004, p. 109)

Brandon Ballengée, *Skate*. Cleared and Stained Clearnose, Raja eglanteria. 2001–2003. Scanner photograph. Specimen preparation in collaboration with the Sci/Art Institute at Hartwick College, Oneonta, New York. High resolution scanning conducted at the Institute for Electronic Arts, School of Art and Design at Alfred University, Alfred, New York. Courtesy of the artist and Archibald Arts.

and across many of the domains that originally fell neatly within categories of the life sciences, the physical sciences, the humanities, the fine arts, and institutional teaching, and this is opening up exciting possibilities for the field. New York artist Brandon Ballengée explains that

> this is something that is growing, there are more scientists that are perhaps learning more about communicating through the arts . . . and vice versa, there are more artists that are pushing the boundaries of different art practices particularly with technology. I consider myself more of a hybrid than a studio artist . . . it's about keeping open and asking questions in both realms. (cited in Mayo, 2004, p. 101)

Making in Communities

If those artists whose practice is mostly circumscribed by *making in systems* are involved in reconfiguring artistic representation from visual forms to other coded forms, those whose practice entails *making in communities* accept that forms of representation exist in what Fred Myers calls "intercultural space" (2002, p. 6). What he means is that artworks produced within a community, and used to communicate and connect with others, do so in ways that are multiple, mutual, and where meaning is continually negotiated according to various perspectives, practices, and positions of power. Therefore, as carriers of meanings, artworks are not objects whose messages are melded within the forms themselves, or entirely embedded in the circumstances of how art is made, or overruled by others who read between the lines of their own design. Although there are more dynamics at work that register the right of others to make a claim on what an artwork might mean, the transactions do not take place in a cultural void. Even if privileged readings can be located and confirmed within particular sources and structures, these can also be easily usurped or misrepresented. This intercultural space is a site where cultural representations reside, interpretations are made, and meanings are communicated, but unless everyone is listening there may be just as much "talking past" each other as there might be in "talking back." These are precisely the circumstances that not only need to be considered, but can also be seen to open up the interpretive space in a culturally responsive way.[6]

There is also something intensely local about knowledge that is grounded in community construction—and local does not mean provincial. The past and the present are never far below the surface, because histories and traditions inform group identity yet do not constrain individual agency. In art making, personal vision and public voice share a loose coalition that not only shapes the dialogue within the community context, but also creates a dialectic with those whose interests are encountered—or so it should be.

There are plenty of cautionary tales of well-intentioned cultural theorists who end up as cultural tourists because they lack an understanding of the interchange between representation, identity politics, and power play. This often results from being blinkered by the authority of discipline interests, or blinded by exotic appeal, and these can lead to superficial encounters and hinder the capacity to see from the position of others. For instance, critiques of disciplines such as anthropology (Clifford, 1988; Marcus & Fischer, 1999) and art history (Harris, 2001; Nochlin, 1988; Pollock, 2001) challenge the way that assumed authority, Eurocentrism, gendered perspectives, and other practices stifle fields of inquiry. In responding to the call for a greater awareness of community in all its complexities, one strategy is to take on the attributes of other disciplines. Hal Foster (1995) highlights this problem with his description of "artist-envy" that he sees in the efforts of some critics of anthropology who seek broader, inclusive forms of cultural representation. Seen in this light, Foster suggests that the artist is naively regarded as "a paragon of formal reflexivity, sensitive to difference and open to chance, a self-aware reader of culture understood as text" (p. 304). On the other hand, Foster describes a trend in contemporary art that promotes the "artist as ethnographer" as a similar move that caricatures anthropology. Here artists and cultural critics are attracted to the concept of "otherness," and how meaning is embedded within objects and their contexts.

These are features that address many of the concerns raised by post-modernism that parallel the move of artists from the studio into the community, and the viewer from a passive to an active participant in artistic encounters. So it is understandable that artists are attracted to ethnographic practice and communities and cultures as sites of inquiry, and vice versa. But as Foster and others caution, there is a problem where the art produced under the guise of site-specific experience can become a "self-fashioning," superficial spectacle that lacks the integrity of depth expected from imaginative and disciplined cultural inquiry. According to Dipti Desai (2002), if an artist takes on elements of ethnographic practice as part of a social activist role, then the implication is that perspective, positionality, and power become part of the discourse.

> At a time when globalization and technological advances rupture national and cultural boundaries, artists are increasingly called upon to work in different sites across the world. The artist as ethnographer model may be more than a recent trend, given these changes. It is therefore necessary to remember, given the differential access to power in our society and world, that experience can only be understood relationally. (p. 321)

Deepali Dewan's (2003) description of the art of New Delhi artist Vivan Sundaram suggests that the caution Desai alludes to appears to be taken into account because the multiplicity of theoretical positions is held within the visual dynamic described.

> Like a scholar-artist he draws from a range of disciplinary languages, including postcolonial theory, art history, popular culture, history, modernism, postmodernism and photography. However, while Sundaram's visual language appropriates from these disciplines, it also comments on them, pointing out their implicit logic. . . . The role of Sundaram [in reference to his work *Great Indian Bazaar,* 1999] as a family member is blurred with the role of the artist as curator/archivist. In a self-reflexive gesture, the work calls into question the nature of historical research using state and national archives which uses a finite group of personal objects to reconstruct a larger collective history, suggesting that the products of artists and historians are perhaps more similar than different. (p. 39)

A similar set of informing conditions shapes the art of Rina Banerjee. Within the conscious political questioning of historical myth making and cultural displacement, Banerjee fuses the science of systematic order and the art of contrast. As a result, her installations and objects combine and contradict as familiar materials are put in unfamiliar settings, and foreign forms are refashioned from their fictional past. The exhibition Yankee Remix[7] invited participating artists to investigate cultural assumptions associated with the meaning given to historical artifacts and everyday collectibles. Rina Banerjee's sprawling installation is full of specimens of shrink-wrapped mementoes that show quixotic and exotic memories to be an infected vision. The discomfort is in the details as we are reminded how the things we surround ourselves with distort as they display. What is intriguing about the Yankee Remix show is the way the artist-theorists and curator-historians shared a goal in critiquing historical perceptions. The artists did what they do best, and created ensembles of visual research that offered arguments, inferences, and insights that invited further questioning.

Rina Banerjee, *Contagious Spaces, Preserving Pinkeye* (2003). Installation of altar, Taj Mahal, and optical sculptures. Commissioned by Massachusetts Museum of Contemporary Art (MASS MoCA) for Yankee Remix. Reproduced courtesy of the artist and MASS MoCA.

The capacity of the visual arts continues to open up new possibilities in ways that reveal insights about problematic practices of the past, and potential directions for the future. In his descriptions of how indigenous artists fashion their own identity construction, Fred Myers (2002) reveals how representation becomes an important "social practice through which indigenous people engage the wider world" (p. 273). In an earlier review of the discourse about the acrylic painting of Central Desert Aboriginal artists shown in 1988 in New York as part of the exhibition *Dreamings: The Art of Aboriginal Australia,* Myers (1995) illustrates how art critics, cultural theorists, and anthropologists talk amongst themselves, but not to each other, and in doing so render the voice of the subject mute. In a followup assessment of this event, Myers (2002, pp. 255–276) positions the debates more clearly from the perspective of the indigenous artists in describing the artworks and performances as forms of social practice. Myers describes how the art forms themselves, be they paintings, artifacts, sand paintings, or performances, are best seen as "events" that are a form of social action. Therefore the works cannot be simply positioned as examples tied to the historical past, or set up as easy targets by critical theorists as instances of ideological shaping by the dominant culture. As agencies of social actions, these representations remain firmly authored by the community of artists and are presented to the wider public on *their* terms. Myers raises questions about Aboriginal cultural production that resonate within broader indigenous issues.

> The questions that ought to be asked about the politics of current forms of Aboriginal cultural production are whether and to what extent local (community-based) social orders are defining themselves—their meanings, values, and possible identities—autonomously in relation to external powers and processes; whether and how they are transformed in relation to new powers and discourses; and whether or how what had been local meanings are now being defined dialectically (or oppositionally) with respect to discourses available from the larger world. (p. 275)

What is especially noticeable in the work of indigenous artists and researchers in recent years is challenging practices that continue to deny position and voice that can rightfully be claimed to be inclusive.[8] For instance, insights into the significance of *making in communities* and the impact on ideas and agency can be paralleled to the question posed in Chapter 1 about the construction of knowledge being raised by indigenous researchers who ask, "Whose research is it?" As Linda Tuhiwai Smith (1999) notes, this process involves "'researching back,' in the same tradition of 'writing back' or 'talking back,' that characterizes much of the post-colonial or anti-colonial literature" (p. 7). To emphasize the communal ownership of knowledge, Tuhiwai Smith acknowledges how important it is to ensure "that research reaches the people who have helped make it." She adds, "two important ways not always addressed by scientific research are to do with 'reporting back' to the people and 'sharing knowledge' [and] both ways assume a principle of reciprocity and feedback" (p. 15). Tuhiwai Smith makes the further point that sharing information and sharing knowledge are not the same. The former is equated with "pamphlet information," which gives surface details. Sharing knowledge, on the other hand, does not rely on language framed in certain ways, such as Western conceptual structures; rather, it is contingent on a respect for voice and making the opportunity to listen. A similar distinction can be drawn in discussing the popular phrase "ways of knowing," which is used as a descriptor to distinguish particular paradigms of thinking that are often associated with different cultural or discipline perspectives. Semali and Kincheloe (1999) make the point that within indigenous communities it is not "knowing" that best characterizes indigenous conceptualizing, but that the value and function of knowledge is best understood as relationships among things. Therefore it is "not as much an expression of knowing as much as it is one of relating" (p. 43). The implication here is that it is not *mastery of* knowledge that is involved in learning but in *relating with* knowledge that is important. This changes the position of how knowledge is created and communicated within communities whereby insider and outsider perspectives become elements within the intercultural space where meaning making occurs. Tuhiwai Smith (1999) explains this perspective as one that relies on a reflexive approach.

> Indigenous research approaches problematize the insider model in different ways because there are multiple ways of both being an insider and an outsider in indigenous contexts. The critical issue with insider research is the constant need for reflexivity. At a general level, insider researchers have to have ways of thinking critically about their processes, their relationships and the quality and richness of their data and analysis. So, too, do outsiders, but the major difference is that insiders have to live with the consequences of their processes on a day-to-day basis for ever more, and so do their families and communities. (p. 137)

There are numerous conceptions of knowledge centered in community-based practices of art making that offer diverse textual references, which communicate to those willing to see and listen.[9] The necessity to be directly involved in creating, claiming, and sharing knowledge is a task undertaken at all levels in indigenous communities and in all forms of representation, and the educational value of these practices hold important lessons for all (Semali & Kincheloe, 1999). As with the hegemonic influence of research, those who would influence visual arts practice often fail to acknowledge the significance of the aesthetic traditions, communication modes, and cultural structures of communities that exist outside the view of the tastemakers of the artworld, or the gatekeepers of the academy. There are, however, many theorists and practitioners who see the arts as forms that are centered in individual and community practices, yet sway and shift in response to changing social and cultural contexts.[10] Molly McGlennen (Ojibwe), for instance, describes how the artist George Longfish seeks to reclaim cultural knowledge lost as a consequence of historical translation.

> Longfish has long asserted that Native people must own their cultural knowledge: "The more we are able to own our religious, spiritual, and survival information, and even language, the less we can be controlled. . . . The greatest lesson we can learn is that we can bring our spirituality and warrior information from the past and use it in the present and see that it still works." This compression of history and present reality subverts linear constructs of time and allows Longfish to reappropriate cultural images and words in order to discern the truth from the lie in a way that has always been innate to Native philosophy and religion. (2004, n.p.)

Invariably these practices include artistic forms that draw on all manner of human expression and take place in a variety of settings as the locus of the aesthetic and educational appeal is now seen to be inclusive and democratic. In keeping with this egalitarian ethic, the methods of inquiry and modes of representation used by the visual arts researcher vary as they can occupy the position of both insider and outsider. This expansive role not only requires the use of artistic forms of inquiry, but can also make good use of narrative structures, oral histories, and "family memory and community recollection" (Bolin, Blandy, & Congdon, 2000, p. 3). When taken beyond the province of education and to the more open setting of the public place, however, community-minded artists often have a hard time dealing with content issues as much as logistics in making their projects happen. Defining the artist as cultural worker is a role that has almost no institutional history with little effort spent on introducing art students to the potential of public projects as a viable form of art practice. Dealing with local histories, communities, bureaucracies, and the demands of collaboration and conflict resolution are not normally part of the studio college curriculum. Plenty of agencies exist to promote public art, and the relatively short contemporary history nonetheless boasts considerable impact as artists and publicly spirited supporters continue to reshape the motivations and methods behind it (Deutsche, 1998; Lacy, 1995). Amongst these pragmatic public projects much

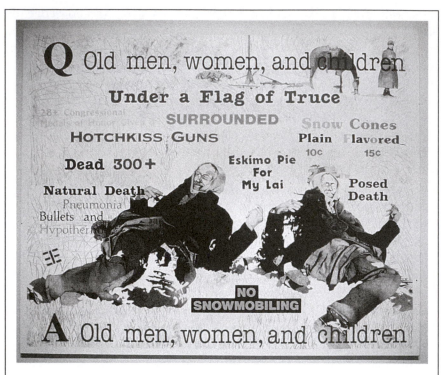

In *Winter Still Life Landscape, South Dakota, 1893,* two images of Chief Big Foot's frozen body mirror one another, with a soldier]and a tent in the distance. Phrases framed as questions and answers, "Old men, women, and children," "Dead 300+," "Posed Death," and "No Snowmobiling," appear as text both framing and cutting through the images. To be sure, humor subversively hints at the absurd; more important, however, the text writes through the narrative that the images create by re-asserting a moment of history with truth. As the onlooker is pulled into the narrative, the story of Wounded Knee is turned on its head. Specifically, Longfish's piece defies fixedness by bringing a sense of "orality" to the experience that necessarily demands perpetual invention, with the speaker and listener, the artist and onlooker as mutual partners in the artistic encounter. And within this ever-changing dialogue, within the remembering of a horrific massacre, spirit enables healing. (Molly McGlennen [Ojibwe], 2004. *George Longfish*, February 28–May 23, 2004, *Continuum 12 Artists*. Smithsonian National Museum of the American Indian)

George Longfish, *Winter Still Life Landscape, South Dakota, 1893*. Acrylic on canvas, 79 × 99 inches. Reproduced courtesy of the artist.

has been done to expand the kind of research artists undertake, yet the distinctions remain that keep institutional practices, artworld process, and public programs mostly at a distance. Perhaps it is a reconfiguration of private studio spaces and the public places as collaborative research sites that might help visual arts researchers respond to the challenge identified by Lucy Lippard (1997).

> With few exceptions, the art schools and university art departments in this country [America] still teach nineteenth-century notions about the function (or functionlessness) of art. Most art students, even sophisticated ones, know little or nothing about the history of attempts to break down the walls. . . . There are very few programs that offer prolonged, in-depth experience working with communities and other "public" entities. Little has been written on the actual day-by-day, year-by-year processes of making public art—what an artist has to go through to execute the "product," which is then reviewed in the art press with minimal understanding of the "public" audience's viewpoint, and in the general press with minimal understanding of the artist's context, hassles, and intentions. (p. 269)

Making in Cultures

As we have seen, for many artists their practice is mediated by systems of making or systems of community, yet for others it is not a collective context that characterizes their art making, but the way they make use of tools or techniques for particular purposes and pursuits. If we consider postmodernism as one of those periodic shakeups of cultural complacency felt across layers of reified theory, and within levels of restrictive practices, it is not so much new content that supplies the shock as it is new ideas about how to do things. With postmodern discourse mostly dealing in theory rather than practice, what is most revealing are the strategies of thought and lines of inquiry used, as these embody the fresh perspectives from this most recent age of ideas.

During modernist times the prevailing construct was "to *see* is to know." This was grounded in an empirical understanding based on direct experience and was mostly achieved by participation in the grand tradition of cultural tourism. To visit and observe sites such as archaeological ruins, historical settings, or the physical abundance of historic museums was essential training for the cultural aesthete. Many art students endured the travails of these travels where knowledge was held within the borders of the ubiquitous art slide and was felt as an experience of art in the dark. During postmodern times we live in a mediated visual world where there is little distinction between the real and the virtual. If we understand the constructions that shape what we see, then "to *know* is to see."[11] Thus there are different ways of knowing and interpreting the world. The critical task is to determine the social impact of these different visions, and the creative task is to create forms of representation that have the capacity to reveal, critique, and transform what we know. This is characteristic of *making in cultures* as artists who pursue a resistant art practice make full use of the potential of visual images to help reveal critical understandings about issues of human concern. The Chinese artist Zhang Dali uses his distinctive visual signature of a profile of a human head to mark up buildings throughout Beijing slated for demolition in the wake of rapid modernization. Zhang Dali uses two forms of graffiti he describes as *Dialogues* and *Demolitions* as a way to alert citizens about the loss of Chinese cultural identity. Dialogues are outlines spray-painted on walls; whereas Demolitions are chiseled and chipped profiles that cut holes in the walls to reveal traditional or contemporary buildings in the background. These empty images are enigmatic reminders of the human scale that was so prominent in the courtyard communities of Beijing.

The task of the artist-theorist within this cultural context therefore is to investigate how image makers and meaning makers come to know the things they do. Obviously the image-based researcher also creates and interprets visual information so a central consideration is to address the need to be critical in assessing how researchers themselves make meanings. This critical imperative implies that the visual image is more than a product that can be isolated or contextualized. Rather, a different set of theoretical parameters is needed to fully understand the way images reveal insights and understandings. This principle is accepted by art historians and cultural theorists who understand the dynamic, interpretive relationships among the object, creator, viewer, and related cultural, political, and institutional regimes that influence how knowledge is both constructed and made problematic (Bal, 1996; Heywood & Sandywell, 1999; Hooper-Greenhill, 2000). Furthermore, the status and meaning of the "visual" undergoes continual change as various means and ends are invoked within the workings of the interpretive communities that surround the visual arts. These discontinuities are evident in the different historical and sociocultural patterns of practice of art writing, art historical inquiry, and curatorial practice.

In considering how art writers and cultural critics respond to traditions and practices of *making in cultures,* it is in relationships rather than images or objects where value is located. It is within the ensemble of art making, interpretive scope, critical perspective, institutional constraints, and cultural influences that meanings are both made manifest and made problematic. In other words, what artists and other communities and collectives create is taken up by art writers and interrogated and repositioned within broader regimes of thought. This cycle of critical analysis continually expands as the robust quality of visual arts can be interpreted with reference to different

Mathieu Borysevicz (1999) describes Zhang Dali's *Dialogue* series this way:

The symbology employed here is figurative; it is the image of a common human denominator, immediately identifiable and therefore highly charged. It is a backdrop that outlines the theater of the street, a shadow cast by China's tremendous population where emergence from the crowd is not only discouraged but is logistically impossible. The image is found in an environment where conformity rules, once through political ideology, but now in the global forces of market and fashion trends. Through its repetition, the head indexes the asphyxiation of individuality in society. Often painted several at a time facing in the same direction, the heads queue up as if to mock the blind herding of the masses. The mass, however, is made of component individuals; they are all originals yet uniform. Likewise, the image is the product of a free hand, not the result of mechanical reproduction; each one is different and yet they are all the same. Zhang Dali's personal story, however, is not the same and these heads attempt, in some way, to narrate that story. (p. 10)

Zhang Dali. *Dialogues*, Spray-painted buildings, Beijing. Reproduced courtesy of the artist. Photograph by Graeme Sullivan.

aesthetic, social, political, and educational ends. The status of the art image or object is therefore best appreciated if seen to be a cultural practice whose genesis is generative of personal and public meaning when opened up to critical discourse by the art writer.

Within this interpretive space where the visual image is squeezed of new meanings, certain canons are disrupted much in the same way that newer reflexive methods of research show up prescribed practices as unable to cope with the complex realities of today. In her investigations of visual culture, Mieke Bal (1996), for instance, dislodges the idea of causality as it is normally associated with the study of art history. An artwork is subject to surrounding influences during its making because it is not merely the end result of a series of actions or temporal events, but is continually re-created in the changing circumstances of the present. The contexts that surround our understanding of art can never really exhaust its meaning. A useful way to understand this notion is to compare interpretive meaning to measurement, as it is understood in scientific research. Quantitative researchers know that all measurement, no matter how precise, contains elements of error or chance that cannot be controlled. The best that can be done in an experiment is to assess the probable ratio of results in any intervention to that of error and hope that there is a significant difference. Consequently, there is no certitude to scientific measurement. In an analogical way, Bal and others (Heywood & Sandywell, 1999; Wolff, 1993) acknowledge that similar circumstances surround the interpretation of visual forms, for there is always a residual interpretive space that opens up opportunities for further meaning making. This does not give a license for endless interpretation, for as with any research activity, the information is in the details and the inference is in the plausibility of the evidence.

A useful example of Bal's approach to thinking in a context, and her questioning of the tendency to lock interpretations within structures of the past, is her analysis of the politics of representation evident in the American Museum of Natural History in New York. In developing a rich semiotic critique of the museum and its location within the physical and cultural language of the city, Bal highlights how the presentation of humanity and nature communicates a narrative "of fixation and the denial of time" (Bal, 1996, p. 16). Examples are given such as the positioning of cultures along timelines depicting "man's rise to civilization," and the less-than-seamless juxtaposition of people and things. An example is the categorization of anonymous non-Western peoples alongside the great names of classical antiquity.

> The time frame initiated, then, is not that of a causal voyage through time. Transforming temporal tourism into knowledge production, the time frame is that of an evolutionism colluding with taxonomy, dividing human cultures into higher and lower, the ones closest to "ours" being the highest. It would be feasible, although not easy, to walk backwards, to undo the telling of this Eurocentric story, but the museum has not provided panels that make such a reversed story readable. (p. 30)

The critical vision presented in these kinds of deconstructive practices run parallel to broader questioning stances concerning representation from personal perspectives, within particular communities, and across cultural divides.[12] Sometimes the struggle is private and puzzling, and although the public historical circumstance may offer an image of change, the rhetoric may often be more than the reality. In considering his African American identity from the position of his curatorial practice, Hamza Walker (2001) describes the contradictions that exist as the social lens is more broadly drawn to reveal a breadth of cultural diversity, but the zoom is backward in time rather than forward, so that the view may be wide but the vision is narrow. For bell hooks (1995), being dispossessed of vision and voice makes it all the more necessary to fashion a critical discourse because "if one could make a people lose touch with their capacity to create, lose sight of their will and their power to make art, then the work of subjugation, of colonization, is complete" (p. xv). The outcome is captured in James Rolling's (2004) evocations of what it is like to be "homeless" and "nameless," which results from a normalizing process that allows one's individual and cultural identity to be defined by others. Direct reference to these dilemmas of identity representation is given by Olukemi Ilesanmi's (2001) commentary on the lyrical, but discomforting, art of Laylah Ali.

> These creatures with large flat heads of color, brown-skinned bodies, and teeth that are hard to ignore as they grin or grimace, ritually make and break allegiances, cut and maim one another, soothe the hurt and make offerings little understood by those of us on the outside of their world. . . . This viewer sees Ali's allegories of power as parables of race as experienced in America. It can't be coincidental that her creatures all have brown skin or that lynching and symbols of team sports, basketball especially, recur in the work. The sleep of reason in the United States has produced monsters that continue to haunt our racial imaginary. The black body as featured star in spectacles of violence and betrayal are peculiarly American entertainment as even a cursory trip down our collective memory lane will reveal. (p. 20)

Making in cultures, when seen from the perspective of identity politics and the cultural diaspora, reveals the hybrid practice of artists working within and across geographies. The physical movement of artists between countries and continents positions them strategically to carry out their imaginative and intellectual critiques. Many pursue a practice that often features curatorial collaborations where the various roles of the theorist and the practitioner easily interchange. Yet within these settings, the issue of cultural representation remains paramount where the curatorial task, according to Alice Yang (1998), involves articulating forms of identity that are "not subjugated to the demands of dominant representation" (p. 97). In discussing the problem of situating contemporary art from China within an exhibition context in the West, Yang sees the task as one that "might free us from the constraints of both the fields of traditional Chinese art history and modern western art criticism, both of which make their claims on Chinese contemporary art, bringing to the enterprise different biases and blinders" (p. 101). Notwithstanding the prevalence of these interpretive constraints, when approached from the perspective of artists, the issues confronted take on board a theoretically profound and culturally rich blend of politics, position, and hybridity. Three short examples drawn from the Asia-Pacific Triennial of Contemporary Art (Webb, 1999) illustrate this point.

Making in Cultures: Artists Participating in the 1999 Asia-Pacific Triennial of Contemporary Art

Mella Jaarsma was born in the Netherlands but trained in Indonesia, where she has been working as an artist since the early 1980s, so she has certain insider's knowledge and an outsider's perspective. An artwork shown in the Asia-Pacific Triennial was titled *Hi inlander (Hello native)*. The piece is a set of performance capes made from the treated skins of chicken, fish, frogs, and kangaroos. It seems Mella Jaarsma is saying something more than posing the question about what it must be like to walk around in someone else's skin. She highlights the uncertainty of identity, one that is not confined or confirmed by location or by origin. One is reminded of how much emphasis we put on identity construction in the visual arts, as we search for self and place. The work of Mella Jaarsma is a jolting reminder about how difficult it is to deal with difference in this quest.

Lee Wen is an artist from Singapore but his performance piece *Journey of a Yellow Man,* has taken him all over the globe in recent years. For several years Lee Wen has painted his whole body yellow and created art events that are usually shown as video documentation of a performance. The most obvious reference can be drawn from the way the yellow paint exaggerates his Chinese background and the varied interpretations this attracts when seen in different cultural contexts. But it's the aspect of the journey that also intrigues. There is almost an alien naïveté and honesty in the way he confronts social and political issues. His work reminds us how difficult it is to see things in a fresh way. Lee Wen reminds the viewer that locating a perspective beyond the safety zone of the acculturated self is a hard road to travel.

Another example is Ah Xian, a Chinese artist now living in Australia who exhibits his work internationally. His dilemma is one shared by many expatriate artists who struggle to reconcile the cultural values of their homeland with that of their adopted country. Ah Xian created a set of porcelain busts titled the *China. China Series.* The irony for Ah Xian is that it was after he left China that he discovered a passion for certain cultural practices and he had to return to China to train with master potters and porcelain painters. According to Ah Xian, one way to confirm the value of the human spirit and to challenge the politics of control is to reinvigorate past histories in new ways. In his hands, porcelain becomes a vehicle through which to think in a distinctive way about the old and the new, the East and the West. This goal sits nicely within the critical minds of artists who transcend cultures, politics, and geographies.

REEMERGENCE OF THE ARTIST-THEORIST ●

Considering the artist as a hybrid identity is a notion that is not inconceivable as the kind of practices that constitute what can happen in the studio can readily be placed anywhere within the discourse of cultural and educational research. This is especially relevant if research trends continue to move beyond the quest for explanatory paradigms as the long dominant positivist practices reveal themselves unable to cope with the breadth and depth of human action. This environment is a particularly rich intellectual space within which to consider the changing role of the artist and the visual image. Originally conceived as an object or icon representative of a time or place, as an informational record, or an idiosyncratic emblem, the image these days is a much more loaded text that carries all sorts of references and inferences. Research into these multiple meanings puts the image under analysis from different perspectives and highlights the robust capacity to reveal insights about individual, historical, cultural, and political content and contexts. Therefore, institutional and discipline traditions, and artworld constituencies, not only serve as interpretive communities that extend the outline of the art experience, but are also sources from which the artist actively draws as the locus of art making expands to embrace theories and practices. This creates an opportunity for the "artist-theorist" to construct a practice that is defined less by one-dimensional features such as stylistic signature, and more by imaginative inquiry that has the potential to be realized in multiple ways. Seen within wide parameters of mission and method, it is not inconceivable to define the visual image as a change agent and the research outcome as one that helps us understand the transformative power of art knowledge. Within the context of research, this implies that the visual image can be seen as a form of data that have the potential to be used as "evidence." As data, a visual image is just raw information—it only becomes evidence when it is interpreted in some way—much in the same way that charcoal is a material that only becomes an artistic medium if it is put to creative use. Consequently, the way artists work is a distinctive human activity that shares the goals of other forms of inquiry.

Artists make informed choices about the imaginative and intellectual approaches they use when they create and respond to art. The process of making insightful decisions when carrying out research *in* art is not predicated on the assumption that there is a prescribed body of knowledge one learns and then applies. The necessity of developing a repertoire of knowledge about relevant technical processes and products is, of course, essential. However, there is little in the way of prevailing explanatory systems of knowledge in the visual arts within which new advances might be framed. The iterative or accumulative model that characterizes the development of knowledge in the human sciences is not so evident. Yet there are cultural boundaries that serve as interpretive frames against which creative outcomes are referenced for the new can only be referenced against the old. Various theories of human processes, communal practices, and cultural agencies obviously abound and these serve as both a grounded set of conditions and an interpretive framework around which inquiry is assessed.

By necessity, the complexity of visual arts research practice *has* to bridge disciplines and in doing so not only opens up new possibilities such as those on offer within the newer information technologies, but also renders mute old arguments that see inquiry as methods bound, rather than issues driven. For the artist-theorist completing projects within the academic setting, the methods deployed in "surrounding" a research problem will be necessarily broad yet grounded in personal and public relevance. Whether undertaking research *in* art or *about* art, the artist-theorist becomes involved in a set of practices that must be defensible. The aim of research in the visual arts, as in other similar forms of exploratory inquiry, is to provoke, challenge, and illuminate rather than confirm and consolidate. Making informed choices about creative ends and means involves selecting, adapting, and constructing ways of working and ways of seeing. To do this one has to construct the tools of inquiry from an array of practices. Yet when working from a base in contemporary art, the conceptions of the discipline are uncertain, the informing parameters are open-ended, but the opportunity for inventive inquiry is at hand. In these circumstances, the artist-theorist is seen to be participating in a transdisciplinary practice. Two brief profiles of contemporary critical practice in the visual arts support this point.

● CRITICAL PERSPECTIVES AND PRACTICES

Unknowing Culture: Fred Wilson

The introduction to Peter Robb's (1998) biography of Caravaggio, *"M,"* begins with a description of a process of inquiry that is intensely human and captures the way that historical research is about trying to make visible that which is mostly unseen. But rather than creating fiction or fantasy, the assembling of evidence in all its messy minutiae is a critical and creative process of reference and inference that results in a plausible and often a provocative representation. This is Robb's account of his research methodology:

> The fragments that tell us what we know about the life and death of the painter I call M float on the surface of a treacherous reality—they're lies to the police, reticence in court, extorted confessions, forced denunciations, revengeful memoirs, self-justifying hindsight, unquestioned hearsay, diplomatic urbanities, theocratic diktat, reported gossip, threat and propaganda, angry outbursts—hardly a word untainted by fear, ignorance, malice or self interest. You have to apply a forensic and skeptical mind to the enigmas of M's life and death. You have to know how to read the evidence. You have to know the evidence is there—you need a feel for the unsaid, for the missing file, the cancelled entry, the tacit conclusion, the gap, the silence, the business done with a nod and a wink. The missing data in M's life and death make up a narrative of their own, running invisible but present through the known facts. (n.p.)

I expect Fred Wilson would delight in the details of Robb's historical digging and relate to the "need to feel for the unsaid." For it is the quest for the unsaid and the unseen that interests Wilson and he has honed his own procedures for inquiry that allow him to reveal historical omissions, distorted tales, and the misrepresented past and present. His critical eye unravels cultural constructions and institutional practices in ways that are disarming and evocative, yet they are assembled from layers of evidence that is under our noses—it's just that we don't see it.

The art practice of Fred Wilson maps loosely over the domain of *making in cultures* as described in this chapter as his work is critical in its resistance to received histories and perceived narratives. The location for much of Wilson's work since the late 1980s has been within the walls of cultural institutions, mostly museums, where walled curatorial structures used to frame the forms of cultural representation presented to the public come under his scrutiny. His critical stance is inherently multivocal and passages of privilege and position, as they are recorded in private perception and documented in public display, are sharply scissored against repressed memories and denied cultural signifiers of "otherness." As Wilson says, "I am most interested in people who are marginal or invisible to the majority, and the larger society's denial of certain issues" (2003, p. 22). His methodology is, in the main, deconstruction, where principles of cultural representation are contested, and systems of institutional practice are dismantled. His research methods comprise comparative critique where proximity and placement create discursive narratives as forms that carry different coded histories as meanings are brought into strong contrast. And all of this occurs within the visual domain of objects, images, and spatiotemporal events that are rendered sharply in the present, as it is the immediacy of our mindset that is assailed. The evidence emerges out of the juxtaposed visual relationships that reveal new impressions and insights that could not have been possible before. What the viewer does with this information and how it might be encoded into experiential forms of understanding is a matter of personal choice. But the palpable effect of an encounter whereby prior knowledge, disturbed complacency, and the impact of a profound visual imprint, suggests that this kind of learning is real indeed.

Part of the impact of the installations created by Wilson can be tracked back to the reflexive quality he is able to invest in his works that reflect the way he "talks back" to the forms he selects and the meanings he invokes. Working in a manner that may require a scrupulous archaeological care for detail in working with objects, and a sensitive ethnographic feel for those who may have used them, Wilson's interpretive aesthetic shapes the statement that brings these together and the context in which they are used to open up further dialogue. As with any field-based researcher, his decision making is mostly self-evident and accrued in ways that could be made more obvious if needed, but an understanding that evidence and the basis for reasoning can be represented in many forms is at the heart of his practice. His work is his art and it is his research.

Wilson's installation, *Speak of Me as I Am,* which was the U.S. representative at the 2003 Venice Biennale, presented elements of historical narrative that tracked the centuries-old presence of African identity in the cultural diaspora around Venice. This work in the American pavilion comprised several installations that brought together in sharp contrast images and objects borrowed from regional collectors and museums. Amidst these Wilson created his own versions and visions by adapting, reconfiguring, editing, and generally recontextualizing the forms around a mostly little known set of narratives about the historical identity of black Africans. In a way, the image reproduced below, *Untitled,* reflects the discourse opened up in that the work spoke to the history and space of Venice as a city-state rather than in direct reference to any institutional or cultural practices. The looming presence was more direct—it was as if the representation of black Africans in and around Venice was an external existence, a bit like the way Venice itself is a museum whose treasures are shown on the outside, along the canals and within the commerce of daily life—the dignity of the everyday to be appreciated and understood on its own terms.

Fred Wilson, *Untitled* (2003). C-print, 13/125. 25 × 31 inches. Reproduced courtesy of the artist.

The Necessity of Visual Dialogue: Fiona Foley

"The absence of evidence is not evidence of absence" (Genocchio, 2001, p. 28). This quote appears early in Benjamin Genocchio's monograph of Fiona Foley. This crisp, lyrical line of text mirrors the sparse, spatial layers of Foley's drawing and painting, and both word and image carry references well beyond what is immediately apparent. The absence refers in part to the physical landscape where the presence of Foley's Aboriginal heritage is held in memories and marks tracked in her artworks. The cultural landscape, on the other hand, exists as a continual expanse of temporal space occupied by Foley's ancestral connections to her Badtjala people. Yet this is fractured by a political landscape where the absence of evidence makes it convenient for many to remain silent about a shameful past and an uncertain present.

As an artist who exhibits and travels extensively throughout the globe, the dialogue Fiona Foley opens up through her art is readily picked up by her indigenous colleagues, which generates debate and discourse of a profound kind. Kindred histories and a clear commitment to the importance of art in narrative traditions, cultural identity, and political activism place artists in a position where their vision and voice can be seen and heard to good effect. The irony, however, is that these richly informing experiences that contribute so much to the integrity of the arguments presented through the art of artists such as Foley mostly falls on deaf ears. The dilemma is that little public debate occurs within mainstream society, and Fiona Foley describes this as another way of remaining silent about indigenous history. In this case, continuing to ignore the present also means a failure to confront the past. Creating profound and challenging art that is displayed in the public arena, sometimes as permanent site-specific art, is only part of the process, and the outcomes wilt unless the community becomes engaged. In speaking about the Australian context, Fiona Foley explains it this way.

> Because there is no analysis of the work it doesn't have a historical con-text, it is not spoken about, therefore there is no history of the work. So important historical moments like that in Australia are "written out" and that's very disturbing for me when the work isn't critiqued in some form. . . . Australia only sees things as a dichotomy of black and white cultures, and everything is reduced to a core between indigenous and nonindigenous, and for me that's not where it's at.[13]

For Foley, the need to maintain the tension is sharpened by the compul-sion to make art. The process carries with it layers of details that swell with direct and indirect reference to historically grounded images and ideas. For this purpose, the historical part of her research process requires Foley to be diligent in scouring limited sources because more formal records and docu-ments generally do not contain the information sought. Other resources, such as old postcards, memorabilia, and everyday artifacts, often serve as more accurate historical traces that hold the clues from which Foley can fashion her critical responses. Here images are wrought in the rawest of form, yet they offer cues that can be read as the narrative threads remind and provoke, ren-der and rouse, and in ways where experience is both seen and felt. A layering of references may be there, or the simplicity of form may signify nothing more than itself, yet there is a particular kind of accessibility in the way that Foley's images or objects speak to all ages. So a playful encounter with spaces, sights, and sounds within a public art piece made by Fiona Foley may delight a child, yet it will also reward a pensive viewer who can take the time to pick up the conversation so that held assumptions are opened up to other options.

Editing out information so as to infuse a simple form with complex con-tent is a way to not only sharpen the historical focus, but it is also an aesthetic decision used to strengthen visual thoughts. On the one hand, this process compiles form and content in a decisive mix in what Benjamin Genocchio

Fiona Foley, *Wild Times Call #2* (2001). Type C photograph. 33 × 40 inches. Series of 7 images edition of 10. Reproduced courtesy of the artist and Roslyn Oxley9 Gallery.

(2001) calls Fiona Foley's "evidentiary aesthetics, a gathering together of signs and signatures . . . a building up of a data-bank of images" (pp. 87–90). The purpose here is relatively clear as the viewer is invited into the narrative. On the other hand, the license to make use of images that do not have a coded heritage means other aspects of inquiry that rely on the meanings she can embody, and the possibilities these open up for the viewer, take over for Foley. In this case, there may be a more poetic and political mix that requires the viewer to work hard to wriggle beneath the irony, metaphor, and incisive humor. The photograph *Wild Times Call #2* shows Fiona Foley as a serious participant among an identifiable group that apparently share a common ancestry; that is, if we accept the assumption that a sepia-toned ethnographic record neatly indexes those in it as people of exotic appeal who can readily be seen to belong together. Are these steadfast Seminole Indians posing in traditional dress within the sanctity of their ancestral home in southern Florida? Maybe not. How different it is when those *making* the photographs rather than those *taking* the photographs are responsible for creating false impressions. As Fiona Foley continually points out in her art practice, the capacity of art to disrupt deep-seated inequities and to disturb long-held biases is palpable. The evidence is contained in the ideas and images, and the claim is in the interpretive power that is supported by the various visual devices used by Fiona Foley in her wry construction.

● CONCLUSION

It is argued in this chapter that conceiving of art practice as research that is grounded in traditions of making can be seen as a viable way to reveal the kind of artistic knowledge that has the capacity to change us. This approach to inquiry runs in sympathy with interpretivist and critical positions in the visual arts and with the ideas and methods from the human sciences that promote the use of visual research methods. For instance, many visual artists today are broadening their practice by using many textual forms to create insightful and imaginative responses to issues of importance to them and others. Although there is no common structure or method to these artworks, there is a critical urgency in the way that ideas of individual public concern are explored and presented. Visual forms are created and critiqued in an investigative and expressive process that communicates visions, arguments, and experiences. The claim made here is that these outcomes of visual arts practice are grounded in an authentic research practice that constructs new knowledge that is individually empowering and culturally relevant.

Although important research practices in the visual arts are found in the studio, in galleries, in communities, on the street, and on the Internet, they have yet to find a rightful place within institutional settings. Thus the issue to be argued is that research in the visual arts incorporates ways of presenting, encountering, and analyzing information that is sufficiently robust to produce new knowledge that can be encountered and acted on. It is possible to consider "the visual" not only as a descriptive or representational form, but also as a means of creating and constructing images that forms an evidential base that reveals new knowledge. Seen from this perspective, the role of visual data in research can be used to move beyond the contribution to explanatory knowledge production, and to a more ambitious state of transformative knowledge construction.

The quest to breach the boundaries of research practice is not without its critics, either from the ire of artworld criticism, or fire from the academic canon, and the dilemma of how to integrate the arts within the academy is not new. As was described in Chapter 1, the institutionalization of visual arts practice has a long and illustrious history. In each era, the formal training of the fine artist invariably created a schism between those within the institution who saw a need to uphold authority, and those from without who challenged it. Many advocates of the training of artists see the marketplace of the art-world as the arbiter that offers professional success, with institutions being mostly responsible for technical training. Those who seek academic status for the profession invariably have to respond to the challenge of setting creative practice on a more grounded discipline foundation. As such, the university exerts its own institutional power. The challenge is how to accommodate these demands yet also maintain a degree of integrity about what constitutes art as a field of study. It is in the area of research where these distinctions become the sharpest.

Part of the legacy of conceptualizing studio art practice as research is the opportunity it gives to reconsider the inextricable relationship between theory and practice. Assembling new historical and critical traditions of fine arts alongside equally diverse studio practices means that the alliance between the artist and the art writer is seen as a shared collaboration that investigates the artwork in a speculative quest to explore the unknown. For the artist, the artwork embodies the questions, ideas, and images, whereby for the art writer, the word becomes the vehicle to advance new realms of investigative possibility. In this case, the coalition between the visual and the verbal is both critical and supportive. New transdiscipline alliances between artists and art writers, and artists and scientists, for instance, are being enacted in those collaborative projects involving the use of digital technologies. The caricatures of the eccentric scientist, the reclusive artist, or the computer nerd have little basis in the reality of the multidisciplinary environment of today. While critical theorists and visual culture critics raise pertinent questions about problematic relationships among art, science, and technology, there is a need to move beyond an analysis that still sees domains of knowledge in paradigmatic terms. In the many situations where artists and scientists are collaborating, there is little talk that sees science as merely a rationalistic endeavor or art as only an expressive activity. These imaginative investigators are working beyond the restriction of defined discipline parameters and are guided by questions, issues, and abstractions where new knowledge is seen as a function of creating and critiquing human experience.

NOTES ●

1. For a review of implications of the digital age and the impact in areas such as visual culture and identity politics, see Darley (2000) and Turkle (1995). For reference to visual artists working across disciplines in the art and sciences, see Casti and Karlqvist (2003), and for within the digital domain, see Lovejoy (1997).

2. For examples of critiques of epistemological and ontological conceptions of research from an indigenous perspective, see Semali and Kincheloe (1999) and Tuhiwai Smith (1999). For examples within the context of visual arts, see Mundine (1996), Myers (2002), and Staikidis (2004).

3. Initially brought to attention through critiques such as Edward Said's (1978) analysis of cultural representation in the late 1970s, the scope and depth of critical artistic investigation of the East-West divide has grown in rich and expansive ways. For examples within the visual arts, see Alice Yang (1998); art exhibition catalogues such as *How Latitudes Become Forms: Art in a Global Age* (Vergne, Kortun, & Hou, 2003); *Beyond the Future: The Third Asia-Pacific Triennial of Contemporary Art* (Webb, 1999); and the journal *Art AsiaPacific* (see http://www.artasiapacific.com). For literary examples, I am indebted to Aphrodite Désirée Navab (2004) for drawing to my attention the work of Iranian American artists and poets (Karim & Khorrami, 1999).

4. The notion of "feedback" is at the heart of many human processes from constructivism to cybernetics where learning is informed by interactions that are used to adapt behavior and direct change.

5. See, for example, the Performance Art Pedagogy of Charles Garoian (1999), in which he incorporates features of performance art, postmodernism, and critical pedagogy that encourages students' embodied learning experiences.

6. For an example of how artworld critics, anthropologists, and cultural theorists talk amongst themselves but not to each other, and in doing so render the voice of the subject mute, see Fred Myers (1995). In the chapter, "Representing Culture: The Production of Discourse(s) for Aboriginal Acrylic Paintings" (pp. 55–95), Myers reviews the discourse about the acrylic painting of Central Desert Aboriginal artists shown in 1988 in New York as part of the exhibition *Dreamings: The Art of Aboriginal Australia*. In a follow-up assessment of this event, Myers positions the debates more clearly from the perspective of the indigenous artists in describing the artworks and performances as forms of social practice (Myers, 2002, pp. 255–276).

7. The exhibition *Yankee Remix: Artists take on New England* (summer 2003 to spring 2004) was a collaboration between the Massachusetts Museum of Contemporary Art (MASS MoCA) and the Society for the Preservation of New England Antiquities (SPNEA). Nine artists—Rina Banerjee, Ann Hamilton, Martin Kersels, Zoe Leonard, Annette Messager, Manfred Pernice, Huang Yong Ping, Lorna Simpson, and Fred Violich—were commissioned to create interpretive works dealing with issues of memory and meaning using artifacts from SPNEA's extensive archival collection.

8. Despite educational theory and practice and moves towards inclusivity, we still render many indigenous people invisible. The book *Dreamkeepers* is fairly typical of cultural travelogues, and the front cover has an extreme close-up image of an Aboriginal man with white ocher daubed across his nose. A comment on the cover suggests that the author, Harvey Arden (1994), "allows the Aboriginal people to speak for themselves. . . ." Yet it is strange how it is only Harvey's name that appears on the cover. On the back cover (and three more times in the opening pages) we are told that the person who *took* the photograph was Mike Osborn. We are never told the name of the person pictured on the front—until page 165—when we find out it is Jack Rogers.

9. The exhibition *The Native Born* (1996) on display at the Asia Society Gallery in New York in 2002, curated by Djon Mundine, challenged Western notions of how typologies of knowledge are constructed. In doing so, Mundine not only presented indigenous relational systems of epistemology, he also positioned the visual image as being central to ontological beliefs about cultural meaning, history, and location.

10. Any list of theorists and practitioners who endorse a view that the visual arts is an inherently cultural, political, and socially embedded educational experience will be very long. Insightful arguments and strategies for inquiry centered around art making as a community practice in all its guises will be found in the writings of Blandy and Congdon (1987); Chalmers (1996, 2002); Congdon, Blandy, and Bolin (2001); Duncum (2002); Freedman (2003); jagodzinski (1997a, 1997b); Krug (2003); McFee (1998); Neperud (1995); Paley (1995); and Stuhr (1994, 2003).

11. I am indebted to Gillian Rose (2001) for highlighting the distinction between the modernist notion of "to see is to know" and the postmodern concept that to "know is to see."

12. For a discussion of the politics of representation within the museum context in general, and the Smithsonian Institution in particular, see Henderson and Kaeppler (1999).

13. Unless otherwise stated, Fiona Foley's quotes are taken from an interview with the author conducted on February 19, 2001, at Teachers College, Columbia University, New York, NY.

PART 3

VISUAL ARTS
RESEARCH PRACTICES

CHAPTER 6

PRACTICE AS THEORY

The prologue of Lev Manovich's *The Language of New Media* (2001) is presented in the form of a visual index. To introduce the main idea of the text, which is a conceptual map of the digital landscape, Manovich uses a device that is very much in keeping with the issues he explores. He selects quotes from throughout the text that describe key concepts and these are placed next to a series of black and white stills taken from the groundbreaking 1929 film *Man with a Movie Camera* by the Russian director Dziga Vertov. The stills resemble the written descriptions where there is a close connection between the content of the image and the information in the written text. The visual image clips and verbal idea quips work in tandem to communicate meaning, yet the correspondence is not neat and symmetrical where one textual form merely illustrates the other. Read individually, and in combination, the list of visual and verbal forms offer different layers of possibilities as meaning is decoded by prompts of recognition that hover between the content cues of the text and the concepts they bring to mind.[1] There is another intriguing element to the device used by Manovich in that the form of the visual index also embodies the content of the book. As a constructed text, the 22 pages of visual and verbal quotes form their own nonlinear narrative. By including visual images to introduce his ideas, Manovich creates something that is more than an index, for he not only matches meanings, but this interface also opens up many other interpretive options. It is this sense of possibility in the way that visual forms can contribute to our understanding that I explore in this chapter.

The expanding landscape of imaginative and critical inquiry pursued by artists, teachers, and cultural commentators is purpose driven where the need to explore new domains for critiquing and creating knowledge is being taken up by expanding demands of personal belief and public need. This transformative process is being shaped by individuals who see structures that define traditional discipline areas not as boundaries or barriers, but as bridges that can link in new ways. Part of the legacy of conceptualizing visual arts practice as research is the opportunity it gives to reconsider the inextricable relationship between theory and practice. Assembling new historical and critical traditions of fine arts alongside equally diverse studio practices means that the alliance between the artist and the art writer is seen as a shared collaboration that interrogates the artwork in a speculative quest to explore the unknown and to renovate the known. For the artist, the artwork embodies the questions, ideas, and images, whereas for the critic, the word becomes the vehicle to advance new realms of interpretive possibility. In this case, the coalition between the visual and the verbal is both critical and supportive. It is not unusual to see artists working as curators and writing as theorists, and art writers taking on the challenge of creating forms and situations that are used to advance views as much as to critique positions.[2] This kind of interchange of roles and practices is loosening conceptual chains and discipline claims, and opening up new possibilities for exchange that are responsive to the imaginative challenge of an intellectual climate that is issues driven rather than content based.

This new transdiscipline alliance between artists and others is clearly seen in connections being forged among artists, sociologists, scientists, and technologists (Rogoff, 2000; Wilson, 2002). For instance, the particular environment of the digital world is proving to be an especially rich setting in which newer conceptions of theory and practice in the arts and sciences are being explored. The caricatures of the eccentric scientist, the reclusive artist, or the computer nerd have little basis in the reality of the multidisciplinary environment of today. Although critical theorists and visual culture critics raise pertinent questions about problematic relationships among art, culture, science, and technology, there is a need to move beyond an analysis that still sees domains of knowledge cloaked in paradigmatic terms (Haraway, 1991; Morgan, 1998). In the many situations where artists and scientists are collaborating, there is little talk that sees science as merely a rationalistic endeavor or art as only an expressive activity. Those imaginative investigators working without the restriction of defined discipline parameters can be seen to be guided by questions, issues, and abstractions where new knowledge is seen as a function of creating and critiquing human experience. By necessity this complex practice *has* to bridge disciplines, and in doing so, not only opens up new possibilities, such as those on offer within the newer information technologies, but also renders mute old arguments that see inquiry as methods bound, rather than issues driven.

Perhaps one of the most appropriate environments for this kind of creative and critical inquiry is within the educational settings where artist-students gain access to personal and professional training. More than anything else, educational study puts into practice the elusive claim that students can learn how to learn. But learning is a destabilizing process that results in the emergence of an individual voice within a collective agency. Therefore, being a student "upsets" in a way that confirms what is known, by continually highlighting what is not. The knowledge one carries is grounded in experience and situations. It is accumulated on the road and under the fingernails, and it is often collected in isolation. Personal knowledge, intuition, and imagination are valuable assets that are sustaining and help offset the dilemma of entering into a community of colleagues where original thinking has mythic status. But this kind of knowledge is not enough. The relentless process of being drawn into a profession is both exhausting and liberating. A premise that informs educational inquiry is that the artist-student becomes proficient in not only appreciating the scope of knowledge that continues to inform the field, but that this understanding is predicated on a critical awareness so that opportunities for changing it are within reach.

A FRAMEWORK FOR VISUAL ARTS RESEARCH PROJECTS ●

This chapter describes the inextricable link between theory and practice and outlines a framework for designing and developing visual arts research projects that are grounded in studio inquiry and embrace broader constituent practices. The basis on which visual arts practice can be conceptualized as research builds on the arguments presented in Part 2, Theorizing Visual Arts Research. The framework shown in Figure 6.1 follows the conceptual structures put in place in previous chapters. The framework of Visual Arts Research (see Chapter 3, Figure 3.1) describes the centrality of the practices that comprise visual arts inquiry, which is the place where research questions, problems, and purposes originate. As an approach that moves seamlessly between the theoretical and the practical, a range of strategies are deployed that I describe as understanding, reflexive, postdiscipline, and visual systems practices. These practices describe some of the ways that visual artists respond to the challenge of using their art practice to undertake creative and critical research.

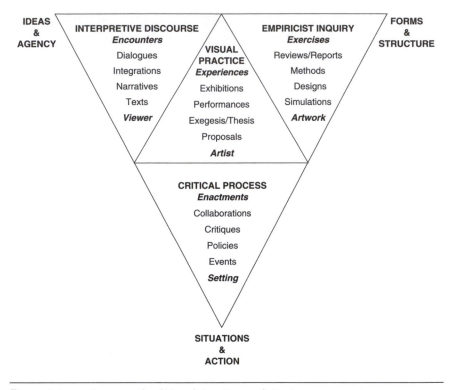

Figure 6.1   Framework of Visual Arts Research Projects

Visual Arts Knowing (see Chapter 4, Figure 4.1) situates the imaginative and intellectual processes that describe a way artists think as they make use of a cognitive coalition of ongoing dialogue between, within, and around the self, artworks, viewers, and settings, where each is used to help create new understandings. This dynamic and reflexive meaning making is described in Chapter 4 as "transcognition," and it captures the movement and purposeful searching of the artistic mind. Seen within the context of research, the alignments and areas of emphasis that artists search out take in the perspectives of "others," be they other artists, theorists, art writers, artworks, viewers, or contexts, and this ensemble provides a structure for referencing and reviewing. The framework of Visual Arts Practices (see Chapter 5, Figure 5.1), acknowledge the theoretical depth and breadth that artists take on through their art making as they assume a multiplicity of roles as meaning makers, cultural commentators, social critics, teachers, and the like. Although grounded within the core experience of artistic making practices where the artist readily adopts the dual role of practitioner and theorist, related domains are engaged as creative inquiry is undertaken. I describe three additional making structures as those that are systemslike, those occurring in relation to community interests, and those that take place within cultural contexts.

As with conceptions of visual arts practice presented in previous chapters, any inquiry will center on art-making practices. I argue that the experience of the artist is the core element in the creation of new knowledge and the potential for new understanding is further enhanced through research projects that may take varied forms such as exhibitions, performances, and publications. The purpose of any inquiry by necessity will connect to an ensemble of allied areas. For instance, if there is a need to invoke an empiricist position, various forms and structures, such as relevant artworks, related perspectives, historical views, methods and media, problems, and proposed models, are the kind of exploratory exercises that might need to be undertaken. On the other hand, if the nature of an inquiry involves more of an examination of the relationship between ideas and agency then the issues and images examined will comprise more of a dialectic connection. Here the interpretivist discourse is sparked by encounters with artistic forms among viewers and the community, and the different narratives and forms of representations created will give rise to alternative conceptions and constructions. Visual arts research also often adopts a critical position as situations and actions are investigated, different strategies enacted, and suitable settings used as sites for inquiry. What follows is a more detailed description of some of the experiences, exercises, encounters, and enactments that can be used to more formally frame visual arts research projects.

VISUAL PRACTICE: *EXPERIENCES* ●

Perhaps the main principle to emerge from the conceptualization of visual arts as research is the relationship between the practices of creating and critiquing. These are pivotal as they form the basis by which new perceptions are imagined, relevant information interrogated, and alternative conceptions realized. Interpretations and representations that arise as a consequence of purposeful, creative pursuits have the potential to produce new understandings because from a position of personal insight and awareness the artist-theorist is well placed to critically examine related research, texts, and theories. In relating the outcomes of creative inquiry to relevant issues in the field, there is a degree of "looking back" involved, as the research process first challenges the artist by the need to create and then uses this new awareness as the critical lens through which to examine existing phenomena. This is somewhat different from traditional research methodology, which in quantitative studies is linear, iterative, and confirmatory, and which in qualitative inquiries, is cyclical, emergent, and discovery oriented. Visual arts research, on the other hand, is dynamic, reflexive, and revelatory as creative and critical practices are used to shed new light on what is known and to consider the possibility of what is not.

Designing and managing research projects therefore require an approach that is not only systematic and rigorous, but also imaginative. Research in visual arts demands that the "big picture" be kept in mind as attention is focused on specific details. This is a strategic process that means decisions are made based on purpose and may require the creative deployment of accepted practices whereby rules get redefined, boundaries crossed, and new applications sought. Although it is important for visual arts researchers to know the language and tactics of research conventions, it is crucial to be aware of the value and necessity of using strategies embedded in the everyday practices of artists and art teachers. We live in an era of hybridity, whether in the arts, education, business, technology, or cultural exchange; consequently, complex contexts are ever present and a significant challenge for today is finding pathways along, through, and around boundaries, both real and perceived. Whether working in the studio, in the museum, in the classroom, or on the Internet, particular approaches prevail, such as visualizing, sensing, intuiting, focusing, reasoning, questioning, grounding, comparing, and interpreting. These are the kind of capacities that characterize the way artists work and are also the attributes needed for conducting effective research in the field. Considering research problems and questions within wider project requirements such as theoretical frameworks, literature reviews, and methodologies, requires a holistic approach. Locating information networks, articulating research problems and questions, and conceptualizing project designs, are part of visual arts research as the structure of a project is visualized and realized. The strategies able to be deployed conform to artistic approaches that focus on the whole and the parts as an inventive analysis is created and an imaginative synthesis is sought. Let me give a synopsis of some basic visualization methods that serve these purposes.

Dimensions of Visualization

A characteristic of visual arts research is that it is multidimensional as many different forms of representation are deployed. Visualization strategies are at the heart of what it is that artists do as they see and know things through images, and this capacity shapes ideas and informs actions. The inextricable links among the mind's eye, the complexity of idea-forming networks, and the habitual transactions with settings and contexts, means that negotiating the visual world is part of everyday experience. A challenge for the visual arts researcher is to be able to frame and claim these processes as critically

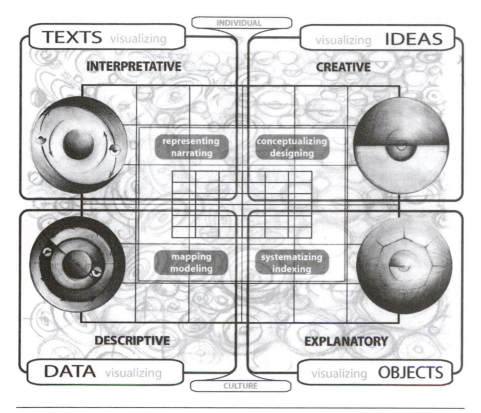

Figure 6.2 Dimensions of Visualization

important kinds of human exchange that have the capacity to change the way we think about how we come to know what we do, and the forms in which information, experience, and understanding can be created and communicated. The visualization of ideas therefore is a conceptual process that is creative, critical, and clinical as speculative questions are raised, issues analyzed, and insights offered. And at all phases of these inquiry processes various visual strategies and methods can be used that not only have heuristic value, but reveal new understanding in ways that cannot be realized using the traditional informational research currency of numbers and words.

Figure 6.2 describes different ways of thinking about how visual strategies might be used in research. These dimensions not only define visualization as a means of building an evidential or documentary base but also are seen as an end themselves in conceiving and conducting research. For instance, the *individual-cultural dimension* divides visualization schemas into those that involve knowledge production, which is culturally embedded, and knowledge construction, which is individually transformative. These dimensions circumscribe four areas of visualization, each addressing somewhat different research needs. Within the quadrants are knowledge schemas that I describe as *Visualizing Objects, Visualizing Data, Visualizing Texts,* and *Visualizing Ideas.* Let me explain these in more detail and give some examples.

Visualizing Objects

Visualizing Objects opens up ways of investigating structures used in communities and cultures that explain systems of operations and how things are organized. Two examples are *systematizing* and *indexing.* For instance, *systematizing* is a holistic and concrete procedure for investigating the entire workings of an entity or a set of related practices. These are often presented as causal networks if information about inputs and predicted effects is known. Systematizing is an "abstracting" process whereby elements, their relationships, sequences, and operations, are able to be documented in different symbolic forms, be they metaphorical or mathematical. For instance, systematizing is used by those researchers who propose explanatory models of human behavior such as Mihaly Csikszentmihalyi's (1990, 1993) theory of flow, or Richard Solso's (1994) explication of visual cognition. These kinds of complex phenomena also lend themselves to visualization as simple and elegant explanatory systems. A classic example is the map created by Charles Joseph Minard that not only *describes* Napoleon's ill-fated invasion of Russia in 1812 that began with 422,000 men, but *explains* why only 10,000 returned.

Indexing is another strategy that is a useful organizational tool that helps visualize objects as typologies, taxonomies, or "trees" situated around certain hierarchical criteria. Further visual discrimination can be applied to distinguish between conceptual levels of information. An example of a visual indexing procedure might be Renata Tesch's (1990) meta-analysis of methods of qualitative data analysis where she collates different approaches around the uses they serve and compiles a connected tree structure that explains the purposes of different approaches to qualitative inquiry.

Visualizing Data

Used as a descriptive strategy, *Visualizing Data* tries to capture the features inherent in socially produced phenomena. In looking to understand the concepts and structures within any ensemble or entity, it is useful to be able to define elements and relationships. This is an analytical process and involves examining structures as parts and as wholes. Two sample strategies are *mapping* and *modeling. Mapping* is a process of locating theories and ideas within existing conceptual frameworks so as to reveal underlying structures and systems of connections. This involves locating key concepts and ideas

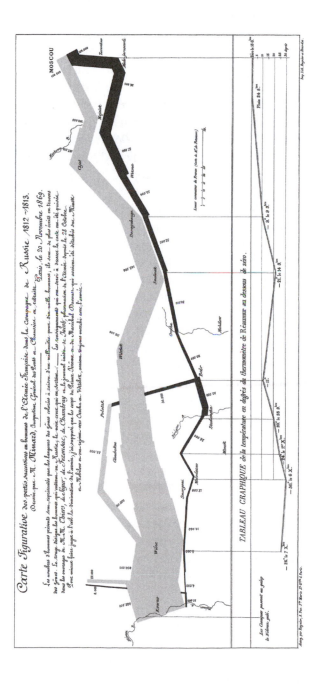

Edward Tufte (1983) highlights the explanatory power of Minard's time-series graphic:

Beginning at the left on the Polish-Russian border near the Niemen River, the thick band shows the size of the army (422,000 men) as it invaded Russia in June 1812. The width of the band indicates the size of the army at each place on the map. In September, the army reached Moscow, which was by then sacked and deserted, with 100,000 men. The path of Napoleon's retreat from Moscow is depicted by the dark lower band, which is linked to a temperature scale and dates at the bottom of the chart. It was a bitterly cold winter, and many froze on the march out of Russia. As the graphic shows, the crossing of the Berezina River was a disaster, and the army finally struggled back into Poland with only 10,000 men remaining. Also shown are the movements of auxiliary troops, as they sought to protect the rear and the flank of the advancing army. Minard's graphic tells a rich, coherent story with its multivariate data, far more enlightening than just a single number bouncing along over time. Six variables are plotted: the size of the army, its location on a two-dimensional surface, direction of the army's movements, and temperature on various dates during the retreat from Moscow.

It may well be the best statistical graphic ever drawn. (p. 40)

Charles Minard, *Napoleon's March to Moscow: The War of 1812.* Edward R. Tufte, *The Visual Display of Quantitative Information,* Courtesy of Graphics Press, 1983.

within some kind of terrain or typology and examples of mapping procedures include file card systems, concept maps, citation logs, idea genealogies, and the like.[3] This form of descriptive mapping is not the kind undertaken by Charles Minard (Tufte, 1983) when he tracked Napoleon's ill-fated Moscow campaign as Minard set himself the more ambitious task of causal explanation. Descriptive mapping, on the other hand, is undertaken by any researcher who defines theoretical frameworks that may influence the issues informing a particular study as this is one way research communities establish conceptual structures around which disciplinary processes are organized. For instance, Laurie Schneider Adams's (1996) introduction to the methodologies of art, maps the approaches used by art historians.[4] The visual arts researcher needs to know about these accepted paradigms if the aim is to be able to question them in new ways.

Modeling, on the other hand, is more process-oriented where information about the relationships among features within a structure is sought. Modeling, therefore, is a more multidimensional reconstructive process and requires the capacity to strip complex phenomena into its constituent parts and to visualize their relationships. Those who critique curriculum models identify how underlying philosophical structures and value systems shape conceptions of art teaching and how these might be translated into meaningful encounters for students in the classroom or the studio (Efland, 1995). On the other hand, established models of accepted practice can be surveyed and found wanting and new regimes proposed. This is the approach taken by James Elkins (2003) with his review of the area of visual culture and his reconstructive call for a broader regime of image analysis that he defines as "visual studies." Elkins not only adds more elements to the content map of visual culture, but he adds different dimensions of inquiry so as to reconfigure the overall conceptual model.

Visualizing Texts

Thinking about *Visualizing Texts* conjures up an image of an idiosyncratic stance whereby personal constructs shape ideas and actions. Yet wider interpretive communities also serve as mediating spaces through which conceptions are reformed that influence views. At the heart of these ideas are the way different agencies create the dialectics and the dialogues that help present new insights. For instance, the reduction and reinterpretation of existing category structures into alternative systems according to other conceptual cues is a type of inductive analysis that is very common in research. Although this kind of reconfiguration helps us synthesize information, perhaps the most value is in the heuristic appeal it holds as a way to see things differently. Furthermore, the plausibility of any interpretive schema can be clarified or confirmed through intersubjective agreement and other consensual strategies. Therefore visualizing texts suggests that the process of engaging critically with received information requires the capacity to "talk back" and this can take many textual forms. Two strategies are relevant here, *representing* and *narrating*.

As an intellectual and imaginative process, *representing* can be defined in many ways for the form or vehicle can be something as basic as an object or artifact, and what is being represented can be as complex as a conception of reality. The basic premise is the acceptance that something created or constructed can stand for something else. The elements involved are inference and meaning: we represent something by giving it form, and infer that it can carry meaning. Within more traditional languages we can ascribe meaning to new forms, be they words or numbers, and through the use of representational tools such as logic and reasoning, or semantics or syntax, we are able to communicate meanings of great simplicity or complexity. On the other hand, the representational forms able to be deployed by the visual artist can also extend beyond codified structures. This broadens the capacity for meaning making by putting the emphasis on re-presentation as much as representation. By this I mean that those responding to visual information are responsible for opening up the interpretive space between the artifact and what it might mean. Part of this power is a consequence of the abstract quality of representations, for they are simplifications and there is no direct correspondence between the representational form and what it represents. Let me give an example.

In her short exposition of the studio critique strategies of the artist, Lucio Pozzi, Lori Kent (2003) describes how a series of diagrams are used by Pozzi as a means of opening up discussion with his students about the progress of their artwork.[5] Using a series of five, sketchy structural signatures, Pozzi is able to draw references to historical issues, use metaphor to tease out possibilities, demolish preconceptions, disrupt complacencies, challenge decision making, and find creative comfort among incongruities. The diagrams themselves become visual thoughts whose representational power takes on meaning when related to creative problems encountered in art making.

A further feature of representation is the idea that the artwork itself is not merely an image or an object that carries meanings, but that it is part of a broader system of cultural forms, and plays an active role in sociopolitical processes. Mitchell (1994) describes representation "as a multidimensional and heterogeneous terrain, a collage or patchwork quilt assembled over time out of fragments" (p. 419). This is a description of representation as a "process" rather than as a "thing." According to Mitchell, representation is best understood "as relationship, as process, as the relay mechanism in exchanges of power, value, and publicity" (p. 420). This is illustrated in Figure 6.1, if the features of interpretive discourse are seen in relation to the other domains of

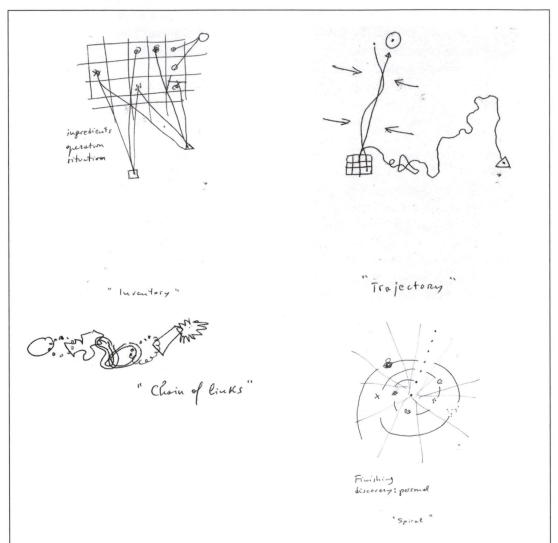

Lori Kent (2003) explains:

Five diagrams, sometimes appearing as insignificant scribbles in a margin, visually communicate an interpretation of some of the most significant ideas about culture and artistic practices in the 20th and 21st centuries. They are used both as a pedagogical tool with college-aged students and an illustrative tool in conversations with mature artists. The diagrams are elemental visual symbols about being an artist, about the choices that artists can make. (p. 5)

The pedagogical purpose of Lucio Pozzi's diagrams is to help students think more clearly and trust their intuitions and ideas as a sustainable source for their own creative pursuits. Reproduced courtesy of the artist.

visual practice, critical process, and empiricist inquiry. As elements in the interpretive process, the viewer and the artwork are part of a wider set of representational agencies and actions, and this adds to the potential power to contribute to individual awareness, social change, and cultural debate.

Another form of textual visualization is *narrative*. Conventional definitions describe narrative as an account of a sequence of events, actions, or ideas that can be fact or fiction. There is something intensely personal about narrative as we have a propensity for storytelling as it renders certain human complexities in a believable form. We are able to locate ourselves within the content of a narrative and the intersubjective features of the text as the experience of the whole overrides questions about the plausibility of the parts. Within narrative frameworks there is also a degree of flexibility that offers more creative and interpretive scope than rule-governed, propositional languages that have preset syntactical and symbolic structures that more or less prescribe meaning. Narrative content can also be weighed down by its own ideological baggage as "grand narratives" can become problematic canonical accounts. Therefore, the interpretive frames that shape the narrative strategies, the fields of reference, and the informing contexts, need to be seen as active agents in how meanings are made. Linda Weintraub's (2003) collection of contemporary art profiles presents much more than narratives about artists' practices, passions, and preferences. Her conceptual stance is grounded in her belief that art practice is continually expanding to embrace all kinds of sociocultural settings, situations, and services, and that this renders any simplistic, narrative moot. As such, questions about the role of the viewer and the function of art in society become more consciously part of the artist's frame of artistic action. Weintraub's interpretive lens is captured in her comment that "free radicals are reproducing in the arts as they are in physical matter [and] because artists are uniquely capable of both initiating and adapting to change, art forms are mutating all around us" (p. 8).

Although Weintraub uses conventional linguistic forms to construct her accounts, it is also possible to consider visual narrative as an interpretive method to construct and critique phenomena. What happens when visual images are introduced as a central element in the narrative structure? In general, the utility of word-picture combinations is a consequence of how they aid illustration and communication. Here meaning is mostly limited to description. However, using visual images as the main component of a narrative means that conceptual, structural, and sequential decisions are formed mostly in pictures, which gives an opportunity to stretch the expressive range of meaning making and open up interpretive possibilities. When considered in the context of a research narrative where the purpose is to construct readings of data that move beyond descriptive accounts and realist tales, the inclusion of visual images also has to contribute to the interpretive conception that frames the narrative. And if visual forms are *not* used as an illustrative device, then visual narrative structures are integrated into the events, issues, and arguments at the outset, not just as an afterthought. This is evident in the approach Michael Emme (2001) uses with his "visual criticism" strategies where the interpretive form is presented as a discrete visual analogue that carries the conceptual content. For Emme, to critique is to create. Drawing on aspects of critical sociology, Emme argues that art criticism can be seen as a form of activism and the pervasive impact of visual images in contemporary culture requires these critical perspectives to be presented as visual processes. Another example of the emphasis on the image used by artists and theorists is the schematic for a visual essay developed by the artist Hugo Ortega López (see Figure 6.3).

Hugo Ortega López (2003) explains:

> Located within an educational academic context there is a need for a fundamental alteration in prevailing patterns of continuity and change. When considering technological innovation and art-making processes, research in the visual arts needs to rely on the production of images and objects that bridge the private domain of studio practice with the public domain of learning. To generate moments of learning between event and audience, we should consider exploring all sequences of intake and output: image to word, word to word, word to image, and image to image. To bridge visual output to practice, image to image has to rely on the "multiple" nature, not the study, of the discipline's process. (p. 3)

Visualizing Ideas

Visualizing Ideas is the final dimension shown in Figure 6.2. Forming ideas is a creative and critical act that relies in part on individual imaginative proclivities, yet the process is also mediated by community contexts. However, when the artist is messing around with ideas, personal vision is paramount. Imaginative and inventive visualizations may emerge in many different forms and be translated as ideas, objects, images, or actions. These forms open up the interpretive space in different ways and each carries particular kinds of inference and reference as expressive and communicative intentions are envisioned. When these private visions are presented in public as artworks or events, or in institutional settings as visual-verbal texts, they are interpreted by sociopolitical agencies such as artworld networks, academic conventions, and discipline traditions. A creative idea, therefore is not only a product of individual visualization, but its degree of originality will be determined by what currently exists within similar genres in the field.

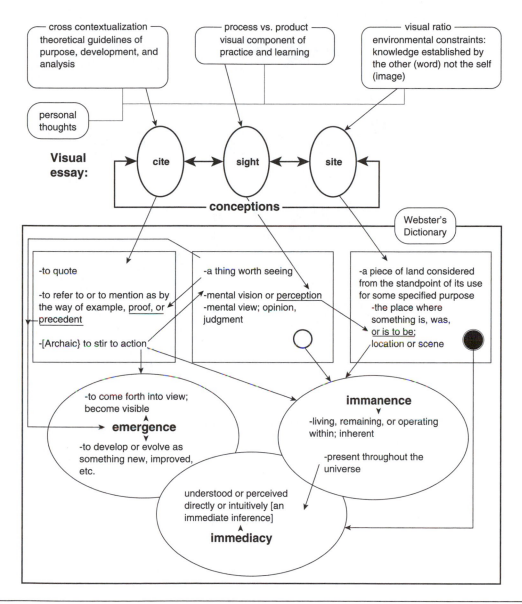

Figure 6.3 Visual Essay

Visualizing ideas can be undertaken in many ways. Two strategies are *conceptualizing* and *designing*. Within a traditional research framework, "concepts" define the way we represent categories of information based on our experiential and empirical understanding. Conceptualizing in this sense involves grounding ways of perceiving things and setting in place structures

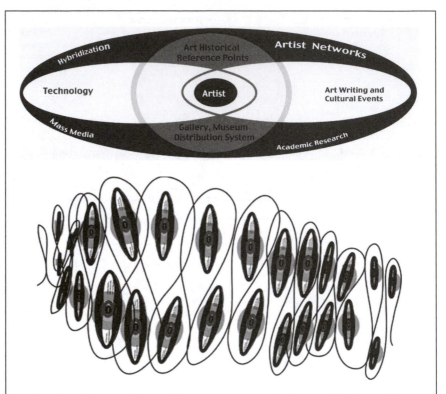

Cultural production does not happen in a vacuum. This model depicts the art object as the artist encoded with contextual data or "cultural DNA." This takes into account the spheres of influence under which an artist produces an art object. The model describes a basic unicellular model in which to understand what happens to an art object as it travels through time in space . . . All cultural objects are embedded in a cultural matrix akin to the "raisin-in-the-pudding" theory of plasma membranes in the body. A membrane is a mosaic structure where lipid bi-layers are impregnated with protein appendages that permeate the lipids. Cultural objects find a place to exist in our atmosphere and are filtered by the spheres of influence that surround them. Cultural objects, like proteins, may transport ideas from one time and place within one cultural milieu to another. (Sherry Mayo, 2004, pp. 6–15)

Sherry Mayo (2004), *Genome Model of the Art Object* (top); *Cultural Matrix, Art Objects in the Cultural Milieu* (bottom).

of ideas and constructs that serve as the interpretive lens we use to make sense of the world around us. As described in Chapter 4, the conceptualizing process advanced here is not one that suggests we rely on a repertoire of coded symbolic meanings from which we draw. Rather, a connectionist model seems to be a more adequate description of artistic thinking whereby concepts and associations emerge from a parallel process of interactions among networks that may be shaped by prior learning, but are also subject to intuitive and opportunistic linking.

It also needs to be added that conceptualizing can be considered to be "situated" whereby the same concepts will carry different meanings for different individuals and this seems especially relevant within the context of visual arts knowing. Conceptualizing therefore plays an important role in creating and critiquing phenomena and the process of constructing mental images can be inventive and individualistic. As Sherry Mayo's "cultural membrane" depicts, when given form, the ideas and concepts enter into the marketplace of an interpretive community and through this mediating process take on additional meanings as conceptual connections are fashioned and fractured. Some processes suitable for conceptualizing ideas include visual versions of linguistic forms such as analogy, metaphor, and homology (Hart, 1998).

Visual analogy compares one thing with another and uses a known starting point as a way to come to understand something that is unknown (the nervous system is like the New York subway; creative self-expression is a "flowering" process). The premise of an analogy is that what is true in one thing is true in another. Analogies therefore help *translate* meaning. An example that uses a verbal means but invokes a visual image is the parallel Peter Plagens (1986) makes in comparing art criticism to a conversation. In his example, Plagens "interviews" a photographic artwork by Lucas Samaras.[6] The piece begins with Plagens, as the art critic, asking questions of the artwork, and a brief extract sets the scene for the two-way conversation that unfolded.

Author: I take it you don't mind being interviewed?

Photograph: Not really. It's not often I have a chance to speak directly. What I have to say is usually conveyed through intermediaries, like dealer and art critics.

Author: That's odd. What a photograph has to say should be obvious to everyone, since it's right there on the surface for everyone to see.

Photograph: Well, part of the trouble is right there. I'm not a "photograph." I'm a work of art.

Author: What's the difference?

Work of Art: At the risk of belaboring the obvious, a photograph can at times be a work of art. But a photograph is, properly speaking, a single-surface, usually unitary, image printed directly from a negative. I may be generically photographic, but as you can see I've been physically manipulated a great deal—you might even call me a collage. Moreover, my brothers and sisters are sculptures, assemblages, pastels, and paintings.

A: I assume you're referring to your siblings in the Samaras family.

W: Yes. We're all very different from each other, but we have our father's vision in common.

A: What would that vision be?

W: You'd have to ask him about that. I can speak only for myself. (p. 255)

Visual metaphor involves creating an image that suggests a resemblance of one thing to something else so as to think of one thing as if it were the same as another (the "cutting edge" of contemporary art). Metaphors are based on the assumption that an image or idea can be used to illustrate another image or idea. Visual metaphors therefore help *transform* meaning by illustrating similarities. In synthesizing descriptions of visual metaphor, Serig (2004) identifies cultural context, the distinctive difference between metaphor and symbol, and the way metaphoric reference is embodied by artists and embraced by viewers, as features that help to transform meanings through artworks. Without an awareness of these qualities, an image such as Man Ray's *Violin d'Ingres* (1924), an iconic back view of a nude with tattooed '*f*' holes, loses some of its ironic appeal.

Visual homology, on the other hand, identifies structural similarities and usually involves seeing a corresponding relationship among forms found in the natural world, in cultures, or the human mind. Consider Howard Gardner's (1983) theory of multiple intelligences that promotes the notion of individual differences in seeing, sensing, and knowing, as corresponding to windows and doors that offer different vantage points for viewing and entering the world. Gardner's multiple intelligences theory is described in terms of a structural equivalent, therefore visual homologies *transcribe* meaning by presenting it as another image. Using another example, a theme evident in several artworks exhibited in the 2003 Venice Biennale was a slightly different take on the ubiquitous investigation of "the human condition" that framed so much artistic inquiry in the visual arts in the 20th century. Rather than delve into the existential depths of what it is to be human, some artists these days are probing the very essence of "the human design" for the 21st century.[7] The artwork of Patricia Piccinini, *We are Family* (2002–2003), is a case in point. Although the correspondences being drawn exhibit obvious visual and structural similarities with human forms, the genetic slippages betray a curiously charming, if somewhat unnerving, future.

The use of analogy, metaphor, and homology, as visual conceptualization devices allows the artist to raise questions about the plausibility of the meanings being expressed. For instance, does the visual analogy help to translate information in a way that increases understanding? With visual metaphors there is the expectation that there is an agreed relationship between the two entities; therefore, does the visual metaphor reveal similarities and does transferring information between the two images serve as a useful bridge upon which further conceptual structures can be built? Assessing the plausibility of visual homologies is akin to asking if there is a structural and conceptual synchronicity between different forms. Do the images used, which are drawn from different visual and theoretical genres, but are based on similar structural principles, identify an equivalence that is conceptually plausible and generative?

Another strategy for the visualization of ideas is *designing*. From a traditional perspective the design process is generally seen to be a problem-solving strategy that moves through a series of phases as a need is identified, constraints considered, concepts and ideas proposed, a prototype designed and tested, and modifications made. The iterative cycle then begins again. But this simplistic process radically distorts the complexity of designing, which, according to Laurel (2003), draws on many different theories, practices, experiences, methodologies, and technologies, to the extent that a distinct field of "design *as* research" is emerging. In his preface to Laurel's anthology, Peter Lunenfeld makes the point that "design research creates a place to braid theory and practice" (2003, p. 10). This is evident in the adaptation of field-based methods such as ethnography and participant observation, as well as critical, interdisciplinary practices that are helping to create a design research culture.

There are many obvious ways to think about designing as a strategy for visualizing ideas as this is the essence of what design practice is all about. An example might be the series of models that the architect Frank Gehry uses in the early phase of design development to visualize ideas such as form, space, movement, and site. In 2002, Gehry displayed at the Guggenheim Museum in New York plans for the proposed Guggenheim to be built on the lower eastside of Manhattan. Many of these models were like sketches in space where crumpled paper served as an approximation of curving, crinkled roof

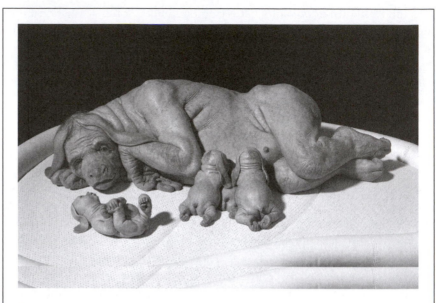

Though the sculpted figures are unusual, they are not the gross, oversexed or nightmarish creations that are familiar from some recent art. Instead they are deeply ambivalent—presented as ordinary beings with impulses to love and play, yet also oddly lifeless, conceding life or animating qualities to the stranger, more deformed aspects of their being, or to other mutant life-forms. Normal become mutant and vice versa . . . Piccinini's art brings a fresh, personal perspective to some of the most difficult ethical issues of our time: What is normal? Who controls life? What is the nature of our relationship with animals? Are some lives worth more than others? What constitutes a family–can it cross species, or be forged in the laboratory? (Linda Michael, 2003, p. 506)

Patricia Piccinini, *The Young Family* (2002). Silicone, polyurethane, leather, human hair, dimensions variable. Reproduced courtesy of the artist and Roslyn Oxley9 Gallery.

structures, and folded card and rough cut blocks marked off areas of mass and space. The sequence began with a "massing model" of blocks that established a sense of scale. Initial "conceptual" models included rapidly drawn scribble-sketches and simple paper and cardboard shapes and forms used to capture Gehry's visual signature. "Study models" followed that documented a higher level of design refinement. These were subsequently modified to form "site models" that took into account broader concerns such as the visual conversations the proposed structure might have with the existing surroundings. At one point a note in the display recorded a comment that "the specific image/metaphor of the building must derive from the immediate context—so let's make it a skyscraper emerging from a fog or a cloud." Toward the end of the sequence, new conceptual models, massing models, and study models, were developed that led to the preliminary master model. The Guggenheim web site described Gehry's approach to visualizing an idea this way:

> This exhibition . . . reveals a unique design process that begins with fluid sketches and simple building blocks. Rarely content with the initial solution, Gehry approaches architecture as an evolving and collaborative process using models as three-dimensional sketches to explore the myriad design possibilities inherent to a given building program. In recent years, the computer technologies used for design and manufacturing applications by his firm have facilitated the realization—on an ambitious new scale—of the gestural quality he has long prized. (Retrieved on March 6, 2004, from http://www.guggenheim.org/exhibitions/past_exhibitions/gehry/exhibition.html)

Exhibitions and Performances

Perhaps the practice most clearly identified with the visual arts is *exhibiting*. Whether held in major museums, commercial galleries, institutional settings, community spaces, or on the Internet, exhibitions provide a public face for the visual arts. As a cultural practice, exhibiting is related to the production and display of art, and the collection and scholarly inquiry about art. This process brings into connection artists, curators, art writers, academics, educators, institutions, and communities, each with a particular reflexive response to artwork. And within this broad ensemble of practices the use of exhibitions as places of visual arts inquiry that is at the public interface is becoming increasingly prominent. On the other hand, when considered within the context of artistic inquiry and community events, *performances* represent an adaptation of contemporary visual arts practice that take on a greater range of textual forms and content. Art events, productions, installations, documentation, and explorations of the body within cultural discourse, pick up on critical perspectives that embrace the self, agency, information, and the politics of practice.

The cultural practices that surround museum exhibitions and other public displays are vast. Since museums became part of the humanist project during the Renaissance, the roles of artists, exhibitions, curators and institutional politics has changed dramatically and today offers considerable opportunity for research and development. Katja Lindqvist (2003) identifies three themes that characterize the emergence of museums as "enterprises" and these help encircle lines of opportunity. Lindqvist tracks the professional involvement of artists as instigators in shaping museum practices; the changing roles of curators and collections; and the recent emergence of the "academic free-lance curator" as a shaper of cultural perceptions. From the time when the artist was elevated in social status, the museum space not only became a place of ideas and ideologies, but the importance of patrons and privilege also contributed to the cultural mix. The more overt marketing of museums as places of cultural reproduction, and the opening up of museum collections to the public, however, created an ambivalence in educational purpose. This was mirrored by the changing roles of the curator, who Lindqvist describes as originally a "professional caretaker of a collection" (p. 37), but who later became not only a content expert and researcher, but also the didactic conduit through which the public was exposed to works of art and culture. The later decades of the 20th century saw the curatorial role become more of a collaborative enterprise in meeting the needs of a broader democracy of culture on the one hand, and increased public accountability on the other. This forged uneasy alliances, where museums became places of innovation, commodity, spectacle, education, and community.

Although there are many cultural and sociopolitical arenas within which exhibition practices are discussed and debated, for my purposes here I am interested in considering exhibitions as sites for visual arts research. Generally this will mean a focus on museum spaces where various constituencies are able to be brought together in a range of ways and for a variety of purposes to explore particular issues surrounding collections, communities, and collaborations. Then there are institutionally situated galleries located in higher education settings that serve a somewhat different function and where considerable opportunity exists for imaginative inquiry and research scope. In this setting, there is a chance to address a different level of innovation and advocacy as the academic environment and local community offer access to diverse cultures. Also operating with a spirit of innovation and collaboration are experimental gallery networks established in virtual environments that are able to make use of loose, collective visions that use technology to help bridge cultures and communities. Thus it is in these museums, galleries, and virtual settings where opportunities exist for reconfiguring the subjects, situations, and sites, for visual arts research.

The possibility that visual arts research might be the kind of activity that has the potential to make good use of these emerging sites of inquiry is probably best exemplified in the performative area of contemporary art. The pervasive impact of information technologies, interactivity, identity politics, cultural diffusion, and educational opportunity, are some of the areas contributing to a theoretically robust area of artistic practice that is rather different to the early performance processes explored by artists who, for example, built on radical Dadaist spectacles. The issues explored and the maneuvers within time and space did break many boundaries and often sharpened the conceptual edge considerably.[8] In recent times, however, the fusion is more comprehensive, such that "the body" is often seen in both literal and metaphoric terms as an entity that is unable to be divided and separated into its parts without distorting basic patterns of operations (Mitchell & Thurtle, 2004). This picks up on the idea that we exist within integrated sets of related systems among human networks and within other connected structures. Furthermore, theorizing the body in this way helps render notions such as essentialism and determinism as overly simplistic ideas that are inadequate in helping get a sense of the complex and connected world in which we live.

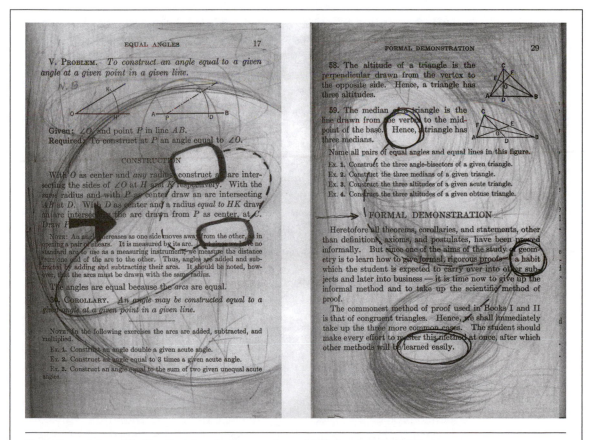

Hugo Ortega López, *Working Back into the Text as a Form of Reflexive Analysis* (2004)

How we manage our reflexive experience and learn within these settings offers considerable potential for artists and teachers, for meaning can be seen to take place through enactment and action. In addition, the learning space disrupts distinctions among artist-objects, viewer-audience, and time-space, such that the encounter is direct and engaging. What Jones and Stephenson (1999) set out to do in their advocacy for performative art experience was to wrestle the interpretive role from some critics and historians who remain safely enmeshed within the cloak of authority and they sought to "open up the process of meaning production" (p. 2). A subtitle of the text by Jones and Stephenson is "performing the text," which draws attention to the active way that "reading back" into the text is a form of performative interpretation. The artist Hugo Ortega López uses a form of graphic choreography to work back into the text. What is created is a partial script that identifies conceptual connections, infers possibilities, and tracks meaning making.

The process of decentering authority is also at the heart of the "performance art pedagogy" approach advocated by Charles Garoian (1999) as he seeks a balance between the mostly prescriptive knowledge encountered in schools, and the understanding that occurs when students directly experience knowledge as an enabling personal construct. Drawing on his experience as a performance artist, and the inherently performative aspects of a teacher's speech and action, Garoian explores the use of many creative and critical languages to enhance individual agency among his students. He adds:

An open form, performance art pedagogy represents a liminal space, an aesthetic dimension, wherein socially and historically constructed ideas, images, myths, and utopias can be contested and new ones constructed as they pertain to students' experiences of reality and their desires to transform that reality. (p. 10)

The importance of performances as reflexive encounters open up possibilities for redefining how visual arts practices can be viewed as sites for inquiry because of the interdependency of the artist, artwork, viewer, and setting.

Exhibition Research Projects

This section describes approaches to visual arts research that use exhibition strategies. Planning and carrying out research requires a critical understanding of a field and ones place within it, as well as a capacity to be able to define problematic issues as researchable questions. Within the visual arts this kind of investigation can be undertaken within the framework of an exhibition project that critiques and presents issues and ideas and makes use of artistic, curatorial, cultural, and related interpretive research practices. When undertaken within institutional contexts, exhibition practices can be part of a broader arena of project-based research where many forms of data generation and analysis can be deployed.

The example shown in Figure 6.4 incorporates an art exhibition and related texts as part of an ensemble of research activities that include a conference event, research presentations, interactive sessions, workshops, and plenary discussions. Designing a research project around the structure of an exhibition-conference gives the visual arts researcher the opportunity to develop a focused program of inquiry that delves into the specifics of an issue. Curating an exhibition around a designated theme brings together artistic responses that can take any number of forms, and these images and objects can be investigated as a discrete source. And of course, the researcher can participate in the show as both artist and curator as these kind of multiple roles are very much in keeping with the diversity of practices pursued by many these days. With sufficient planning it is also possible to consider the benefits that might accrue if the exhibition is also available to a wider geographic audience who have access to it through the Internet. This increases the possibility of using the exhibition to generate responses to add to those that can be collected from gallery visitors. By having the exhibiting artists also participate in the conference program adds to the potential to dig deeper into topics by accessing another source of artists' input. As a performative event, the related conference generates an array of documented information that exists in many textural forms and this not only gives the participants a range of experiences, it also helps the visual arts researcher establish a broad and trustworthy data base. In sum, the potential exists with an exhibition research project to design and carry out a study that uses elements of artistic experience that are central to what it is we do, and incorporates reliable methods that have credence in the research community. Such a study can be a discrete event that explores a particular research issue, or be seen as a nested study within a larger research project.

Exegesis and Thesis

As I described in Chapter 3, an *exegesis* is the term usually used to describe the support material prepared in conjunction with an exhibition, or some other research activity that comprises a visual arts research project. Debates about whether or not it is necessary to compile contextual material circles around issues about where the theorizing used to create new knowledge might be located, be it within any artworks produced, or as arguments

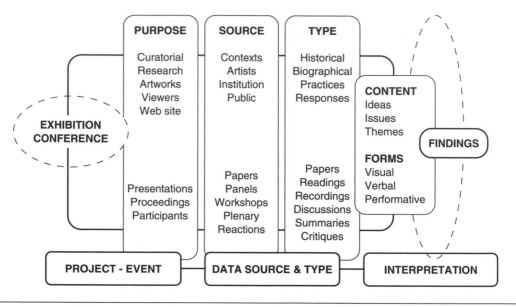

Figure 6.4   Exhibition Research Project

that can be framed in an exegesis. In most instances, this will be a "nonde-bate" because an underlying assumption about visual arts theorizing is that it is a diverse practice that can take many forms and any in-depth thesis will, by necessity, need to be articulated in diverse ways. This also suggests that an exegesis is not merely a form of documentation that serves preliminary pur-poses, records in-process activity, or displays outcomes: *It is all of these.* An additional set of parameters to be invoked will be those institutional prac-tices deemed necessary to conform to established research expectations; after all, this kind of artistic inquiry is undertaken within the academic art-world. As has been argued in this book, however, institutional constraints are only an impediment if they cannot be used to advantage, and to do so requires knowledge of the culture of research so as to be able to claim a place within it. Furthermore, if the role of the "artist-theorist" is seen to best describe the visual arts researcher, then the task of taking up the challenge of serious inquiry will require extensive study and documentation in order to achieve the creative and critical outcomes expected.

Strategies for preparing a visual arts exegesis or thesis vary considerably. More formal expectations will be found within those institutional programs that are experimenting with these research practices as part of advanced graduate degrees. In Chapter 3, I discussed some developments in this area in connection with "practice-based research" in visual arts and design, and these programs are beginning to produce a corpus of projects that offer promising directions. On the other hand, the scope of development of research structures at the level of the master of fine arts (MFA) seems much less ambitious. The main research experience is seen to be the "capstone" or culminating project and the structure will generally revolve around a series of works being prepared for exhibition. The scope of these projects will vary according to programmatic and institutional demands, yet a review of MFA and bachelor of fine arts (BFA) requirements will reveal little has changed in this area in recent decades. The most noticeable developments are within those institutions that have actively incorporated the artistic and technological challenge of new media as part of visual arts programs. It remains to be seen whether the innovative, opportunistic practices being pursued by contemporary artists and the issues raised in this book will sharpen the challenge of inquiry that confronts visual artists working in institutional settings.

EMPIRICIST INQUIRY: *EXERCISES* ●

Visual arts inquiry can be described as a practice of "researching," which for Brent Wilson (1997), is a quest for new knowledge that is shaped in part by questioning what is known and by offering new conceptions that relate to "what *is,* with what *might* be and what *ought* to be" (emphasis in the original, p. 1). The kind of visual arts research strategies that might be expected to be used when conducting inquiries in an empiricist tradition include *Reviews* and *Reports, Methods, Designs,* and *Simulations* (see Figure 6.1). In essence, these are research exercises that focus on, among other things, forms and structures, and these can be found in a great variety of data sources and data types. The procedures used will vary depending on research interests, and in the sections below I summarize some sample strategies.

Undertaking visual arts research is contingent on finding out what others have done and is a basic requirement of scholarship. Within the research traditions of the social sciences compiling *Reviews* and *Reports* as part of the literature review process serves this function. As a primary component of research practice, reviewing is often seen as a way of mapping "what was done." Building on foundations, adding pieces to a jigsaw, and other structural images are used to describe the function of reviews. But this offers a limited view at best. After all, the review process provides the opportunity to look backwards and forwards at the same time. As others have persuasively argued, reviews have an interpretive function that is crucial to scholarly practice.[9] Investigating how information is presented and how it acquires the status of knowledge in a field requires one to use a series of critical and strategic methods. The views, theories, definitions, and arguments found in related literature provide a basic starting point for critiquing research. For example, as a research tool, definitions help identify the boundaries and contexts within which certain ideas and concepts are used. In evaluating definitions, one not only considers their adequacy and consistency, but whether the underlying premise can withstand scrutiny; after all, definitions can unknowingly privilege a position to the detriment of a more inclusive view. The critical, reflective review should shake the foundations as much as shape them, and blur the borders as much as bind them. In this sense, the task of completing a visual arts literature review is similar to the curatorial effort required to mount a challenging thematic art exhibition. As such, the exhibition not only comprises a selection of artworks that are placed within a particular context, but it offers an original interpretation that brings new insights into the field.

Methods of empirical inquiry make up long lists of approaches in the research literature and comprise all kinds of strategies for collecting and analyzing information. Having a working knowledge of the underlying methodological assumptions of different forms of research and associated procedural techniques will allow most methods to be adapted in imaginative, yet rigorous, ways. Being a slave to method is not a consequence that works very well in visual arts where eclecticism, ingenuity, and pragmatism make better companions. *Designs* or *simulations,* on the other hand, can help to conceptualize how research ends and methodological means might be integrated within a broader set of goals. By designs, I refer to both the process and product of research, for most inquiries undertaken in the visual arts will be projectlike, shaped by overall questions and issues, and comprise a series of interdependent activities. Simulations may help refine other options if, for example, time and space variables are involved and access to suitable computer software is available to explore possibilities. Whereas a useful strategy for organizing the structure and sequence of research proposals is to create visual abstracts, more complex projects might be better conceived as computer graphic simulations. The constraint of reducing a research project to a set of components and their relationships within a single diagram or a simulated model can have both theoretical and logistical appeal and serve as a very useful focusing device (Tonfoni, 1994).[10]

The capacity to analyze and synthesize requires the ability to think in new ways. Managing new ideas involves a process of finding and analyzing information, identifying areas of omission, and designing options to follow up. Locating relevant information is an eclectic procedure of trawling for ideas that are relevant to research interests and needs. The process of analysis simply means systematically breaking down something into its parts. The data used for analysis is information and it comes in many structures and forms. Visual information is interpreted as evidence of ideas, arguments, propositions, interpretations, summaries, conclusions, and is communicated using various symbolic texts such as diagrams, images, words, numbers, objects, and films. Designing research projects is a scholarly practice that is informed in part by what is known, yet it is also critical in that conceptualizations are based on an idea structure of one's own making.

INTERPRETIVE DISCOURSE: *ENCOUNTERS* ●

When visual arts research incorporates discursive methods to explore dimensions of meaning and issues related to ideas and agency, many of the language-based strategies associated with the interpretivist research paradigm come into play (see Figure 6.1). The arts and humanities and the human sciences are fields that use a range of meaning-making approaches to construct landscapes of knowledge. Making sense of this vast and ever-changing terrain requires one to accept that meanings are made rather than found. Consequently, ideas and visions are individually and socially constructed, yet mediated by different domains that maintain an ongoing tension between the old and the new. In this way, peers and discipline interests serve as both moderators and muses. Although there are accepted bodies of knowledge within any scholarly community, there is usually the possibility, indeed the necessity, to move beyond existing boundaries. The capacity to interpret what is happening in a field requires the ability to think in new ways.

All research practice includes a phase where information is encountered and critiqued in order to create representations that will assist further inquiry. Responding to information in an insightful fashion through constructive *dialogue* means that private views need to enter into public discourse, for it is within the interpretive community of the field that alternative visions are most keenly felt. In shaping this discussion, a deconstructive phase where assumptions are reviewed will be followed by a synthesis or *integration* of the parts identified in the analysis. Here one creates a new set of conceptual signposts that forge new connections and conceptual relationships. Yet there will be logic and sound reasoning to any arguments made, as the evidence assembled will support the interpretations made. The means used to report research may take on different *narrative* forms, for often it is in bringing personal accounts into the public domain that rich connections are made and new paths revealed. Furthermore, the visual arts researcher has access to a range of *texts* in which to represent experiences and this helps to open up new opportunities for dialogue.

Although this process is readily adaptable to deconstructive and reconstructive encounters with texts, what might it look like for the visual arts researcher who wants to revision studio practice and open it up to constructive dialogue within an interpretive community? In addition, is it possible to see visual arts practice not only as an interpretable or representational form, but as a means of coming to understand something in a way that other research traditions cannot? To do so requires theorizing studio art experiences so as to reveal a history of personal preferences and practices and to identify points of content and process connection, collaborative potential, and community relevance. The purpose, in part, is to reveal an individual artistic profile that can be used as a confident basis from which to shape a research profile. As a visual arts researcher, the possibility of crafting a research practice that models personal proclivities based on studio experiences means that doing research *in* the visual arts, and *about* the visual arts, becomes much more viable. Theorizing one's studio art practice for the purpose of identifying preferred ways of doing research, and for interpreting research interests, involves three stages that include a *reflective* process, a *contextualization* procedure, and a *reflexive* activity.

Theorizing Studio Art Practice: Reflection, Contextualization, and Reflexivity

Reflection Activity: *Artistic Connections*

Reflect on your existing artistic lifestyle and respond to the questions below.

- What systems, agencies or groups are you part of? For instance, how many "caps" do you wear?—schools/institutions; communities/cultures; groups/formal/informal; professional associations; ad hoc collectives.
- How do you communicate with these groups? What do you talk about? Are there any common issues, ideas, or actions that characterize your interest across these groups? What role does your art practice play in how you participate in all/some of these groups?

How can you locate your art practice in relation to the following statement?
When artists make works of art they participate in a particular set of organized processes which are both historically and socially determined. (Michael Carter, 1990, p. 35)

Contextual Activity: *Ideas Network*

Use whatever visual or verbal means you are comfortable with and construct a network of "others" whose ideas, art, or actions, influence your art practice in some way. This activity is similar to bibliographic analysis where documented sources and citations listed in a research article can be mapped to reveal underlying theoretical alliances.

In your case, however, your artwork, as an emblem of your art practice, is the topic of analysis. There are two stages to this process.

- The first identifies a network of artworld references.
- The second level of analysis is to find those researchers who share a content interest, or who use a similar method of inquiry but work in a different discipline.

Reflexive Activity: *Anatomy of an Artwork*

Make a quick sketch/description of an artwork you have created. Reflect on your artistic history and the ideas network constructed and respond to the questions below.

- What is the piece about?
- What factors were considered in determining the content and form of the piece?
- Why did you make it?
- What impact do you think your work has on others? How do you know?

What is your response to the following statement?
Every artifact is the result of multiple determinants or factors . . . consequently the amount of information that could be relevant to an explanation is enormous. (Walker & Chaplin, 1997, p. 4)

CRITICAL PROCESS: *ENACTMENTS* ●

Chapter 4 opened with reference to a Maxine Greene saying by which she reminds us that although art can't change things, it can change people, who can change things. The activist role of the visual arts as a form of critical and creative inquiry and human agency has a long, if somewhat checkered, history and continues to be used by artists to take on sociocultural and geopolitical issues. The image-laden world of today and the technological diversity in how visual culture is produced and presented offers a landscape of form and content that is hard to resist, if even more difficult to penetrate to lasting effect. Yet it is precisely through the network opportunities opened up by the digital age in institutional settings where the nexus between academic possibility and artworld connections can be expected to thrive. The critical perspective that directs much research activity in higher education, and the arguments made in this book that visual arts research can take a leading role in this practice, suggests that the time is right to claim a more formal space within this discourse.

A characteristic of critical practice, whether cultural, political, pedagogical, or whatever, is that an activist position involves *collaborative* processes that are at once local and global, and theoretical and practical, as situations and actions are enacted through artistic practice (see Figure 6.1). A collective sense can also give rise to agreed upon, if ad hoc, *policies* that can be used to guide frameworks of practice that can be compared and contrasted to existing theoretical paradigms. Sharing similarities and highlighting differences can be both an astute political process and a necessary academic practice, and these kinds of positions readily lend themselves to visual arts research. Many of the strategies previously discussed are relevant as diverse content interests mean that the referencing circles are vast, as is access to a dizzying array of technical sources and art media. Consequently, the methods, *events,* and *settings* that might be encompassed in visual arts research can be positioned within a range of research frameworks if needed.

Perhaps the most prominent research practice within this domain of inquiry is the *critique.* I discussed the studio critique earlier as a component of critical teaching practice; however, a broader research brief requires a much more comprehensive strategy to incorporate a critical perspective. For instance, investigating how information is presented and how it acquires the status of knowledge in a field requires one to use a series of critical and strategic methods. Knowledge is seen to be a consequence of experience, reasoning, and inquiry, and to further our understanding there is a need to not only conduct research but to also critique what is done by others. The views, theories, and arguments presented in the field in the form of ideas and images provide a basic starting point for research. Arguments reflect how researchers believe knowledge is acquired and constructed. As a result of conducting studies, researchers give reasons about why something is so. These reasons are based on evidence assembled from the research methods used. Obviously, different research methods will yield evidence in different forms and the reasoning will be grounded on different criteria.

Hart (1998) notes, however, that at a basic level, there are two main components of an argument: the *claim* and the *evidence.* If one argues by making a claim and then assembling the evidence, then a deductive stance is taken. On the other hand, compiling evidence from which a claim is made is an inductive process. In the visual arts, where evidence in research is varied and complex, there are several ways to evaluate arguments. A philosophical approach might deploy formal logic and the conventions of reasoning to assess whether the conclusions drawn are in accordance with the premises (reasons). Several other strategies for evaluating arguments can be applied. Drawing on Hart (1998), distinctions can be seen among inferences, assertions, and suppositions made in arguments. For example:

Supposition: Is the claim made an assumption? ("Left-handed people are artistic.")

Assertion: Is a claim made about the existence or cause of something without supporting evidence? ("I am left-handed, therefore I am artistic.")

Inference: Are conclusions based on some observation or knowledge claim? ("I've noticed that many artistic people are left-handed.")

The analysis of arguments may reveal fallacies. Fallacies give rise to conceptual deceptions that may be unintended and often unknown until revealed through critique. Identifying similarities and differences among ideas, concepts, definitions, interpretations, and theoretical views is one of the most common methods of analysis used in research. A basic requirement is to locate common points or areas of overlap whereby views can be compared and contrasted. In essence, one is looking for common interests and different views.

As a research process, adopting a critical perspective results in the construction of a set of meanings about a topic. The topic is usually a combination of concepts and issues assembled from an analysis of ideas and information drawn from various sources. What makes this process of meaning making a critical exercise is that there are gaps revealed in frameworks of knowledge and these gaps can become the focus for follow-up research. And as with all forms of inquiry, basic criteria need to be met to ensure the investigation is systematic and rigorous. This, of course, does not mean that the imagination is denied. Indeed, the opposite is the case.

CONCLUSION ●

In his devilish critique of the contemporary art world Robert Morgan (1998) takes clear-sighted aim at market-driven art practice and theory-laden art production. His critique of the "tail wagging the dog" phenomenon questions the extrinsic factors that shaped much of the artworld activity in recent decades. What is missing for Morgan is clear and consistent evidence of an inner-driven approach to art practice that takes on the challenge of culture on the artist's terms. His definition of what an artist is centers squarely on the capacity to use art in a personally relevant and culturally significant way that embodies both transformation and resistance.

> To be an artist—regardless of how one's success is measured—has always been a matter of intelligence, passion, constraint, shrewdness, and wit. This implies a position of resistance, but not out of denial. The power of art lies in its oblique angle to the accepted cultural norm. Artists define themselves as artists in terms of both their attraction and repulsion to this norm. The crucial issue here is in finding what sustains the necessity of one's liberation, because artists will move in relation to this necessity more than in the pursuit of ideas. (p. 8)

Although I endorse Morgan's view that the compulsive vision of the artist is an individual and cultural necessity, I do not see this as being antagonistic to the pursuit of ideas. Nor do I subscribe to the view that theories of art and theories of art making are mutually exclusive. What I take from my conversation with Morgan's text is his passion for the centrality of the artist as the site of profound human experience. Furthermore, it is the participation in this experience that Morgan sees as the primary role of the art writer. Again I resonate with the call for autonomy rather than ideology, and the reliance on visual evidence on which to ground experience. Yet I am hopeful that the complex artworld links that Morgan sees as severed might be seen as sturdy in the unlikely setting of the academy.

What I have attempted to do in this chapter is to build on my argument that promotes art practice *as* research in institutional settings. Both the artworld and the academy can be seen as critical sites where the individual and cultural significance of the visual arts has the potential to be fully realized. By proclaiming the role of studio experience as the keystone event around which consequent inquiries can be pursued, all that is central to the art experience and all that is available through related theories and domains of inquiry can be brought to bear on the ideas, issues, and interests at hand. And the range of options open to the visual arts researcher is considerable through the forms and structures, ideas and agency, and situations and actions that can be explored and adapted within purposeful and imaginative inquiry. In drawing attention to the importance of visualization as a creative and critical research tool, it is obvious that the visual artist is already well equipped to undertake serious and sustained research that is important, credible, and capable of adding new insights to the stock of human knowledge. By taking on the challenge of research within the framework of the academy, and doing so according to the integrity of visual arts practice, perhaps the artist-theorist can claim the right to create and critique issues of human significance on arts' terms. And perhaps this is also a way to meet Robert Morgan's goal that "artists have the power to redefine culture in their own terms" (1998, p. xxii).

NOTES ●

1. I am reminded of the writings of Ken and Sylvia Marantz (1992), who for years have been promoting children's picture books as works of art that are profound sites of meaning making where both the distinctions and seamless connections among words, pictures, design, and production provide opportunities for rich and renewable aesthetic experiences.

2. Many artists and art writers have taken up both pencil and pen and transposed roles. The modernist image of the Renaissance person, or the 19th-century cultural esthete, as a skilled practitioner and expert authority has been replaced by collaborative actions and cross-discipline projects that are less about maintaining essential practices and more about exploring new possibilities and practicalities.

3. For an excellent overview of the use of mapping as an analytical process in scholarly writing see Chris Hart's text, *Doing a Literature Review: Releasing the Social Science Research Imagination* (1998), Chapter 6, "Mapping and Analyzing Ideas."

4. A strategy I have found useful in describing the survey approach to art historical methodologies presented by art writers such as Laurie Schneider Adams (1996) is to align the various methods presented in the text with selected covers from *The New Yorker* magazine. It is not difficult to find cover art examples of formalism, iconography, semiotics, psychoanalysis, autobiography, poststructuralism, and the like.

5. Lucio Pozzi's diagrammatic analysis builds on the instructional spirit reflected in Paul Klee's *Pedagogical Sketchbook* (1953), first published in 1925 as part of a series produced at the Bauhaus. In her introduction, Sibyl Moholy-Nagy highlights Klee's capacity for making the familiar strange so as to see in new ways.

His forms are derived from nature, inspired by observation of shape and cyclic change but their appearance only matters in so far as it symbolizes an inner actuality that receives meaning from its relationship to the cosmos. There is a common agreement among men on the place and function of external features: eye, leg, roof, sail, star. In Paul Klee's pictures they are used as beacons, pointing away from the surface into a spiritual reality. Just as a magician performs the miraculous with objects of utter familiarity, such as cards, handkerchiefs, coins, rabbits, so Paul Klee uses the familiar object in unfamiliar relationships to materialize the unknown. (Emphasis in the original, p. 7)

6. Peter Plagens has been the art critic for *Newsweek* since 1989. The conversation-interview example of his art writing first appeared in *Aperture*, March 24, 1983, pp. 150–153 and was later published in his collection of art criticism, *Moonlight Blues: An Artist's Art Criticism* (1986), pp. 255–262.

7. See, for example, the traveling exhibition *Gene(sis): Contemporary Art Explores Human Genomics,* which features contemporary art created in response to

developments in human genomics. The curator, Robin Held (2004), says the artwork not only responds to important questions being raised, but also what is exhibited "addresses concrete audience needs: finding a means of comprehending highly technical material with potentially profound social implications; fostering public dialogue among populations; and enabling high level collaboration between fine arts and hard sciences" (pp. 277–278). See also http://www.gene-sis.net/artists_kac.html (last accessed on December 9, 2003).

8. I remember seeing a Carolee Schneemann installation in the early 1980s at Ohio State University. The concept she explored was one I found exceptionally powerful; it added to my expanding repertoire of examples where artistic insight helped clarify a particular educational problem. In one of her pieces, Schneemann referenced the umbrella as an androgynous form that could be both female (when opened) and male (when closed). I couldn't help think about the ubiquitous use of the term the "arts umbrella" that was a popular educational slogan at the time, and remains so today. I commented in an editorial not long after about the inanity of trying to create a new curriculum species that had no real connections to arts experiences in the outside world, and the folly of using an image of an androgynous umbrella where there was little chance of procreation, let alone creation.

9. For a discussion of the role of different types of reviews, especially those used in peer reviewing, see the fall 2001 issue of *Studies in Art Education*, 43(1) and the *Review of Educational Research*, 1998, 68(4).

10. In his text, *Writing as a Visual Art*, Graziella Tonfoni (1994) describes the writing process that is so central to research as a kind of formalism that can be modeled on the visual arts. He devises visual symbols that serve as graphic devices used to analyze texts, and visual objects and "imagining textual machines" (p. 141) as structures for visualizing writing as a creative and constructive process.

EPILOGUE: CONCLUSIONS AND BEGINNINGS

I began this book with a claim that the imaginative and intellectual work undertaken by artists is a form of research. I also make the point that the kind of research artists do in studios, classrooms, communities, and in cyberspace, shares commonalities with what our colleagues do in the humanities and in the social and physical sciences. This is a quest for knowledge and understanding, and in this creative pursuit no one holds copyright on ideas: where to find them, how to find them, or what to do with them. What is valued is human insight and how we might use it. Therefore I argue that although we can agree this is an important goal, we also need to agree that it can be achieved in different ways. For the visual artist this means making art that has the capacity to transform us, and thereby change the world around us. And if you happen to be making art within an educational setting, then there is a responsibility to be able to use your imaginative and intellectual drive to respond to our incessant need to know, and to do so in a way that meets the rigor demanded of practices undertaken in institutional communities. In a practical sense, this means that different paths can be used to get to the same place, and while there is a need to locate forms of artistic inquiry within certain scholarly frameworks, there is no need to be a slave to them. But as I point out in this book, the quest to claim a place for visual arts, as a critically important area of human knowing, requires strong arguments, which is an ongoing challenge.

As well as presenting a case for art practice *as* research, part of the project undertaken in this book is to dispel myths. Perhaps the most persistent is the inane misconception that the arts are a warm, fuzzy, feel-good part of our lives that are nice but unnecessary. The power of the arts to stop us in our tracks certainly captures the intensity of this body-snapping experience, but this only partly reveals what is going on in the mind. Yet the complexity of this elusive human experience causes most researchers to ignore it for it is assumed we don't have the "instruments" to measure it. But this attitude is as silly as the old cartoon that shows a drunk kneeling in the gutter under the lamplight looking for his keys. When asked where he lost them he replies, "Somewhere over there in the dark." To the incredulous bystander's question, "But why aren't you looking over there?" he replies, "Because I can see here." It seems we've also been looking in the wrong place—to find out what is important about the visual arts there is a need to start with art. Artists know this. Art writers know this. Art educators know this. And to enlighten others will not only take advocacy and political guile, but also credible evidence, convincing argument, sound research, insightful practice, valid theory, and powerful art.

● CHIPPING AWAY

If a purpose of this book is to begin to craft an argument that art practice is research, then the chapters chip away at the corner of this granitelike task. In doing so, some assumptions are buried, old shibboleths dusted off, and new arguments chiseled out. The result is a series of claims I use as the foundation for each chapter, which I summarize below.

Part 1: Contexts for Visual Arts Research establishes the historical, cultural, conceptual, and educational basis of the book. Several arguments are presented that position the visual arts as a historically rich and conceptually robust area of inquiry.

- First, the creation and critique of art in recent centuries is shown to occur within a changing set of interrelated circumstances that must be considered if the cultural and educational potential of the visual arts is to be realized.
- Second, it is argued that if the institutionalization of the visual arts does not maintain a primary link between contemporary art practice and the culture of the academy, the possibility of sustained development is diminished.
- Third, to present a viable argument that the visual arts provide a way of coming to know the world that is real and relevant, there is a need to be knowledgeable about methods of inquiry used in the sciences so that similarities and differences can be cogently articulated.
- Finally, if the impact of the visual arts as a powerful cultural and educational agency of human insight is to be further developed, there is a need to argue from a perspective that is grounded *in* the visual arts and adapted to wider systems of theory and practice.

Part 2: Theorizing Visual Arts Practice establishes a basis on which visual arts practice can be seen to be a form of inquiry that is sound in theory, robust in method, and capable of generating important creative and critical outcomes. Several arguments are made.

- First, theorizing is an approach to understanding that occurs at all levels of human inquiry and involves creative action and critical reflection.
- Second, visual arts practice is a form of human understanding whose cognitive processes are distributed throughout the various media, languages, and contexts used to frame the production and interpretation of images.
- Third, conceiving of visual arts practice as a form of transformative research makes full use of the potential of visual images to reveal insights about issues of human concern.
- Fourth, the visual image is part of cultural practices, individual processes, and information systems that are located within spaces and places; is evidence of mediated processes; and is indicative of visual regimes that may be tangible or invisible.
- Finally, the contemporary artist adopts many patterns of practice that dislodge discipline boundaries, media conventions, and political interests, yet still manages to operate within a realm of cultural discourse as creator, critic, theorist, teacher, activist, and archivist.

The purpose of *Part 3: Visual Arts Research Practices* is to provide strategies to assist with conceptualizing and planning visual arts research projects. The challenge is to describe guidelines that have sufficient utility, yet resist the tendency to prescribe methods. Chapter 6 presents these arguments.

- First, current descriptions of discipline structures, research paradigms, and methods of inquiry do not accommodate the full range of ways in which humans engage with issues, ideas, theories, and information.
- Second, doing art is a basic, generative practice of creative and critical investigation from which many derivative forms of inquiry can be developed and applied.
- Third, undertaking original research by investigating what others have done and thereby constructing new interpretations of what has been ignored is a major characteristic of critical and creative inquiry.
- Fourth, beyond the studio space, digital environments, cultural collaborations, and community-based opportunities are creating new places for creative and critical inquiry.
- Fifth, conducting informative and imaginative inquiries into issues and ideas that have personal and public relevance is an inherently educational process.

- Finally, visual arts research comprises practices that are theoretically robust, idea based, process rich, purposeful, and strategic, and make use of adaptive methods and inventive forms whose uniqueness is best seen as connected to, yet also distinct from, traditional systems of inquiry.

● UNCERTAIN CONCLUSIONS

An ongoing conundrum throughout this book is the acceptance that contradiction, conflict, and opposition are useful states of mind. Indeed, these attitudes are necessary in adopting a creative and critical stance for doing visual arts research. In practical terms, whether producing artworks, or planning research, there is a need to reconcile differences and rationalize difficulties. As with art and research, however, it is often from experiences that are both simple and complex, precise and uncertain, that the most insightful outcomes are revealed, and the most important questions arise. Thus it is not necessary to assume that theories are neat, practices are prescribed, all outcomes can be predicted, or that meanings can be measured. The messy resistance of new understanding relies on the rationality of intuition and the imagination of the intellect, and these are the kind of mindful processes used in art practice as research.

REFERENCES

Abrams, M. H. (1971). *The mirror and the lamp: Romantic theory and the critical tradition*. New York: Oxford University Press.

Adams, L. S. (1996). *The methodologies of art: An introduction*. Boulder, CO: Westview Press.

Alvesson, M., & Sköldberg, K. (2000). *Reflexive methodology: New vistas for qualitative research*. London: Sage.

Amundson, R., Serlin, R. C., & Lehrer, R. (1992). On the threats that do *not* face educational research. *Educational Researcher, 21*(9), 19–23.

Anderson, M. L., Auping, M., Cassel, V., Davies, H. M., Farver, A. J., Miller-Keller, A. & Rinder, L. R. (2000). *2000 Whitney Biennial Exhibition*. New York: Harry N. Abrams.

Apple, M. (1990). *Ideology and curriculum* (2nd ed.). London: Routledge.

Apple, M. W. (1993). *Official knowledge: Democratic education in a conservative age*. New York: Routledge.

Apple, M. W. (1996). *Cultural politics and education*. New York: Teachers College Press.

Apple, M. W. (1999). *Power, meaning, and identity: Essays in critical educational studies*. New York: Peter Lang.

Arden, H. (1994). *Dreamkeepers: A spirit-journey into aboriginal Australia*. New York: HarperCollins.

Arnheim, R. (1969). *Visual thinking*. Berkeley: University of California Press.

Arnheim, R. (1974). *Art and visual perception: A psychology of the creative eye* (Rev. ed.). Berkeley: University of California Press.

Austin, J. H. (2003). *Chase, chance, and creativity: The lucky art of novelty*. Cambridge: MIT Press.

Awoniyi, S. (2002). Premises for a question about memory. *Selected working papers in art & design* (Vol. 2). Retrieved September 14, 2003, from http://www.herts.ac .uk/artdes/research/papers/wpades/vol2/awoniyifull.html

Bachelard, G. (1969). *The poetics of space* (Maria Jolas, Trans.). Boston: Beacon Press.

Bal, M. (1996). *Double exposure: The subject of cultural analysis*. New York: Routledge.

Ball, M. S., & Smith, G. W. H. (1992). *Analyzing visual data*. Newbury Park, CA: Sage.

Banks, J. A. (Ed.). (1996). *Multicultural education: Transformative knowledge & action*. New York: Teachers College Press.

Banks, M. (2001). *Visual methods in social research*. London: Sage.

Barber, B. R. (1996). *Jihad vs. McWorld: How globalism and tribalism are reshaping the world*. New York: Ballantine Books.

Barnard, M. (2001). *Approaches to understanding visual culture.* New York: Palgrave.

Barone, T. (2001). Science, art, and the predispositions of educational researchers. *Educational Researcher, 30*(7), 24–28.

Barone, T., & Eisner, E. W. (1997). Arts-based educational research. In R. M. Jaeger (Ed.), *Complementary methods for research in education* (2nd ed., pp. 73–116). Washington, DC: American Educational Research Association.

Barrett, T. (1994). *Criticizing art: Understanding the contemporary.* Mountain View, CA: Mayfield.

Barrett, T. (1996). *Criticizing photographs: An introduction to understanding images* (2nd ed.). Mountain View, CA: Mayfield.

Barthes, R. (1968). *Elements of semiology* (A. Lavers & C. Smith, Trans.). New York: Hill and Wang.

Bechtel, W., & Abrahamsen, A. (1991). *Connectionism and the mind: An introduction to parallel processing in networks.* Cambridge, MA: Blackwell.

Beittel, K. R. (1979). Unity of truth, language, and method in art education. *Studies in Art Education, 21*(1), 50–56.

Benjamin, W. (1968). The work of art in the age of mechanical reproduction. In W. Benjamin, *Illuminations* (H. Arendt, Ed. and Intro.; & H. Zohn, Trans.) (pp. 219–253). New York: Schocken Books.

Berger, J. (1972). *Ways of seeing.* London: British Broadcasting Corp.

Binstock, J. P. (1996). American Kaleidoscope. In J. Days Serwer, *American kaleidoscope: Themes and perspectives in recent art.* Washington, DC: Smithsonian American Art Museum. Retrieved on May 14, 2004, from http://www.american art.si.edu/collections/exhibits/kscope/tanseyexhframe.html

Bird, E. (2000). Research in art and design: The first decade. *Selected working papers in art & design* (Vol. 1). Retrieved September 14, 2003, from http://www.herts .ac.uk/artdes/research/papers/wpades/vol1/bird2full.html

Blandy, D., & Congdon, K. G. (Eds.). (1987). *Art in a democracy.* New York: Teachers College Press.

Bloom, A. D. (1987). *The closing of the American mind.* New York: Simon and Schuster.

Bloom, L. (Ed.). (1999). *With other eyes: Looking at race and gender in visual culture.* Minneapolis: University of Minnesota Press.

Bolin, P. E., Blandy, D., & Congdon, K. G. (Eds.). (2000). *Remembering others: Making invisible histories of art education visible.* Reston, VA: National Art Education Association.

Borysevicz, M. (1999). Zhang Dali's conversation with Beijing. In M. Maggio, *Zhang Dali*. Beijing: CourtYard Gallery.

Brockman, J. (Ed.). (1995). *The third culture: Beyond the scientific revolution.* New York: Touchstone.

Brosterman, N. (1997). *Inventing kindergarten.* New York: Harry N. Abrams.

Brown, M., & Korzenik, D. (1993). *Art making and education. Disciplines in art education: Context of understanding.* Urbana: University of Illinois Press.

Brown, N. C. M. (2000). The representation of practice. *Selected working papers in art & design* (Vol. 1). Retrieved September 14, 2003, from http://www.herts .ac.uk/artdes/research/papers/wpades/vol1/brown2full.html

Brown, N. C. M. (2003). Art as a practice of research. *Proceedings of the 31st InSEA World Congress, August, 2002. InSEA Member Presentations: Papers and Workshops CD-ROM.* New York: The Center for International Art Education, Inc., Teachers College, Columbia University.

Brown, T., & Jones, L. (2001). *Action research and postmodernism: Congruence and critique.* Buckingham, UK: Open University Press.

Bruner, J. (1996). *The culture of education.* Cambridge, MA: Harvard University Press.

Bullough, R. V., Jr., & Pinnegar, S. (2001). Guidelines for quality in autobiographical forms of self-study research. *Educational Researcher, 30*(3), 13–21.

Burton, J. M. (2001). The configuration of meaning: Learner-centered art education revisited. *Studies in Art Education, 41*(4), 330–345.

Burton, J. M., Horowitz, R., & Abeles, H. (2000). Learning in and through the arts: The question of transfer. *Studies in Art Education, 41*(3), 228–257.

Cahnmann, M. (2003). The craft, practice, and possibility of poetry in educational research. *Educational Researcher, 32*(3), 29–36.

Candlin, F. (2000). Practice-based doctorates and questions of academic legitimacy. *Journal of Art and Design Education, 19*(1), 96–101.

Candlin, F. (2001). A dual inheritance: The politics of educational reform and PhDs in art and design. *Journal of Art and Design Education, 20*(3), 302–310.

Caranfa, A. (2001). Art and science: The aesthetic education of the emotions and reason. *Journal of Art and Design Education, 20*(2), 151–160.

Carrier, D. (1987). *Artwriting.* Amherst: University of Massachusetts Press.

Carrier, D. (2003). *Writing about visual art.* New York: Allworth Press.

Carroll, N. (2001). *Beyond aesthetics: Philosophical essays.* Cambridge, UK: Cambridge University Press.

Carter, M. (1990). *Framing art: Introducing theory and the visual image.* Sydney: Hale & Iremonger.

Casti, J., & Karlqvist, A. (Eds.). (2003). *Art and complexity.* Amsterdam: Elsevier.

Chalmers, G. F. (1996). *Celebrating pluralism: Art, education, and cultural diversity.* Los Angeles: Getty Education Institute for the Arts.

Chalmers, G. F. (2002). Celebrating pluralism six years later: Visual transculture/s, education, and critical multiculturalism. *Studies in Art Education, 43*(4), 293–306.

Chang, C. Y. (1982). Christo. Excerpted from "Dialogue" an unpublished interview. In E. Johnson (Ed.), *American artists on art from 1940 to 1980* (pp. 196–200). New York: Harper & Row.

Cheetham, M. A., Holly, M. A., & Moxley, K. (Eds.). (1998). *Subjects of art history: Historical objects in contemporary perspective.* New York: Cambridge University Press.

Chiu, M. (2003). Chen Zhen. *ART AsiaPacific, Quarterly Journal, 37,* 33.

Choi Caruso, H. Y. (2004). Art as a political act: Expressions of cultural identity, self-identity and gender in the work of two Korean/Korean American women artists (Yong Soon Min, Suk Nam Yun) (Doctoral dissertation, Teachers College, Columbia University, 2004). *Dissertation Abstracts International, A64*(12), 4319 (UMI No. 3117836).

Chomsky, N. (1980). *Rules and representations.* New York: Columbia University Press.

Christo & Jeanne-Claude. (2000). *Most common errors.* Paris: Editions Jannick.

Cizek, G. J. (1995). Crunchy granola and the hegemony of the narrative. *Educational Researcher, 24*(2), 26–28.

Clark, R. (1996). *Art education: Issues in postmodernist pedagogy.* Reston, VA: National Art Education Association.

Clifford, J. (1988). *The predicament of culture: Twentieth-century ethnography, literature, and art.* Cambridge, MA: Harvard University Press.

Clifford, J., & Marcus, G. E. (Eds.). (1986). *Writing culture: The poetics and politics of ethnography.* Berkeley: University of California Press.

Coffey, A., & Atkinson, P. (1996). *Making sense of qualitative data: Complementary research strategies.* Thousand Oaks, CA: Sage.

Cohen, L., Manion, L., & Morrison, K. (2000). *Research methods in education* (5th ed.). London: Routledge Falmer.

Cole, A. L., & Knowles, J. G. (Eds.). (2001). *Lives in context: The art of life history research.* Walnut Creek, CA: Alta Mira Press.

Congdon, K. G., Blandy, D., & Bolin, E. P. (Eds.). (2001). *Histories of community-based art education.* Reston, VA: National Art Education Association.

Costantino, T. E. (2002). Problem-based learning: A concrete approach to teaching aesthetics. *Studies in Art Education, 43*(3), 219–231.

Coveney, P., & Highfield, R. (1995). *Frontiers of complexity: The search for order in a chaotic world.* New York: Fawcett Columbine.

Creswell, J. W. (2003). *Research design: Qualitative, quantitative, and mixed method approaches* (2nd ed.). Thousand Oaks, CA: Sage.

Crossley, N. (1996). *Intersubjectivity: The fabric of social becoming.* London: Sage.

Csikszentmihalyi, M. (1988). Society, culture and creativity: A systems view of creativity. In R. J. Sternberg (Ed.), *The nature of creativity: Contemporary psychological perspectives* (pp. 325–339). New York: Cambridge University Press.

Csikszentmihalyi, M. (1990). *Flow: The psychology of optimal experience.* New York: Harper & Row.

Csikszentmihalyi, M. (1993). *The evolving self: A psychology for the third millennium.* New York: HarperCollins.

Danto, A. C. (1981). *The transfiguration of the commonplace: A philosophy of art.* Cambridge, MA: Harvard University Press.

Danto, A. C. (1986a). *Encounters & reflections: Art in the historical present.* New York: The Noonday Press.

Danto, A. C. (1986b). *The philosophical disenfranchisement of art.* New York: Columbia University Press.

Danto, A. C. (2001a). Introduction. In P. G. Meyer (Ed.), *Brushes with history: Writing on art from* The Nation, *1865–2001* (pp. xxi–xxviii). New York: Thunder's Mouth Press/Nation Books.

Danto, A. C. (2001b, May 28). In the bosom of Jesus. *The Nation,* 30–34.

Darley, A. (2000). *Visual digital culture: Surface play and spectacle in new media genres.* London: Routledge.

Davies, B. (1992). Women's subjectivity and feminist stories. In C. Ellis & M. G. Flaherty (Eds.), *Investigating subjectivity: Research on lived experience* (pp. 53–76). Newbury Park, CA: Sage.

de Freitas, N. (2002). Towards a definition of studio documentation: Working tool and transparent record. *Selected working papers in art & design* (Vol. 2). Retrieved September 14, 2003, from http://www.herts.ac.uk/artdes/research/papers/wpades/vol2/freitasfull.html

Dennett, D. (1995). Intuition pumps. In J. Brockman (Ed.), *The third culture: Beyond the scientific revolution* (pp. 181–197). New York: Touchstone.

Denzin, N. K. (1989). *Interpretive biography.* Thousand Oaks, CA: Sage.

Denzin, N. K., & Lincoln, Y. S. (Eds). (1998). *The landscape of qualitative research: Theories and issues.* Thousand Oaks, CA: Sage.

Desai, D. (2002). The ethnographic move in contemporary art: What does it mean for art education? *Studies in Art Education, 43*(4), 307–323.

Deutsche, R. (1998). *Evictions: Art and spatial politics.* Cambridge: MIT Press.

Dewan, D. (2003). Vivan Sundaram. *ART AsiaPacific Quarterly Journal, 37,* 39.

Dewey, J. (1938). *Logic, the theory of inquiry.* New York: H. Holt.

Diamond, C. T. P., & Mullen, C. A. (Eds.). (1999). *The postmodern educator: Arts-based inquiries and teacher development.* New York: Peter Lang.

Diderot, D., & d'Alembert, J. R. (1751/1965). *Encyclopedia* (N. S. Hoyt & T. Cassirer, Trans.). Indianapolis, IN: Bobbs-Merrill.

Douglas, A. (2000). Research through practice: Positioning the practitioner as researcher. *Selected working papers in art & design* (Vol. 1). Retrieved September 14, 2003, in http://www.herts.ac.uk/artdes/research/papers/wpades/vol1/douglas2.html

Dow, A. W. (1899/1998). *Composition. A series of exercises in art structure for the use of students and teachers* (13th ed.) (Joseph Masheck, New Intro.). Berkeley: University of California.

Draper, J. W. (1852). *Text-book on chemistry: For the use of schools and colleges.* New York: Harper & Brothers.

Dubuffet, J. (1988). *Asphyxiating culture and other writings* (Carol Volk, Trans.). New York: Four Walls Eight Windows, 14–15.

Duncum, P. (2002). Theorizing everyday aesthetic experience with contemporary visual culture. *Visual Arts Research, 28*(2) 4–15.

Duncum, P., & Bracy, T. (Eds.). (2001). *On knowing: Art and visual culture.* Christchurch, NZ: Canterbury University Press.

Eagleton, T. (1992). Capitalism, modernism and postmodernism. In F. Frascina & J. Harris (Eds.), *Art in modern culture: An anthology of critical texts* (pp. 91–100). London: Phaidon.

Edwards, S. (Ed.). (1998). *Art and its histories: Academies, museums, and canons of art.* New Haven, CT: Yale University Press.

Efland, A. D. (1990). *A history of art education: Intellectual and social currents in teaching the visual arts.* New York: Teachers College Press.

Efland, A. D. (1995). Change in the conceptions of art teaching. In R. W. Neperud (Ed.), *Context, content, and community in art education: Beyond postmodernism* (pp. 25–40). New York: Teachers College Press.

Efland, A. D. (2002). *Art and cognition: Integrating the visual arts in the curriculum.* New York: Teachers College Press.

Egan, K. (1999). *Children's minds, talking rabbits & clockwork oranges: Essays on education.* New York: Teachers College Press.

Eisner, E. W. (1991). *The enlightened eye: Qualitative inquiry and the enhancement of educational practice.* New York: Macmillan.

Eisner, E. W. (1993). Forms of understanding and the future of educational research. *Educational Researcher, 22*(7), 5–11.

Eisner, E. W. (1999). Rejoinder: A response to Tom Knapp. *Educational Researcher, 28*(1), 19–20.

Eisner, E. W. (2002). *The arts and the creation of mind.* New Haven, CT: Yale University Press.

Eisner, E. W. (2003). On the art and science of qualitative research in psychology. In P. M. Camic, J. E. Rhodes, & L. Yardley (Eds.), *Qualitative research in psychology: Expanding perspectives in methodology and design* (pp. 17–29). Washington, DC: American Psychology Association.

Eisner, E. W., & Peshkin, A. (Eds.). (1990). *Qualitative inquiry in education: The continuing debate.* New York: Teachers College Press.

Elkins, J. (1999). *The domain of images.* Ithaca, NY: Cornell University Press.

Elkins, J. (2003). *Visual studies: A skeptical introduction.* New York: Routledge.

Emme, M. J. (2001). Visuality in teaching and research: Activist art education. *Studies in Art Education, 43*(1), 57–74.

Emmison, M., & Smith, P. (2000). *Researching the visual: Images, objects, contexts, and interactions in social and cultural inquiry.* London: Sage.

Eve, R. A., Horsfall, S., & Lee, M. E. (Eds.). (1997). *Chaos, complexity, and sociology: Myths, models, and theories.* Thousand Oaks, CA: Sage.

Feldman, A. (2003). Validity and quality in self-study. *Educational Researcher, 32*(3) 26–28.

Feldman, D. H., Csikszentmihalyi, M., & Gardner, H. (1994). *Changing the world: A framework for the study of creativity.* Westport, CT: Praeger.

Fernie, E. (1995). *Art history and its methods: A critical anthology.* London: Phaidon.

Feyerabend, P. K. (1991). *Three dialogues on knowledge.* Oxford, UK: Blackwell.

Feyerabend, P. K. (1993). *Against method* (3rd ed.). New York: Verso.

Fineberg, J. (1997). *The innocent eye: Children's art and the modern artist.* Princeton, NJ: Princeton University Press.

Flick, U. (2002). *An introduction to qualitative research* (2nd ed.). London: Sage.

Foster, H. (1995). The artist as ethnographer? In G. E. Marcus & F. R. Myers (Eds.), *The traffic in culture: Refiguring art and anthropology* (pp. 302–309). Berkeley: University of California Press.

Fox, G. T. (2001). Creating research questions from strategies and perspectives of contemporary art. *Curriculum Inquiry, 31*(1), 33–49.

Frayling, C. (Ed.). (1997). *Practice-based doctorates in the creative and performing arts and design.* Lichfield, UK: UK Council for Graduate Education. Retrieved October 26, 2003, from http://www.ukcge.ac.uk/report_downloads.html

Freedman, K. (2003). *Teaching visual culture: Curriculum, aesthetics, and the social life of art.* New York: Teachers College Press.

Gablik, S. (1984). *Has modernism failed?* New York: Thames and Hudson.

Gablik, S. (1991). *The reenchantment of art.* New York: Thames and Hudson.

Gahan, C., & Hannibal, M. (1998). *Doing qualitative research using QSR NUD•IST.* Thousand Oaks, CA: Sage.

Gardner, H. (1973). *The arts and human development.* New York: John Wiley & Sons.

Gardner, H. (1982). *Art, mind and brain: A cognitive approach to creativity.* New York: Basic Books.

Gardner, H. (1983). *Frames of mind: The theory of multiple intelligences.* New York: Basic Books.

Gardner, H. (1993). *Creating minds.* New York: Basic Books.

Garoian, C. R. (1999). *Performing pedagogy: Toward an art of politics.* Albany: State University of New York.

Gell-Mann, M. (1994). *The quark and the jaguar: Adventures in the simple and the complex.* New York: W. H. Freeman.

Gell-Mann, M. (1995). Plectics. In J. Brockman (Ed.), *The third culture: Beyond the scientific revolution* (pp. 316–332). New York: Touchstone.

Gell-Mann, M. (2003). Regularities and randomness: Evolving schemata in science and the arts. In J. Casti & A. Karlqvist (Eds.), *Art and complexity* (pp. 47–58). Amsterdam: Elsevier.

Genocchio, B. (2001). *Fiona Foley: Solitaire.* Annandale, NSW: Piper Press.

Geuss, R. (1981). *The idea of a critical theory: Habermas and the Frankfurt school.* Cambridge, UK: Cambridge University Press.

Gierstberg, F., & Oosterbaan, W. (Eds.). (2002). *The image society: Essays on visual culture.* Rotterdam, the Netherlands: NAI.

Giroux, H. A. (1981). *Ideology, culture, and the process of schooling.* Philadelphia: Temple University Press.

Giroux, H. A. (1983). *Critical theory and educational practice.* Victoria, Australia: Deakin University.

Giroux, H. A. (1997). *Pedagogy and the politics of hope: Theory, culture, and schooling.* Boulder, CO: Westview Press.

Giroux, H. A., & McLaren, P. (Eds.). (1989). *Critical pedagogy, the state, and cultural struggle.* Albany: State University of New York Press.

Gleick, J. (1988). *Chaos: Making a new science.* London: Sphere Books.

Golomb, C. (1974). *Young children's sculpture and drawing: A study in representational development.* Cambridge, MA: Harvard University Press.

Golomb, C. (1992). *The child's creation of a pictorial world.* Berkeley: University of California Press.

Goodman, N. (1978). *Ways of worldmaking.* Indianapolis, IN: Hackett.

Goodman, N. (1984). *Of mind and other matters.* Cambridge, MA: Harvard University Press.

Gould, S. J. (1981). *The mismeasure of man.* London: Penguin.

Gould, S. J. (1991). *Bully for brontosaurus: Reflections in natural history.* New York: W. W. Norton.

Gowan, J. C., Demos, G. D., & Torrance, E. P. (1967). *Creativity: Its educational implications.* New York: John Wiley & Sons.

Gray, C. (1998). Inquiry through practice: Developing appropriate research strategies. In P. Strandman (Ed.), *No Guru, No Method?* Discussions on Art and Design Research, University of Art & Design, Helsinki, Finland: UIAH. Retrieved on September 14, 2003, from http://www2.rgu.ac.uk/criad/cgpapers/ngnm/ngnm.htm

Gray, C., & Pirie, I. (1995). "Artistic" research procedure: Research at the edge of chaos? Paper presented at "Design Interfaces" conference, European Academy of Design, University of Salford, April 1995. In *Proceedings of Design Interfaces Conference* (Vol. 3). Retrieved September 14, 2003, from http://www2.rgu.ac.uk/criad/cgpapers/ead/ead.htm

Green, H. (Ed.). (2001). Research training in the creative and performing arts and design. Lichfield, UK: UK Council for Graduate Education. Retrieved December 14, 2003, from http://www.ukcge.ac.uk/report_downloads.html

Greenberg, C., & Sylvester, D. (2001). The European view of American art. In P. G. Meyer (Ed.), *Brushes with history: Writing on art from* The Nation, *1865–2001* (pp. 227–232). New York: Thunder's Mouth Press/Nation Books.

Greene, M. (1995). Texts and margins. In R. W. Neperud (Ed.), *Context, content, and community in art education: Beyond postmodernism* (pp. 111–127). New York: Teachers College Press.

Greene, M. (2003). The arts and social justice. In P. Sahasrabudhe (Ed.), *Art education: Meaning dimensions and possibilities.* Keynote addresses. The 31st InSEA World Congress, August 2002 (pp. 21–25). New York: The Center for International Art Education, Teachers College, Columbia University.

Gross, P., & Levitt, N. (1994). *Higher superstition: The academic left and its quarrels with science.* Baltimore: Johns Hopkins University Press.

Guba, E. G., & Lincoln, Y. S. (1998). Competing paradigms in qualitative research. In N. K. Denzin & Y. S. Lincoln (Eds.), *The landscape of qualitative research: Theories and issues* (pp. 195–220). Thousand Oaks, CA: Sage.

Guilford, J. P. (1950). Creativity. *American Psychologist, 5,* 444–454.

Guilford, J. P. (1956). Structure of the intellect. *Psychological Bulletin, 53,* 267–293.

Habermas, J. (1971). *Knowledge and human interests* (J. J. Shapiro, Trans.). Boston: Beacon.

Haraway, D. J. (1991). *Simians, cyborgs, and women: The reinvention of nature.* New York: Routledge.

Harris, J. (2001). *The new art history: A critical introduction.* London: Routledge.

Harris, M. (Ed.). (1996). *Review of postgraduate education.* Bristol, UK: Higher Education Funding Council for England. Retrieved December 22, 2003, from http://www.hefce.ac.uk/Pubs/hefce/1996/m14_96.htm

Hart, C. (1998). *Doing a literature review: Releasing the social science research imagination.* London: Sage.

Held, R. (2004). Gene(sis): Contemporary art explores human genomics. In R. Mitchell & P. Thurtle (Eds.), *Data made flesh: Embodying information* (pp. 263–278). New York: Routledge.

Henderson, A., & Kaeppler, A. L. (Eds.). (1999). *Exhibiting dilemmas: Issues of representation at the Smithsonian.* Washington, DC: Smithsonian Institution Press.

Heywood, I., & Sandywell, B. (Eds.). (1999). *Interpreting visual culture: Explorations in the hermeneutics of the visual.* London: Routledge.

Hirsch, E. D. (1987). *Cultural literacy: What every American needs to know.* Boston: Houghton and Mifflin.

Hirschfeld, L. A., & Gelman, S. A. (Eds.). (1994). *Mapping the mind: Domain specificity in cognition and culture.* Cambridge, UK: Cambridge University Press.

Hockney, D. (2001). *Secret knowledge: Rediscovering the lost techniques of the old masters.* New York: Viking Studio.

Hoffmann Davis, J. (2003). Balancing the whole: Portraiture as methodology. In P. M. Camic, J. E. Rhodes, & L. Yardley (Eds.), *Qualitative research in psychology: Expanding perspectives in methodology and design* (pp. 199–217). Washington, DC: American Psychology Association.

hooks, b. (1995). *Art on my mind: Visual politics.* New York: The New Press.

Hooper-Greenhill, E. (2000). *Museums and the interpretation of visual culture.* New York: Routledge.

Hubbard, G. A. (1963). The Development of the visual arts in the curriculums of American colleges and universities. *Dissertations Abstracts International, 24*(01), 171 (UMI AAT 6304607).

Hughes, R. (1993). *Culture of complaint: The fraying of America.* New York: Oxford University Press.

Ilesanmi, O. (2001). Laylah Ali. In *Freestyle* (pp. 20–21). New York: The Studio Museum in Harlem.

Irwin, R. L., & Miller, L. (1997). Oral history as community-based participatory research: Learning from First Nations women artists. *Journal of Multicultural and Cross-Cultural Research in Art Education, 15,* 10–23.

Irwin, R. L., Stephenson, W., Robertson, H., & Reynolds, J. K. (2001). Passionate creativity, compassionate community. *Canadian Review of Art Education, 28*(2), 15–34.

Itten, J. (1964). *Design and form: The basic course at the Bauhaus* (John Maass, Trans.). New York: Reinhold.

Jaeger, R. M. (Ed.). (1997). *Complementary methods for research in education* (2nd ed.). Washington, DC: American Educational Research Association.

jagodzinski, j. (1997a). *Postmodernism dilemmas: Outrageous essays in art & art education.* Mahwah, NJ: Lawrence Erlbaum.

jagodzinski, j. (1997b). *Pun(k) deconstruction: Experifigural writings in art & art education.* Mahwah, NJ: Lawrence Erlbaum.

Jeffri, J. (2002). *Changing the beat: A study of the worklife of jazz musicians* (3 vols.). NEA Research Division Report #43. Washington, DC: National Endowment for the Arts.

Jencks, C. (1989). *What is post-modernism?* (3rd ed.). New York: St. Martin's Press.

Jipson, J. A., & Paley, N. (Eds.). (1997). *Daredevil research: Re-creating analytic practice.* New York: Peter Lang.

Jones, A., & Stephenson, A. (Eds.). (1999). *Performing the body: Performing the text.* London: Routledge.

Karim, P. M., & Khorrami, M. M. (1999). *A world between: Poems, short stories, and essays by Iranian-Americans.* New York: George Braziller.

Kellner, D. (1989). *Critical theory, Marxism, and modernity.* Cambridge, UK: Polity Press.

Kemmis, S., & McTaggart, R. (Eds.). (1988). *The action research planner* (3rd ed.). Victoria, Australia: Deakin University.

Kent, L. A. (2001). *The case of Lucio Pozzi: An artist/teacher's studio critique method* (Doctoral dissertation, Teachers College, Columbia University). *Dissertation Abstracts International, A62*(05), 1687 (UMI No. 3014892).

Kent, L. (2003). *Lucio Pozzi: Diagrams.* Italy: Edizioni Bacacay.

Kepes, G. (1944). *Language of vision.* Chicago: Paul Theobald.

Kincheloe, J. L., & McLaren, P. L. (1998). Rethinking critical theory and qualitative research. In N. K. Denzin & Y. S. Lincoln (Eds.), *The landscape of qualitative research: Theoretical issues* (pp. 260–299). Thousand Oaks, CA: Sage.

King, M. (2002). From Max Ernst to Ernst Mach: Epistemology in art and science. *Selected working papers in art & design* (Vol. 2). Retrieved September 14, 2003, from http://www.herts.ac.uk/artdes/research/papers/wpades/vol2/kingfull.html

Kirk, J., & Miller, M. L. (1986). *Reliability and validity in qualitative research.* Newbury Park, CA: Sage.

Klee, P. (1948). *On modern art.* London: Faber and Faber.

Klee, P. (1925/1953). *Pedagogical sketchbook.* London: Faber and Faber.

Krug, D. (1992/1993). The expressive cultural practices of a non-academically educated artist, Ellis Nelson, in the micro and macro environment. *Journal of Multicultural and Cross-Cultural Research in Art Education, 10/11,* 20–48.

Krug, D. H. (2003). Symbolic culture and art education. *Art Education, 56*(2), 13–19.

Kuhn, T. S. (1970). *The structure of scientific revolutions.* (2nd ed. Enlarged). Chicago: University of Chicago Press.

LaChapelle, J. R. (1991). In the night studio: The professional artist as an educational role model. *Studies in Art Education, 32*(3), 160–170.

Lacy, S. C. (Ed.). (1995). *Mapping the terrain: New genre public art.* Seattle, WA: Bay Press.

Lankford, E. L. (1992). *Aesthetics, issues and inquiry.* Reston, VA: National Art Education Association.

Laurel, B. (Ed.). (2003). *Design research: Methods and perspectives.* Cambridge: MIT Press.

Lave, J., & Wenger, E. (1991). *Situated learning: Legitimate peripheral participation.* New York: Cambridge University Press.

Lawrence-Lightfoot, S. (1983). *The good high school: Portraits of character and culture.* New York: Basic Books.

Lawrence-Lightfoot, S., & Hoffmann Davis, J. (1997). *The art and science of portraiture.* San Francisco: Jossey-Bass.

Light, P., & Butterworth, G. (Eds.). (1993). *Context and cognition: Ways of learning and knowing.* Hillsdale, NJ: Lawrence Erlbaum Associates.

Lindqvist, K. (2003). *Exhibition enterprising: Six cases of realization from idea to institution. School of Business research report no. 2003:5.* Stockholm, Sweden: Stockholm University School of Business.

Lippard, L. R. (1997). *The lure of the local: Senses of place in a multicentered society.* New York: The New Press.

Logan, F. M. (1955). *Growth of art in American schools.* New York: Harper & Brothers.

Lovejoy, M. (1997). *Postmodern currents: Art and artists in the age of electronic media* (2nd ed.). Upper Saddle River, NJ: Prentice Hall.

Lunenfeld, P. (2003). Preface: The design cluster. In B. Laurel (Ed.), *Design research: Methods and perspectives* (p. 10–15). Cambridge: MIT Press.

MacLachlan, G., & Reid, I. (1994). *Framing and interpretation.* Carlton, Australia: Melbourne University Press.

MacLeod, K. (2000). The functions of the written text in practice based PhD submissions. *Selected working papers in art & design* (Vol. 1). Retrieved September 14, 2003, from http://www.herts.ac.uk/artdes/research/papers/wpades/vol1/macleod2.html

Maffei, S., & Zurlo, F. (2000). Designing a competence. *Selected working papers in art & design* (Vol. 1). Retrieved September 14, 2003, from http://www.herts.ac.uk/artdes/research/papers/wpades/vol1/maffei1.html

Manovich, L. (2001). *The language of new media.* Cambridge: MIT Press.

Marantz, S., & Marantz, K. (1992). *Artists of the page: Interviews with children's book illustrators.* Jefferson, NC: McFarland.

Marcus, G. E. (1998). What comes (just) after "post"?: The case of ethnography. In N. K. Denzin & Y. S. Lincoln (Eds.), *The landscape of qualitative research: Theories and issues* (pp. 383–406). Thousand Oaks, CA: Sage.

Marcus, G. E., & Fischer, M. M. J. (1999). *Anthropology as cultural critique: An experimental moment in the human sciences* (2nd ed.). Chicago: University of Chicago Press.

Marshall, C., & Rossman, G. B. (1999). *Designing qualitative research* (3rd ed.). Thousand Oaks, CA: Sage.

May, T. (Ed.). (2002). *Qualitative research in action.* Thousand Oaks, CA: Sage.

Mayo, S. L. (2004). *Emergent objects at the human-computer-interface (HCI): A case study of artists' cybernetic relationships.* Unpublished doctoral dissertation, Teachers College, Columbia University, New York.

McFee, J. K. (1998). *Cultural diversity and the structure and practice of art education.* Reston, VA: National Art Education Association.

McGlennen (Ojibwe), M. (2004). *George Longfish.* Continuum 12 Artists, National Museum of the American Indian's George Heye Center, April 2003 to November 2004. Smithsonian National Museum of the American Indian.

McNiff, S. (1998). *Art-based research.* London: Jessica Kingsley.

McTaggart, R. (Ed.). (1997). *Participatory action research: International contexts and consequences.* Albany: State University of New York Press.

Meyer, P. G. (Ed.). (2001). *Brushes with history: Writing on art from* The Nation, *1865–2001.* New York: Thunder's Mouth Press/Nation Books.

Michael, L. (2003). We are family. In F. Bonami & M. L. Frisa (Eds.), *50th International art exhibition: Dreams and conflicts—The dictatorship of the viewer* (pp. 506–507). Ca' Giustinian, San Marco: La Biennale di Venezia.

Miller, D. (Ed.). (1985). *Popper selections.* Princeton, NJ: Princeton University Press.

Minor, V. H. (1994). *Art history's history.* Englewood Cliffs, NJ: Prentice-Hall.

Mirzoeff, N. (1999). *An introduction to visual culture.* London: Routledge.

Mitchell, R., & Thurtle, P. (Eds.). (2004). *Data made flesh: Embodying information.* New York: Routledge.

Mitchell, W. J. T. (1994). *Picture theory: Essays on verbal and visual representation.* Chicago: University of Chicago Press.

Mithaug, D. E. (2000). *Learning to theorize: A four-step strategy.* Thousand Oaks, CA: Sage.

Morgan, R. C. (1998). *The end of the art world.* New York: Allworth Press.

Morgan, R. C. (1999). Omniscient eyes: Selected works by Angiola Churchill. In F. Farina & R. C. Morgan (Eds.), *Angiola Churchill: The trickster*. Milan: Lattuada Studio.

Morrow, R. A. (1994). *Critical theory and methodology.* Thousand Oaks, CA: Sage.

Mundine, D. (1996). The native born. In. B. Murphy (Ed.), *The native born: Objects and representations from Ramingining, Arnhem Land* (pp. 29–111). Sydney, Australia: Sydney Museum of Contemporary Art.

Myers, F. R. (1995). Representing culture: The production of discourse(s) for Aboriginal acrylic paintings. In G. E. Marcus & F. R. Myers (Eds.), *The traffic in culture: Refiguring art and anthropology* (pp. 55–95). Berkeley: University of California Press.

Myers, F. R. (2002). *Painting culture: The making of an aboriginal high art.* Durham, NC: Duke University Press.

Nadaner, D. (1998). Painting in an era of critical theory. *Studies in Art Education, 39*(2), 168–182.

National Commission of Excellence in Education. (1983). *Nation at risk: The imperative for educational reform*. D. Pierpont Gardner (Chairman), A Report to the Nation and the Secretary of Education, United States Department of Education. Washington, DC: National Commission of Excellence in Education.

Navab, A. D. (2004). *Unsaying life stories: A comparative analysis of the autobiographical art of four Iranians*. Unpublished doctoral dissertation, Teachers College, Columbia University, New York.

Neperud, R. W. (Ed.). (1995). *Context, content, and community in art education: Beyond postmodernism.* New York: Teachers College Press.

Newbury, D. (1996). Knowledge and research in art and design. *Design Studies, 17*(2), 215–219.

Newell, A., & Simon, H. (1981). Computer science as empirical inquiry. In J. Haugeland (Ed.), *Mind design: Philosophy, psychology, artificial intelligence* (pp. 35–66). Cambridge: MIT Press.

New South Wales Department of Education. (1952). *Curriculum for Primary Schools.* Sydney, Australia: Author.

N. N. (Elizabeth Pennell). (2001). The impressionists in London. In P. G. Myer (Ed.), *Brushes with history: Writing on art from* The Nation, *1865–2001* (pp. 80–86). New York: Thunder's Mouth Press/Nation Books.

Nochlin, L. (1988). *Women, art, and power and other essays.* New York: Harper & Row.

Ortega López, H. A. (2003). *The visual essay of art making research: Prototypes and considerations.* Unpublished manuscript, Teachers College, Columbia University, New York.

Paley, N. (1995). *Finding art's place: Experiments in contemporary education and culture.* New York: Routledge.

Panek, R. (1999, February 14). Art and science: A universe apart? *New York Times,* Arts & Leisure, pp. 1, 39.

Parsons, M. (1992). Cognition as interpretation in art education. In B. Reimer & R. A. Smith (Eds.), *The arts, education, and aesthetic knowing* (pp. 70–91). Chicago: The National Society for the Study of Education.

Parsons, M. (1995). Art and culture, visual and verbal thinking: Where are the bridges? *Australian Art Education, 18*(1), 7–14.

Pearse, H. (1992). Art education theory and practice in a postparadigmatic world. *Studies in Art Education, 33*(4), 244–252.

Pellegrin, M. (1999). *Reflections and intentions.* Venice, Italy: Arsenale Editrice.

Perkins, D. (1992). *Smart schools: From training memories to educating minds.* New York: Free Press.

Perkins, D. (2000). *The eureka effect: The art and logic of breakthrough thinking.* New York: W. W. Norton.

Pevsner, N. (1973). *Academies of art, past and present.* New York: De Capo Press.

Phillips, D. C. (1990). Subjectivity and objectivity: An objective inquiry. In E. W. Eisner & A. Peshkin (Eds.), *Qualitative inquiry in education: The continuing debate* (pp. 19–37). New York: Teachers College Press.

Phillips, D. C., & Burbules, N. C. (2000). *Postpositivism and educational research.* Lanham, MD: Rowman & Littlefield.

Pink, S. (2001). *Doing visual ethnography: Images, media, and representation in research.* London: Sage.

Pinker, S. (1994). *The language instinct.* New York: W. Morrow.

Pinker, S. (1997). *How the mind works.* New York: W. W. Norton.

Pirsig, R. M. (1974/1999). *Zen and the art of motorcycle maintenance: An inquiry into values.* New York: HarperCollins.

Plagens, P. (1986). *Moonlight blues: An artist's art criticism.* Ann Arbor, MI: UMI Research Press.

Pollock, G. (2001). *Looking back to the future: Essays on art, life and death.* Amsterdam: G+B Arts International.

Popper, K. R. (1968). *Conjectures and refutations: The growth of scientific knowledge* (2nd ed.). New York: Harper Torchbooks.

Prosser, J. (Ed.). (1998). *Image-based research: A sourcebook for qualitative researchers.* London: Falmer Press.

Reed-Danahay, D. E. (Ed.). (1997). *Auto/ethnography: Rewriting the self and the social.* Oxford, UK: Berg.

Rees, A. L., & Borzello, F. (Eds.). (1986). *The new art history.* London: Camden Press.

Refsum, G. (2002). Bete comme un peintre? Contribution to an understanding of the knowledge base in the field of visual arts. *Selected working papers in art & design* (Vol. 2). Retrieved September 14, 2003, from http://www.herts.ac.uk/artdes/research/papers/wpades/vol2/refsumfull.html

Reichardt, C. S., & Rallis, S. F. (Eds.). (1994). *The qualitative-quantitative debate: New perspectives.* San Francisco: Jossey-Bass.

Reilly, L. (2002). An alternative model of "knowledge" for the arts. *Selected working papers in art & design* (Vol. 2). Retrieved from http://www.herts.ac.uk/artdes/research/papers/wpades/vol2/reillyfull.html

Reimer, B. (1992). What knowledge is of most worth in the arts? In B. Reimer & R. A. Smith (Eds.), *The arts, education, and aesthetic knowing* (pp. 20–50). Chicago: The National Society for the Study of Education.

Reiss, J. H. (1999). *From margin to center: The spaces of installation art.* Cambridge: MIT Press.

Ricoeur, P. (1981). *Hermeneutics and the human sciences: Essays on language, action, and interpretation* (J. B. Thompson, Ed., Trans., & Intro.). Cambridge, UK: Cambridge University Press.

Robb, P. (1998). *M: The man who became Caravaggio.* New York: Henry Holt.

Rogoff, I. (2000). *Terra infirma: Geography's visual culture.* London: Routledge.

Rogoff, B., & Lave, J. (Eds.). (1984). *Everyday cognition: Its development in social context.* Cambridge, MA: Harvard University Press.

Rolling, J. H. (2004). Messing around with identity constructs: Pursuing a poststructural and poetic aesthetic. *Qualitative Inquiry, 10*(4), pp. 548–557.

Rose, G. (2001). *Visual methodologies.* London: Sage.

Rowley, S. (Ed.). (1994). *Research and postgraduate studies in the visual arts and design proceedings.* NCHADS Research Seminar, 15–6 April 1994, College of Fine Arts, UNSW.

Rumelhart, D. E. (1998). The architecture of mind: A connectionist approach. In P. Thagard (Ed.), *Mind readings* (pp. 207–238). Cambridge: MIT Press.

Ryle, G. (1949). *The concept of mind.* London: Hutchinson House.

Sacca, E. J. (1989). Typologies in art education: How to live with them and how to live without them. *Visual Arts Research, 15*(2), 58–70.

Said, E. W. (1978). *Orientalism.* New York: Pantheon Books.

Salomon, G. (1991). Transcending the qualitative-quantitative debate: The analytic and systemic approaches to educational research. *Educational Researcher, 20*(6), 10–18.

Schank, R. C., & Abelson, R. P. (1977). *Scripts, plans, goals and understanding: An inquiry into human knowledge structures.* Hillsdale, NJ: Lawrence Erlbaum Associates.

Scheffler, I. (1991). *In praise of the cognitive emotions and other essays in the philosophy of education.* New York: Routledge.

Scheurich, J. J. (1997). *Research method in the postmodern.* London: The Falmer Press.

Schleifer, R., Con Davis, R., & Mergler, N. (1992). *Culture and cognition: The boundaries of literary and scientific inquiry.* Ithaca, NY: Cornell University Press.

Schön, D. A. (1983). *The reflective practitioner: How professionals think in action.* New York: Basic Books.

Schön, D. A. (1987). *Educating the reflective practitioner: Toward a new design for teaching and learning in the professions.* San Francisco: Jossey-Bass.

Scrivener, S. A. R. (2000). Reflection in and on action and practice in creative-production doctoral projects in art and design, the foundations of practice-based research: An introduction. *Invited Working Papers in Art & Design* (Vol. 1). Retrieved September 14, 2003, from http://www.herts.ac.uk/artdes/research/papers/wpades/vol1/scrivener2.html

Semali, L. M., & Kincheloe, J. L. (Eds.). (1999). *What is indigenous knowledge? Voices from the academy.* New York: Falmer Press.

Sengupta, S., Dietz, S., Nadarajan, G., Bagchi, J., & Narula, M. (2003). Translocations. In P. Vergne, V. Kortun, & H. Hou (Eds.), *How latitudes become forms: Art in a global age* (pp. 40–57). Minneapolis, MN: Walker Art Center.

Serig, D. A. (2004). *Generative visual metaphors in art: Understanding the conceptual landscape.* Unpublished manuscript, Teachers College, Columbia University, New York.

Silverman, D. (2001). *Interpreting qualitative data: Methods for analyzing talk, text and interaction* (2nd ed.). London: Sage.

Singerman, H. (1999). *Art subjects: Making artists in the American university.* Berkeley: University of California Press.

Smith, J. K., & Heshusius, L. (1986). Closing down the conversation: The end of the quantitative-qualitative debate among educational researchers. *Educational Researcher, 15,* 4–12.

Smith, N. R. (1993). *Experience and art: Teaching children to paint* (2nd ed.). New York: Teachers College Press.

Smith, P. (1996). *The history of American art education: Learning about art in American schools.* Westport, CT: Greenwood Press.

Smith, S., & Watson, J. (Eds.). (2002). *Interfaces: Women, autobiography, image, performance.* Ann Arbor: The University of Michigan Press.

Snow, C. P. (1959/1993). *The two cultures and the scientific revolution.* New York: Cambridge University Press.

Solomon R. Guggenheim Museum (2001). *Frank Gehry, Architect*, May 18–September 4, 2001. New York: Solomon R. Guggenheim Museum. Retrieved on March 6, 2004, from http://www.guggenheim.org/exhibitions/past_exhibitions/gehry/exhibition.html

Solso, R. L. (1994). *Cognition and the visual arts.* Cambridge: MIT Press.

Soucy, D., & Stankiewicz, M. (Eds.). (1990). *Framing the past: Essays on art education.* Reston, VA: National Art Education Association.

Stafford, B. M. (1994). *Artful science: Enlightenment entertainment and the eclipse of visual education.* Cambridge: MIT Press.

Stafford, B. M. (1996). *Good looking: Essays on the virtue of images.* Cambridge: MIT Press.

Staikidis, C. (2004). Where lived experience resides in art education: A painting and pedagogical collaboration with Mayan artists. Unpublished doctoral dissertation, Teachers College, Columbia University, New York.

Sternberg, R. J., & Wagner, R. K. (Eds.). (1994). *Mind in context: Interactionist perspectives on human intelligence.* New York: Cambridge University Press.

Stewart, I. (1995). *Nature's numbers: The unreal reality of mathematics.* New York: Basic Books.

Strand, D. (1998). *Research in the creative arts.* Canberra, ACT: Commonwealth of Australia.

Strauss, A., & Corbin, J. (1990). *Basics of qualitative research: Grounded theory procedures and techniques.* Newbury Park, CA: Sage.

Stronach, I., & MacLure, M. (1997). *Educational research undone: The postmodern embrace.* Buckingham, UK: Open University Press.

Stuhr, P. (1994). Multicultural art education and social reconstruction. *Studies in Art Education, 35*(3), 171–178.

Stuhr, P. (2003). A tale of why social and cultural content is often excluded from art education—and why it should not be. *Studies in Art Education, 44*(4), 301–314.

Sullivan, G. (1993). Art-based art education: Learning that is meaningful, authentic, critical, and pluralist. *Studies in Art Education, 35*(1), 5–21.

Sullivan, G. (1994). *Seeing Australia: Views of artists and artwriters.* Annandale, Australia: Piper Press.

Sullivan, G. (1996). Critical interpretive inquiry: A qualitative study of five contemporary artists' ways of seeing. *Studies in Art Education, 37*(4), 210–225.

Sullivan, G. (1998). *Critical influence: A visual arts research project with Jayne Dyer and Nikki McCarthy.* CD-ROM. Sydney, Australia: College of Fine Arts, University of New South Wales.

Sullivan, G. (2001). Artistic thinking as transcognitive practice: A reconciliation of the process-product dichotomy. *Visual Arts Research, 27*(1), 2–12.

Sullivan, G. (2002). Ideas and teaching: Making meaning from contemporary art. In Y. Gaudelius & P. Speirs (Eds.), *Contemporary issues in art education* (pp. 23–38). Upper Saddle River, NJ: Prentice Hall.

Sullivan, G. (2004). Studio art as research practice. In E. W. Eisner & M. D. Day (Eds.), *Handbook of research and policy in art education* (pp. 795–814). Mahwah, NJ: Lawrence Erlbaum Associates.

Sullivan, G., & Hochtritt, L. (2001). *Christo & Jeanne-Claude: The art of gentle disturbance.* New York: The President and Trustees of Teachers College, Columbia University.

Tashakkori, A., & Teddlie, C. (1998). *Mixed methodology: Combining qualitative and quantitative approaches.* Thousand Oaks, CA: Sage.

Tashakkori, A., & Teddlie, C. (2003). *Handbook of mixed methods in social and behavioral research.* Thousand Oaks, CA: Sage.

Taylor, C. (1989). The work of art as hermeneutic process: An artist "takes on" Heidegger. *Visual Arts Research, 15*(2), 52–57.

Tesch, R. (1990). *Qualitative research: Analysis types and software tools.* Basingstoke, Hampshire, UK: The Falmer Press.

Thelen, E., & Smith, L. B. (1994). *A dynamic systems approach to the development of cognition and action.* Cambridge: MIT Press.

Tonfoni, G. (1994). *Writing as a visual art*. Oxford, London: Intellect Books.

Torrance, E. P., & Myers, R. E. (1970). *Creative learning and teaching*. New York: Dodd, Mead.

Tufte, E. R. (1983). *The visual display of quantitative information*. Cheshire, CT: Graphic Press.

Tuhiwai Smith, L. (1999). *Decolonizing methodologies: Research and indigenous peoples*. Dunedin, NZ: University of Otago Press.

Turkle, S. (1995). *Life on the screen: Identity in the age of the Internet*. New York: Simon & Schuster.

Valovic, T. S. (2000). *Digital mythologies: The hidden complexities of the Internet*. New Brunswick, NJ: Rutgers University Press.

Valpy, A. J. (1838). *Paley's moral and political philosophy* (American Ed.). Philadelphia: Uriah Hunt.

van Leeuwen, T., & Jewitt, C. (Eds.). (2001). *Handbook of visual analysis*. Thousand Oaks, CA: Sage.

Varnedoe, K. (1998). *Jackson Pollock*. New York: The Museum of Modern Art.

Vasari, G. (1568/1993). *Lives of the artists*. (George Bull, Trans., 1965). London: The Folio Society.

Vergne, P., Kortun, V., & Hou, H. (Eds.). (2003). *How latitudes become forms: Art in a global age*. Minneapolis, MN: Walker Art Center.

Walker, H. (2001). Renigged. In *Freestyle* (pp. 16–17). New York: The Studio Museum in Harlem.

Walker, J. A., & Chaplin, S. (1997). *Visual culture: An introduction*. Manchester, UK: Manchester University Press.

Wallace, D. B., & Gruber, H. E. (1989). *Creative people at work*. New York: Oxford University Press.

Webb, J. (Ed.). (1999). *Beyond the future: The third Asia-Pacific triennial of contemporary art*. Brisbane, Australia: Queensland Art Gallery.

Webb, J. (2000). Research in perspective: The practice of theory. *Selected working papers in art & design* (Vol. 1). Retrieved September 14, 2003, from http://www.herts.ac.uk/artdes/research/papers/wpades/vol1/webb2.html

Weintraub, L. (2003). *Making contemporary art: How today's artists think and work*. London: Thames and Hudson.

Weisberg, R. W. (1993). *Creativity: Beyond the myth of genius*. New York: W. H. Freeman.

Weitzman, E., & Miles, M. B. (1995). *Computer programs for qualitative data analysis*. Thousand Oaks, CA: Sage.

West, T. G. (1997). *In the mind's eye*. New York: Prometheus Books.

Wilson, B. (1997). The second search: Metaphor, dimensions of meaning, and research topics in art education. In S. D. La Pierre & E. Zimmerman (Eds.), *Research methods and methodologies for art education* (pp. 1–32). Reston, VA: National Art Education Association.

Wilson, F. (2003). Interview with Kathleen Goncharov. In *Speak of me as I am* (pp. 20–25). Cambridge: MIT List Visual Arts Center.

Wilson, S. (2002). *Information arts: Intersections of art, science and technology.* Cambridge: MIT Press.

Wimsett, W. K., & Beardsley, M. (1946/1971). The intentional fallacy. In G. Dickie (Ed.), *Aesthetics, an introduction* (pp. 110–121). Indianapolis, IN: Pegasus.

Wolff, J. (1993). *The social production of art* (2nd ed.). New York: New York University Press.

Wolmark, J., & Gates-Stuart, E. (2002). Research as cultural practice. *Selected working papers in art & design* (Vol. 2). Retrieved September 14, 2003, from http://www.herts.ac.uk/artdes/research/papers/wpades/vol2/wolmarkfull.html

Yang, A. (1998). *Why Asia? Contemporary Asian and Asian American art.* New York: New York University Press.

Young, J. O. (2001). *Art and knowledge.* London: Routledge.

Zurmuehlen, M. (1990). *Studio art: Praxis, symbol, presence.* Reston, VA: National Art Education Association.

INDEX

ABOUT THE AUTHOR

Graeme Sullivan, Associate Professor of Art Education, Department of Arts and Humanities, Teachers College, Columbia University, joined the faculty in January 1999. He received his PhD from The Ohio State University, Columbus, Ohio, in 1984 and taught at the University of New South Wales, Australia, from 1988 until taking up the position at Columbia Teachers College. Since the early 1990s, his research has involved an ongoing investigation of critical-reflexive thinking processes and research practices in the visual arts. This focus on artistic practice has been applied in different contexts where the quest is to reposition the role and influence of art in the educational life of individuals. He has published widely in the field of art education, and in 1990 the National Art Education Association (NAEA) awarded him the Manual Barkan Memorial Award for his scholarly writing. He is the author of *Seeing Australia: Views of Artists and Artwriters* (1994), he has fulfilled many professional roles, and he is the immediate past editor of *Studies in Art Education,* the research journal of the NAEA. He maintains an active art practice, and his *Streetworks* continue to be created and installed in different cities and sites.